Flash Advertising

Flash Advertising

Flash Platform Development of Microsites, Advergames, and Branded Applications

Jason Fincanon

Routledge
Taylor & Francis Group

LONDON AND NEW YORK

First published 2010 by Focal Press

This edition published 2015 by Focal Press

Published 2017 by Routledge
2 Park Square, Milton Park, Abingdon, Oxon OX14 4RN
711 Third Avenue, New York, NY 10017, USA

First issued in hardback 2017

Routledge is an imprint of the Taylor & Francis Group, an informa business

© 2010 Jason Fincanon. Published by Taylor & Francis.

Notices
Practitioners and researchers must always rely on their own experience and knowledge in evaluating and using any information, methods, compounds, or experiments described herein. In using such information or methods they should be mindful of their own safety and the safety of others, including parties for whom they have a professional responsibility.

Product or corporate names may be trademarks or registered trademarks, and are used only for identification and explanation without intent to infringe.

Library of Congress Cataloging-in-Publication Data
Fincanon, Jason.
  Flash advertising : flash platform development of microsites, advergames, and branded applications / Jason Fincanon.
    p. cm.
  ISBN 978-0-240-81345-5
1. Computer animation. 2. Flash (Computer file) 3. Web sites–Design. 4. Internet advertising. I. Title.
  TR897.7.F479 2010
  006.6'96–dc22   2010025536

British Library Cataloguing-in-Publication Data
A catalogue record for this book is available from the British Library.

ISBN 13: 978-1-138-42637-5 (hbk)
ISBN 13: 978-0-240-81345-5 (pbk)

Typeset by: diacriTech, Chennai, India

Dedication

To my wife and children. You give me focus, direction, passion, and joy in everything you do. I love you and thank you for making my life so wonderful and fun.

CONTENTS

FOREWORD

You visit a Web site. An ad takes over your screen. This has happened before, but this time it actually looks like an ad for a legitimate product, not like the creepy ads you often see at the top of your favorite social networking site. Not only does this ad look legit, it has a huge red button that for some strange reason is beckoning; no, demanding that you press it. So, you do. This, my friends, is the power of Flash advertising. In reality, this magic probably only happens once for every thousand times an ad is seen. However, the beauty of the Internet is that this ad will be seen twenty million times.

Advertising is big business and it is no secret that advertising on the Internet is quickly becoming the mother lode. While you may not think this has much to do with you, Jason would disagree. Advertising on the Internet means jobs and this book will teach you everything you could possibly need to know to get started with Flash advertising. I know this for a fact. Jason was my mentor when I first got into the industry. The methods, concepts, and procedures that Jason details in this book are all things that he taught me during many an all-nighter at one of the largest interactive shops in the United States. His approach has been tested and streamlined in the most demanding of environments. It's been years since we have worked together, but I can now proudly say that my company uses Jason's experience to our advantage. Not only do we use his approach in our Flash media development, we actually hand out his book as training material for new Flash media developers. At the risk of sounding like an infomercial being seen in the middle of the night, this is the real deal.

This is the second edition of *Flash Advertising*. One of the main changes in the industry since the first edition is the adoption rate of the Adobe Flash Player. Now that most PC users have Flash Player version 9 or greater installed, ads developed with Action-Script 3 are being used with much greater frequency. This is a big deal to people developing cutting-edge Flash ads and microsites. This latest edition will show you how to make the step up to ActionScript 3 from ActionScript 2. If you are new to ActionScript in general, this edition will provide you with the building blocks you need to get off to a good start.

Jason is an enthusiast in his family life, in his hobbies, and in his work. He loves Flash and will show you how much fun it can be to work with Flash advertising. As an active contributor to the Flash community, Jason believes in the open exchange of ideas. It's with this sense of community that he authors this book. Developing Flash advertising is a great way to make a living, and Jason shares this enjoyment in his writing. So, read this book and learn from one of the first and the best.

—Christopher Long, Partner, Ovrflo Media, Inc.

ACKNOWLEDGMENTS

In addition to the thanks I gave in the first edition of this book, I'd like to add a few names to the list and reiterate a few from before. So here they are in no particular order (Thanks guys!):

Chris Long

James Wilson

Danh Ta

Jamie Fishler

Danny Dura

Dan Ferguson

Chris Griffith (check out his book *Real-World Flash Game Development*)

John Keehler

Katie McCracken

James Hering

Elizabeth Basham

Special thanks also goes out to:

Ovrflo Media (*http://www.ovrflomedia.com*)

Blockdot (*http://www.blockdot.com*)

Eyeblaster (*http://www.eyeblaster.com*)

Click Here (*http://www.clickhere.com*)

ABOUT THE AUTHOR

With experience working with the Flash Platform since graduating from The Art Institute of Dallas in 1998, Jason has spent the majority of his career building Flash-based websites, games and applications while working for employers ranging from interactive advertising agencies to branded entertainment and advergaming companies. During his time in these industries, Jason has had the opportunity to work on projects for clients such as Patrón Tequila, GameStop, Hyundai, Fruit of the Loom, National Pork Board, Travelocity, Florida Department of Citrus, Nokia and many others. Outside of work, he also stays involved in the Flash Platform community by co-managing Flash Dallas, an official Adobe Flash User Group, and maintaining a Flash and Flex related blog that can be found at *http://www.jasonfincanon.com*.

INTRODUCTION

Advertising online has come to have a not-so-favorable reputation with Internet users. Combine that reputation with the often uninformed opinion that Flash is for creating nothing more than exceptionally annoying banners or Web site intros and preloaders that are so bloated in file size they need their own preloaders and you've got a recipe for disaster. On the other hand, when done correctly, Flash can be (and is) used to create some of the most eye-catching, awe-inspiring, mind-blowing, award-winning work on the Web.

A major contributor to the unfortunate misconception of this combination is the fact that there *IS* work out there that fits directly within its own reputation. However, with a little forethought and planning, those same ads could be very quickly redesigned with the outcome of much better user reception and interaction. If the work that is causing the bad reputation for Flash advertising can be made better, then so can the reputation itself. Just as its predecessor, this book was written in hopes of doing exactly that. It was written to help educate and inform individuals, teams, departments, and even companies on the ins and outs of creating advertising with Flash.

INTRODUCTION

1

FLASH ADVERTISING OVERVIEW

CHAPTER OUTLINE

Flash Advertising. DOI: 10.1016/B978-0-240-81345-5.00001-3

The use of the Flash Platform in advertising has been around for many years now, and it continues to thrive even in the face of the development of other "Flash killer" technologies. Its use is far from limited to the stereotypical banner ad that people tend to think of when the word "advertising" is used in the interactive realm. In fact, the Flash Platform is used for everything from banners to corporate Web sites, from personal portfolios to client specific online news channels, and in many cases, it may even be used for desktop applications that are designed to promote your client's brand.

The Flash Platform has matured and grown into a powerful set of tools over the years, but there are still plenty of ads and sites out there that tend to leave some people with a bad impression, and it's up to us to change their minds. So how do we change the minds of these people and wow them at the same time? We can start by following a few simple design rules, anticipating interaction and animation issues, targeting the correct audience, and steering away from the things we find annoying or wouldn't want to see ourselves.

As the platform has grown, so has online advertising. There was a time when you had to choose between a static .jpg and an animated .gif for your banners, but that time has long since past. The option to use the Flash Platform has enabled interactive advertising agencies, as well as individual developers, to create much more engaging and entertaining advertising in many different forms. It has also opened up a channel for more interactivity and the ability to do things like gather user information from within an ad itself.

So with the lines between the computer desktop, the Internet, the television, and mobile devices blurring more and more every day, it has become increasingly important to give users better, more memorable, more interactive experiences in everything they do online, including viewing your clients' brands by way of advertising. After all, if they remember the experience you provided, they'll remember the brand and be more likely to buy from your client in the future. And after they buy from your client, your client will be happy and will most likely return to you for more projects (and, of course, more projects mean more income).

So let's take a quick look at what we'll be covering in this first chapter where I'll first cover a little bit about the book itself and then why you should use the Flash Platform for advertising, as well as the options and considerations placed in front of you when doing so. The sections contained within this chapter are as follows:

- What This Book Is and Is Not
- Supporting Web site
- The Flash Platform
- Why Use the Flash Platform for Advertising
- Types of Ads
- Interactive Standards and the Interactive Advertising Bureau

- Advertising Templates In Flash
- Ad Specs
- Deadlines
- Microsites
- Quality Control
- Version Control

What This Book Is and Is Not

This book should be thought of and read as a sort of guide into the world of advertising with the Flash Platform. While its intention is to prepare you for the flow of projects as they come in your door and work their way to living online for millions of users to interact with, you should also understand that different places of employ-ment will all have their own internal workings and processes to follow. With that said, there are also several constants and considerations that are absolutely unchanged from one advertising agency to the next; items like standard banner specs or file optimization.

On the flip side, this book should not be thought of as a strictly code-oriented book that developers might read to learn Flash itself. While it does contain ActionScript for the developers, it also contains a lot of information that is not specific to any single discipline. With that being the case, anyone from Flash Platform Developers to Media Directors to Account Managers can most likely find some sort of usable information within these pages.

Supporting Web site

The supporting Web site for this book can be found at http://www .flashadbook.com. On this Web site, you can find information about the chapters, share your thoughts and questions, and download many of the files from the book. Now before we dive in, let's briefly talk about the Flash Platform and some of the tools that will be used in this book.

The Flash Platform

Until recently, when you talked to someone about Flash design and/or development, you were most likely talking about Flash itself. Whether you were talking about building a Flash Web site, a Flash animation or any other "Flash" work, it's a good bet that the project in question was to be designed or developed using the Flash IDE. However, using the word Flash to describe a project may need a little more clarification now due to the emergence of what is now known as the Adobe Flash Platform (Fig. 1.1).

Figure 1.1 The Adobe Flash Platform.

The current short description on Adobe's Web site states, "The Adobe Flash Platform is an integrated set of technologies surrounded by an established ecosystem of support programs, business partners, and enthusiastic user communities." The site also lists the technologies included in the Flash Platform as Flash Player, Adobe AIR, Flex, Flash Builder, Flash Professional, Flash Media Server, and LiveCycle Data Services ES. I'll be touching on some, but not all of these technologies in this book.

We're obviously going to be working with Flash, and if you don't already have it installed on your computer, you can get a trial version from the Adobe Web site. I'll also touch on Flash Builder 4 a little, though it's not a part of the Flash Platform, and I'll be using Photoshop as well. Each of these can be downloaded from the following locations:

- Flash – http://www.adobe.com/products/flash/
- Flash Builder – http://www.adobe.com/products/flashbuilder/
- Photoshop – http://www.adobe.com/products/photoshop/

Okay, now that you've got your tools, I'd like to continue with some extremely brief descriptions of each one. If you're already familiar with them, please feel free to skip ahead to the next section.

Flash Professional

Flash (Fig. 1.2) is where this all started many years ago (under a different name) and it has come a long way over all those years. It's been around for a while and I believe (or at least hope) that it will continue to grow for many more years to come. After all, it has an entire platform named after it, right? Flash, in the sense of this particular paragraph/section, is an IDE used to develop, animate, and compile your work to usable files such as .swf files, executable (.exe) files, Adobe AIR applications, and even more recently, iPhone apps.

Figure 1.2 The Adobe Flash Professional CS5 launch screen.

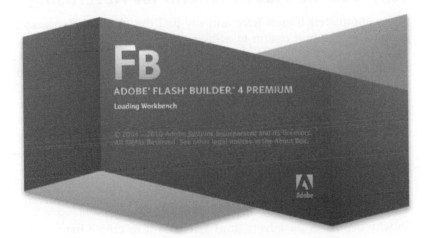

Figure 1.3 The Adobe Flash Builder 4 Premium launch screen.

Flash Builder

Flash Builder (Fig. 1.3), which was previously named Flex Builder, is an IDE built by Adobe for the purpose of working with the Flex framework. The reason for the recent name change with version 4 was to tie it in more closely with the Flash Platform while also drawing a clear line of distinction between the IDE and the framework. The Flex framework itself also moved up in version number (to version 4) and includes new namespaces, components, and other tools to make your work as a designer or developer a whole lot easier while helping you complete tasks and projects much more quickly. Again, Flash Builder is available from the Adobe Web site: http://www.adobe.com/products/flashbuilder/

AIR

Adobe AIR is a runtime that not only allows you to build and deploy branded desktop games and applications with HTML, Ajax, Flash, and/or Flex, but it also allows you to do so across multiple operating systems. This means that you can build your game or application one single time and have one single installer for many users regardless if they are on Windows, Mac, or Linux. As a developer, you can build your applications with Adobe products like Flash or Dreamweaver or you may choose to use your favorite text editor in conjunction with the free AIR SDK to package your applications. For lots more information about Adobe AIR, check it out on Adobe's Web site: http://www.adobe.com/products/air/

Why Use the Flash Platform for Advertising

I'll be completely honest here and say that the Flash Platform isn't going to be the best option to achieve your goals 100% of the time. As with any technology, you should avoid using it just for the sake of using it. Instead, you should assess the project at hand to decide if the Flash Platform is the best option to go with. In some cases, you may want to use AJAX. In other cases, you may want to use nothing more than plain 'ol HTML. The point is that you should choose what best serves the needs of your client. With all of that said, this is a book about creating Flash advertising, so we'll go ahead and make the assumption your work calls for it.

Banners

So why use Flash for advertising? Why use it to create banner ads for your client's service or product? The short answer: Brand interaction through features is not available with other options. With a static .jpg or even an animated .gif banner, you might have a good enough image to get a user to click and go to the intended destination, but that's pretty much all you have – an image. With Flash, you have the ability to engage your audience with your client's brand. You can use smooth animation and interaction to tell a story. You can build an ad with tabs for different "pages" within your banner. You can build a banner that gives users even more interactive elements once they interact with it for the first time. You can even show a television commercial or other video inside your ad.

Let's look at an automobile manufacturer as an example. Your client, Typical Motors, wants you to build a round of online advertisements that will allow the end user to begin choosing options on their newest model. They want people to see the ad, make choices from dropdown menus about what color and trim package they would like on the car, submit the form, and be taken to the "build your own" section of the manufacturer's Web site where the selections made in the banner will carry over. By allowing users to fill out the form in the banner, you've allowed them to complete a portion of the task before they even get to the site.

So why wouldn't you just build the banner out with HTML? That would be a great option if we were only talking about a form and two, maybe three, frames of images and text. However, your client wants more than that. They want to see several different images of the car smoothly cross-fade from one to the next on user interaction. They also want to see 360° views of that car and offer users an option to watch their new TV spot directly inside the banners, and the Flash Platform is the best way to provide them with these features.

Microsites

So what about microsites? In addition to the banners, Typical Motors wants to launch a site specifically for the new car. They would like to see an interactive 360° view of the car, an image gallery page, a video page, maybe a driving game featuring the new car, and several other features. This is, of course, in addition to the information you would expect to find on a car site like a specs page or the manufacturer's suggested retail price of the car. They would also like to see a nice, fresh, creative approach to page transitions. Now you could probably accomplish some of those tasks with anything like Ruby, PHP, .NET, or several others, but in order to give them the full experience they seem to be looking for, I'd suggest designing and building them a microsite using the tools available in the Flash Platform.

Branded AIR Applications

An AIR application gives your client an opportunity to stay with the potential customer after they have left the microsite and even the browser itself. You may choose to build something like a branded game, a video player, an inventory tracker, or even an application that would enable a customer to configure, order, and buy a new car. You may even extend the functionality of that application to remind the customer of things like scheduled maintenance or alert them to things like safety recalls. By adding in long-term features like those, you raise the likelihood that each user who has installed the application will leave it on their machine, continue to use it, and continue to be exposed to your client's brand.

Mobile Devices

A lot has changed in the realm of Flash and mobile devices since the last edition of this book. One of the biggest changes is the fact that Flash Player 10.1 is available on several devices such as the Palm Pre, Motorola Droid, and Google Nexus One phones. That is, of course, in addition to the millions of devices that already support Flash Lite. On top of that, you can now build your content in Flash CS5 and have it compiled to an iPhone application. Don't confuse that to mean that the Flash Player is on the iPhone or that Flash content will play on the iPhone because it won't (at least not at the time I'm writing this). And just in case you're wondering about this crazy Flash-to-iPhone business, let me give you a quick and dirty example of how to do it.

The first thing you'll need to do is to create a new Flash file by simply choosing "New" from the File menu and then selecting "iPhone OS" from the resulting menu and choices (Fig. 1.4). Once you have your new .fla, you simply build out your app almost as if you were building it for use on the Web. I say *almost* because there are definitely some constraints and features that need to be taken into consideration.

Before I go into detail, let's get back to the banner ads. While covering the banner example for Typical Motors I mentioned forms, videos, animation, and a few other things that need to be considered. What I haven't talked about yet is the different ad formats that are available for you to choose from. Let's get to that now.

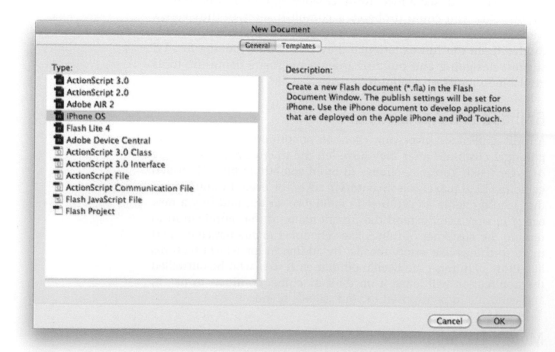

Figure 1.4 Flash CS5's new iPhone OS document option.

Types of Ads

When it comes to creating online banner ads, you have options for the format in which you will build them and the top-level, bird's eye view of those options are standard Flash and rich media.

Standard Flash

I'm going to stick with Typical Motors for now and we're going to tone down their ads to simple animations with nothing more than a couple of images and some text. Because we aren't going to include any high-profile extras like video, this is a good time to use what's generally called a standard Flash ad. Standard ads are the most basic of all the Flash ads you'll build. They're simple, straightforward, and get the message across. Your standard Flash ads will usually consist of a small animation, a couple of lines of copy with a call to action such as "click here to visit our site," and one or more clickable areas. These ads are usually constrained to a file size limitation of 30–40k and are served by either an ad-serving company or directly by the site on which the ad is running (see more on ad-serving companies and site-serving ads in Chapters 6 and 7). Keep in mind that while some sites allow you to utilize more file size, standard banners are not the place to try to squeeze in anything like audio or video.

Rich Media

If you're looking to have audio or video in your ads, or if you feel you'll need more than the 30–40k file size allowed by standard Flash ads, you'll need to move them over to a third-party rich-media company (I will discuss several of them in Chapter 6). These companies have technologies in place that allow you to have much more file size, interactivity, video, audio, and so forth. They allow you to build a much richer experience. In addition to the features I've just mentioned, you'll need the rich-media companies to serve your banners if you plan on creating anything like expandable or floating ad units. Again, I'll discuss more about those later in the book but as a quick explanation, both of those banners do exactly what you'd think: Expandable ads expand to a larger size when a user rolls over or clicks on them and floating ads "float" over the main content of the page.

| ALERT!

When you are planning and working on a banner campaign, always remember that choosing rich-media banners over standard Flash ads can cost more. However, also remember that the added benefits of rich-media banners may very well be worth the extra expense.

Cost Can Be an Issue

So why wouldn't I design my ads to run with a rich-media company every single time? I mean, if I were going to be constrained to a file size, I'd rather be constrained to 100k than 30k. How about the ability to have additional loads in the form of Flash files, images, XML, or several other options? Why give that up? What about the video I want to stream into my ads? The answer is cost, my friend, cost! When you upsize that meal at the drive-thru or when you buy the car with the larger engine, you expect to pay more because you get more, right? The same concept applies here. The difference is that you aren't spending your own money now; you're spending your client's money. Another concept that fits perfectly is the concept of not using a technology just for the sake of using that technology. Pitch your ideas to your client and let them know which ones will require them to "upsize their order." They will let you know which one they are happy with, as well as which one they feel comfortable spending their money on.

Interactive Standards and the Interactive Advertising Bureau

Because we just got finished talking about ad formats and since I mentioned a usual file size limit of 30–40k, let's spend a minute on online advertising standards. The Interactive Advertising Bureau (IAB) is an association whose goals are not only to campaign for interactive marketing and advertising, but also to prove its effectiveness. In addition, they also lead the charge to get the industry organized with a voluntary set of standards and guidelines for interactive marketing.

The voluntary guidelines you'll find from the IAB are those that most sites and agencies currently follow. They include, but are not limited to, ad units, e-mails, pop-ups, and rich-media. By familiarizing yourself with their voluntary guidelines and standards, you'll know valuable information pertaining to important topics dealing with your work. Topics include ad formats (width and height), recommended file sizes, animation lengths, and audio/video controls.

I'll go into a little more detail about the IAB in just a bit. You can also find more information and IAB guidelines on everything from ad units to rich media to e-mail to pop-ups on their Web site located at http://www.iab.net (Fig. 1.5).

> **TIP**
>
> The Bandwidth Profiler in Flash is a very useful resource when it comes to keeping your banners within the file size allowed by your specs. It also comes in quite handy for seeing how your microsites will download and

Figure 1.5 The IAB Web site.

play with various settings, such as a user with a 56k dial-up modem versus a user with a faster internet connection like DSL or cable. To get to the Bandwidth Profiler, simply test your Flash movie by pressing both the Command (Ctrl on PC) button and the Enter button on your keyboard. Once your test movie is playing, press both the Command (Ctrl on PC) button and the B button to toggle the Bandwidth Profiler on and off. I'll get a little more in depth with the Bandwidth Profiler in Chapter 3.

Advertising Templates in Flash

A quick word on the advertising templates that come packaged with Flash (Fig. 1.6). While I personally don't use them, it's worth mentioning that they are built at some of the industry standard sizes as far as height and width. By starting your

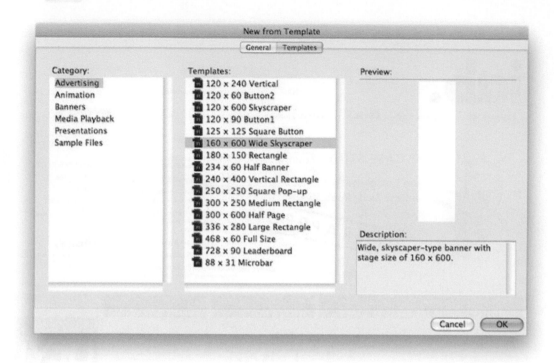

Figure 1.6 The advertising templates available in Flash Professional CS5.

project with one of these, you'll save yourself the step of resizing the stage. There isn't a whole lot to them, but you can use them as a starting point or you can modify them to suit your needs and save your own custom templates. For example, you might start a new file from the 300 × 250 advertising template, change the frame rate from 24 frames per second to 18 frames per second (the IAB standard), and bump the player version to whatever your project specs call for. Once you have made the modifications you need and you are satisfied with the properties of your new file, select "Save as Template" from the File menu, name your file, and you've got a new custom template made for you, by you.

Ad Specs

Rules, rules, rules. Everywhere you turn, there are rules telling you what you can and can't do and ad banners are no exception. Almost every major site your ads may run on has a section where you can get their specs. If you can't find a link that takes you to their advertising area, simply contact the site to let them know you need their advertising specs and there should be no problem obtaining them. The information you are after are things like the maximum file size your ad can be when published to the final .swf, the amount of time you are allowed to run animation, and the number of times your banner can loop before finally coming to a stop. Another thing to watch out for is a maximum frame rate. Although most sites may not have the maximum frame rate listed in their specs, some do, and your work can very easily get kicked back to you if you exceed it.

Keep It Down (Your File Size That Is)

The sites that your ads will run on don't want to bog down their readers' bandwidth with banners that exceed the file size in their specs and you don't want the banners to take too long to start playing. If you built an ad that was 500k, your audience would have to wait for it to load before they ever got to see the product. Sure, with that much file size you'd probably have a pretty amazing banner, but your end goal to intrigue users and get them to interact with your ad could be lost in all of it. As I mentioned earlier, most sites usually stick with a maximum file size of 30–40k. There are, of course, exceptions where some sites will accept a higher file size like 50k. Another fairly consistent spec is timing and looping. A lot of sites prefer to set a time limit of 15 or 30 s with a maximum of three loops.

More IAB

Because we're on the subject of specs, let's expand on the information about the IAB from a little earlier. As I was mentioning before, the IAB has voluntary guidelines for what they call Interactive Marketing Units (IMUs). These guidelines are updated as needed by the IAB's Reimagining Interactive Advertising Taskforce. The taskforce is made up of leaders from creative agencies, media agencies, and publishers, and they review the Ad Unit Guidelines each year. Table 1.1 shows some of the sizes in the guidelines at the time of writing this book.

Remember that Table 1.1 is only a partial list and the sizes listed within it may have changed by the time you are reading this. To make sure you have the most up-to-date guidelines, visit the IAB's Ad Unit Guidelines page on their Web site at http://www .iab.net/. While you are there, be sure to also take a quick look around at the other guidelines for more advertising options like Pop-up Guidelines, Rich Media Creative Guidelines, and Digital Video Ad Format Guidelines & Best Practices. Obviously, the latter is where you'll find information on running audio and video in your banners.

Table 1.1 Just a Few of the IAB Recommended Banner Specs

Banner size	Recommended maximum initial download fileweight	Recommended animation length (s)
300 × 250 (Medium rectangle)	40k	15
180 × 150 (Rectangle)	40k	15
468 × 60 (Full banner)	40k	15
728 × 90 (Leaderboard)	40k	15
160 × 600 (Leaderboard)	40k	15

Deadlines

So let's jump right in to talking about deadlines and their importance because they can make or break your client list. When a project is set up and your client "signs off" on you doing the job for them, there will be a time associated with having that work finished and pushed live on the Internet. If you are not the actual person who agreed to and set this deadline, then that person most likely has a pretty good idea of how long it will take you to create the work and you'll be held to that date. Now I won't candy coat this issue by saying that there are never going to be any problems or stress with tight deadlines. Quite frankly, most deadlines will be at least a little bit tight, and there will be times when you'll need to work some late hours in order to meet those deadlines. So how big of a deal is it when you start missing your deadlines? Well, on top of the potential embarrassment of not delivering the work when you promised the client you would, you could be facing any one of several levels of consequences from a small warning all the way up to losing your client. The severity of the consequences may depend on several factors like the policies of your place of employment or how many deadlines you've missed in a given amount of time. Just try to remember that deadlines are an extremely important part of a project and they should be taken as such.

TIP

Your rest and energy levels can play a key role in meeting deadlines. There comes a point in a long, long workday that your productivity level actually drops due to fatigue. It may happen after 12 hours or it may happen after 18 hours, but that drop in productivity can have you working even longer into the night without accomplishing anything and possibly even creating problems in your code. Sometimes, the best thing to do is walk away, go home to get some rest, and try again the next day.

Aim Ahead of Schedule

One suggestion I would like to make is to aim ahead of your deadline. If you have 4 weeks to complete a microsite, try to have it finished in 3 weeks. If you have 3 days to build a round of banners, see if you can knock them out in 1 1/2 days. If you are the Flash developer on the project, your first deadline will most likely be to get your project handed over to quality control. The quicker you can get it to them, the less crunched they are on time and the better they can do their job. The next deadline you will probably face is the deadline to have the bugs that are found by quality control worked out. This deadline usually ties right in with the launch or campaign start date. Imagine if you turned the project over to quality control 2 days early, they find a few issues, report them to you, and you fix them right away. Now you look again at your final deadline, and yes, you've just completed the project 3 full days ahead of schedule. What client isn't going to want the reassuring comfort that you and your team have everything so completely under control?

ALERT!

Remember that other than quality control, you are usually the last to have your hands in a project before it goes live to the world. Because that is the case, your deadlines are extremely important. Don't miss them.

Creeping Scope

Another good reason to stay ahead of the game when it comes to your deadlines is scope creep. The best way I can describe this phenomenon is the same as it has been explained to me in the past: *Scope creep* is the inevitable process in which the client or stakeholder, after agreeing to initial deliverables, discovers what those deliverables truly need to be. This process usually occurs gradually over time and only becomes evident once the project is nearing completion. If it's not managed well, scope creep can very easily translate into many extra work hours. However, by expecting it to happen, you can be prepared to watch for the signs ahead of time.

You're Not Alone

Because we've talked about your deadlines as the Flash developer, let's talk about another deadline: The deadline to have the layouts and artwork delivered to you. After all, how can you start building a banner or site if you don't have the needed assets? If someone other than yourself is doing the creative/art side of the project, they should be given a date by which they need to have these assets to you. The probability of you making your deadline is partially dependent on them making theirs. However, you should keep in mind that some companies may choose to utilize different approaches to these particular deadlines. For example, your employer may have a bit of a loose schedule in this area to allow the timelines of different disciplines to overlap. This would mean that while layouts are due to you by a certain date, those layouts may only include select pages of a microsite. This method allows the creative talent to keep working on the design of the underlying areas while you start developing the main functionality of the site. The result is a site that has had more attention given to the details and more details given to the site. And we all know the old saying about the details, right?

Keep In Touch

While working with these overlapping work times, it is extremely important that you stay in close contact with the creative person. As you'll quickly learn, this is because parts of the site that have not yet been designed may be affected by the functionality you are programming into the main area of the site or vice versa. While developing the main functionality, let the creative person know what you are doing as you are doing it. Let them know exactly how you're developing the site and ask them to explain the underlying sections that could be affected. What you are trying to avoid here is spending a couple of hours coding only to find out that you need to change it in such a way that you are nearly starting over.

Microsites

What exactly is a microsite? Well, it's smaller than a full Web site but bigger than a banner, and it can be anything from pure information to a full multimedia experience. With microsites you can concentrate on that one specific product or idea that your client wants to push. Because it is being built for that single product, the site can have its own look and feel that doesn't necessarily have to match that of the client's main Web site. A microsite can be designed to portray how elegant the product is. It can be built to give users a feel for how fun the product is. It can have its own soundtrack so users can hear how exciting the product is. The possibilities are limited only by your creativity, your client's approval, and the end goal of the campaign.

Design to the Campaign

Remember that it's a good idea to tie the design of your microsite in with any other advertising that is going on in the campaign at the same time. This means that you would want to take a look at something like the television commercials or print ads and you would want to use some design elements from them. The new Typical Motors car is a very nice one. It's extremely elegant, refined, and generally top of the line in luxury and comfort, and it's being advertised as such offline. So let's take that slick, expensive-looking background from the magazine ad and incorporate it into the site. And let's take the smooth, elegant, classical track from the television commercial to use as background music on the site.

A lot of times when you build a microsite, you'll also build banners to go with it. You've probably guessed that the banners are intended to drive traffic to the microsite and that's exactly what they'll do. In addition to the banners, there should also be a piece on the client's main Web site that promotes and drives even more traffic to the new microsite.

Microsites are usually highly amusing projects and you generally have more creative freedom with them than you do with banners. This is the place where you'll have more opportunities to code some new effects or try out that cool new feature that's only available in the newest version of the Flash Player.

> **Inside Advertising**
>
> It's very common to use materials online that were originally created for offline production. Essentially anything that was created for print, television, radio, or outdoors (billboards, and so on) can be used in one form or another in your online campaign efforts.

> **TIP**
>
> If you know that you are going to be working on a microsite for a client, try to get approval to publish out to the latest version of the Flash Player. If they won't agree to that, ask for the next version down. Being able to publish out to the latest version is beneficial for all parties involved: Creative departments get to design with new features in mind, Flash programmers get to work directly with those new features, and clients get cutting-edge microsites that people talk about and pass around to their friends. In addition to those benefits, you'll be helping the penetration rates of that version of the Flash Player. The quicker the penetration rates rise, the easier it is to convince a client that it's safe to use.

Quality Control

Before I start with this section, I'd like to offer a quick bit of clarification: Quality control may go by many other names such as quality assurance or quality testing. However, for consistency, I will always refer to it as quality control within this book. And now that you're aware of that piece of information, let's talk about it.

Much like version control (which I'll talk about next in this chapter), quality control is a step that some developers (and even companies) choose to skip for some reason. The unfortunate choice that is sometimes made against quality control is one that can cost everyone involved and it can cost them dearly. Imagine if you created a piece of work and didn't test it even a single time. You're probably good enough so that one piece of work would be fine and so would the next 10. However, what if you hadn't had your morning coffee yet? Or what if you were at the end of an 18 hour work day? You might just miss something and end up sending your work to the client, bugs and all. Now imagine that you *did* test your work but because you're so close to the project, you missed an error and sent it out anyway. The best solution to all of this is to check your own work and then have someone else check it again.

Test Yourself

You should be testing your own work as it progresses and again after it is complete. Among other things, this testing is another advantage to aiming ahead of your deadlines. If you finish up with the animation and coding with time to spare, you can (and always should) test it out before sending it on to quality control. If you find a bug at this point, that's one less you'll have to fix after you hand it off (not to mention that you will have helped make the quality controller's job a little easier). The fewer bugs you pass to quality control and the fewer bugs you have to fix at the end of the project, the earlier it can be approved to go live and the quicker everyone can either go home or move on to the next piece of work. I'll go into more detail on quality control as it pertains to banners and microsites individually in their respective chapters later on in the book. For now though, how about a bit of an overview?

TIP

It's always a good idea to test as you work. Each time you create a new piece of functionality for a project, don't just test that one piece. Instead, do at least a quick run through of the project to make sure that your new functionality didn't break other pieces or sections.

The Reason for Quality Control

So what is the focus of quality control? The answer to that question is in the first word of the job title itself: quality. The work you do should be held to the highest standard and quality control is there to help make sure that it is. By making sure your work stays within the specifications that have been set and by attempting to actually break anything and everything you create, they are making your work virtually unbreakable while also making sure it doesn't get kicked back from the hosting company or sites on which it will run. You personally benefit from this process as well, because in the future, you will remember what broke, how it broke, and what you did to fix it. With this information, you become better and better as a Flash developer and/or designer because you have the practice that they say makes perfect and you have made the mistakes from which you can learn. So while doing your absolute best to avoid creating bugs, welcome those that are reported to you as new opportunities to advance your knowledge even if only a little.

You're Still Not Alone

I also have a piece of information that may help you sleep a little easier at night: Not all bugs will rest on your shoulders alone. For example, there may be issues that come up that involve changing something in the original layout of the work. When these issues arise, be sure to get the creative talent involved with the change. It is, after all, their design you'll be altering and it probably shouldn't be altered without the knowledge of the original creator of the work. Another example might be if there is someone else working on the database from which you are pulling information for a microsite. If something needs to be changed that involves the code that person wrote, they obviously need to be informed and involved in the change. Speaking of changes, what happens when you make a change and you later find out that you need to undo that change? Well, hopefully you've got some kind of version control system in place.

Version Control

Have you ever realized that you hadn't saved in quite a while just as the program you're working in was crashing? Have you ever worked on a file for several days or even weeks? Have you ever had one of those files get corrupted or accidentally deleted? How about a coworker? Have you ever opened a file to find that a coworker had changed almost everything in the file and saved it before realizing they had the wrong file open? How about you? Have you ever accidentally messed up any files in any way? Were you able to get your files back and roll them back to the condition they were in when they worked oh so well? If you answered no to that last question and yes to any of the others, then you, my friend, need to get some sort of version control in place and you need to get it in place as soon as possible. Once you have it in place, make sure that your entire team is using it as well.

ALERT!

If you aren't using any kind of version control, I highly recommend that you start using it immediately. The simple practice of using version control has been known, on several occasions, to actually save a project that would have otherwise been lost to problems like accidental deletion and/or miscommunication between developers. Being able to save these projects can also save you from potentially losing your client as well.

Options

When it comes to version control, you have many proprietary (such as Microsoft's SourceSafe) and free solutions (such as Subversion or Git; Figs. 1.7 and 1.8). Each of them has their individual advantages and disadvantages, but the end goal to all of

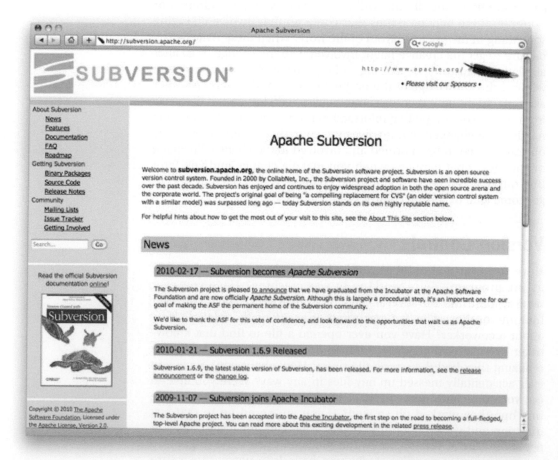

Figure 1.7 The Subversion Web site.

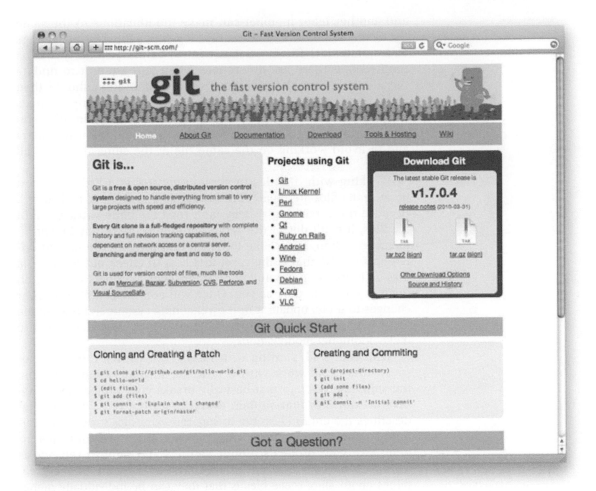

Figure 1.8 The Git Web site.

them is the same: to save past versions of your work in case you lose the current version or you need to revert back to an older one. A very basic example of simple version control would give a file a version number of 1 on its initial creation. If that file is then modified, the version number is bumped up to 2. The next change would increment the version number again, and so on.

You may work a little differently with version control depending on the file you're actually modifying. For example, if you're working on an .as file, you won't need to check out or lock the file in the versioning system unless you absolutely don't want anyone else working on it at the same time. This is because the .as file is, in essence, a text file in which the versioning system should be able to read and decipher differences. In other words, you and another team member can make modifications to the same file at the same time. If the other developer finishes his or hers and updates the file in version control before you do, you'll be notified that there are differences when you attempt to update the file with your changes. Your versioning system should then show you the differences and allow you to make any changes needed before actually updating the file. With that said, it's good practice to keep good communication between team members and to avoid working on the same file at the same time if at all possible.

Working with .fla files in version control is a little different because .fla files are binary files (as are .jpg, .png, .psd, and so on). Because the versioning system can't read the code written within .fla files, it can't detect the actual differences that may be within them even though it is able to detect that the files are indeed different. Because that is the case, it is best to check out or lock .fla files so there is no possibility of other team members working on them at the same time as you. Once you are finished making your changes to a file, update it in the versioning system and release the lock to allow other developers access to it in case they need to make additional modifications.

With that said, starting with Flash Professional CS5, you can save, open, and work with a new file format called XFL. The uncompressed XFL format basically breaks your project apart into several .xml files that contain everything from one .xml file that describes the entire Flash file to separate .xml files for each individual symbol in your library. It also contains more .xml files for items like your project's mobile settings and publish settings as well as folders for external images, and so on. One of the great things about all of these files is that they can be individually managed in source control, which actually allows more than one person to work on a single Flash file at the same time! In addition to that awesomeness, XFL files support live updates of editable assets. What does that mean? It means that while one developer is working in the main Flash file, another developer (or designer) could do something like edit the .xml file for a button or other library asset. Once that developer is finished with that asset and saves the .xml, the changes are reflected in Flash.

ALERT!

Always check in or unlock your files in version control once you're finished working on them. Because some version control solutions won't let anyone access files except for the person who has them checked out, it's important to release the control of those files in case you leave the office or end up being out sick the following day. If you leave the files locked, it will make it more difficult for your team to continue working on them in your absence.

A Version Control Story

John and Mary work for an interactive advertising agency and they have been working on a microsite for one of their biggest clients. Things have gone smoothly throughout the life of the project and they are almost ready to send it to quality control when John notices a problem during one of his own quality tests. He isolates the issue, notes the steps taken to recreate the problem, and opens the .fla file that he believes actually contains the error. After navigating to the line of code he suspects as the bad line, he makes his change and publishes the .swf file. Because it's the end of the day and John has a flight to catch for an out-of-town vacation, he saves his work, shuts down his computer, and leaves.

The next morning, Mary passes the project over to quality control as soon as she gets to work. Within an hour, she starts receiving numerous notifications of bugs in the site; bugs in areas she thought she had tested the day before. Mary opens the site in her Web browser and starts to navigate to the sections that contain the reported issues, and sure enough, there are a lot of areas that have mysteriously decided to break. Because the final deadline for this project is fast approaching, Mary feverishly opens the source .fla files and starts to search for the cause of each bug. As she digs through the code in each file, she comes across a couple of possible culprits and makes changes to those lines. After making each change, Mary tests the file and finds that the errors still exist. She goes back to the code and, without undoing her previous changes, she tries other options that only end up creating more bugs in areas she isn't currently testing. By the end of the day not only has Mary not been able to solve the original problem, but more have surfaced in her attempts. It has gotten late and Mary is tired and frustrated so she decides to call it a night and try again tomorrow.

The next morning Mary feels rested and refreshed. As she opens the files to take another run at fixing the bugs, she realizes there is one more thing she didn't think of before. She finds her way to the line of code she presumes is causing a problem and discovers that her new suspicion is correct. She makes the change, publishes the .swf files and tests for the problem, which is now corrected. However, since Mary made so many changes to the code yesterday that she failed to remove, the site is now broken in many other areas and she has to try to remember where each modification is in the site. After hours of work, Mary finally resolves all of the issues that were reported to her by quality control and the site is ready to go live … a day late.

What Happened?

When John made his change before leaving town, he misspelled the name of a variable that was extremely important to the rest of the site. Because he was in a rush to catch his plane, he failed to check his work and ended up creating more issues than previously existed. Since Mary was unaware that John had made the change, she went directly to the code that was actually indirectly affected by the change and accidentally created even more bugs in the site.

How Could It Have Been Avoided?

On top of the lack of communication between the team members (especially on John's part), the entire string of events and resulting errors could have been avoided by simply using version control. When John made his change, he should have included a note with the file he updated on the version control server. That note would have let the team know what change he made and in which file he made that change. Even if Mary didn't see the note to the team, she would have been able to "roll back" her files to the state they were in before she started making her changes that created so many more issues. When she rolled them back, the files would only contain the initial error created by John and she would be able to make that single change to launch the site on time.

Conclusion

As I mentioned at the beginning of this chapter, there will be aspects of your work that will remain constant from project to project and there are considerations to keep in mind as you move between those projects. Once you start to recognize which aspects are reoccurring and to which ones you need to give special attention and thought, you can start fine-tuning your plan each time you start a new piece of work. One benefit to the constants is that because you know that every project is going to go through a quality control process, you'll start catching your bugs before they even happen, which can actually improve your coding skills. Also, as time progresses, you will start to be able to tell if a banner will fit within the file size limitations set by the project specs just by looking at the design layout, which brings us to Chapter 2.

2

DESIGNING BANNER ADS

CHAPTER OUTLINE

While designing for banner ads and designing for microsites can be a very similar process, there are still differences between the two. For example, you have a much larger virtual canvas and file size to work with in microsites, but you are constrained to specific widths, heights, and file sizes in banners. Another difference is that your microsites can (and should, in most cases) be broken up into multiple files, but you are generally only allowed a single file with standard Flash banners and a limited amount of additional external files with rich-media banners.

Because of these differences, I'm going to split the topic of design into different areas of the book. In this chapter, I'll be talking about banners. I'll go into designing for microsites in Chapter 8, aptly titled "Designing Microsites," and I'll touch on a couple of

Flash Advertising. DOI: 10.1016/B978-0-240-81345-5.00002-5

design tips for AIR applications later in Chapter 11. Until then, the sections you'll find here are as follows:

- Conception
- Campaign Goal
- Branding and Selling
- Designing to Move

Conception

Inside Advertising

Every great design that achieves its goal has meaning and planning behind it and that planning is usually done by a planner. Although the job title may differ from workplace to workplace, the job itself is essentially the same: to research products, brands, target audiences, clients, and client competition. The research may consist of many different approaches, such as focus groups or even getting your hands on the actual product to test it out. Once the research is complete, a plan is put in place to create a "map" for the campaign. Included in the map is a creative brief, and that's where the design ideas are generated. The creative brief is basically a rundown of all of the information that pertains to the audience, the look and feel of the brand, and the goal of the campaign.

Before you have a final design for a banner, you should create two or three layouts for the client to choose from. These layouts, also known as *concepts*, can generally be viewed as the different directions in which the final design can go.

Many different techniques can be used to find the best look for a banner, and each designer will have his or her own individual ways of coming up with ideas. With that said, one suggestion to try after reading over the creative brief for the project is to jump right in and start getting creative. Your first impression and your first thoughts about the project at this point are oftentimes going to be very close (if not dead on) to where they need to be for designing your concepts. Try to use your "off the cuff" emotions to drive the initial design, or another way to look at it is to follow your first instincts because they usually work best. Once you get going, you'll hopefully find that your work is feeding your ideas as you go.

Now that I've offered up the thought of basically flying by the seat of your pants in your design, I'm going to attempt to bring you back down to Earth a little because there is some thought that needs to be put in to your designs. While much of that thought can be found in the creative brief, some of it will require a little research and client/brand interaction of your own.

Know Your Client

Knowing your clients on a little bit of a personal level can work wonders in the design of your work, and you should do your best to talk directly with them as much as you can without going overboard. Of course, when you talk to them for the first few times, it will most likely be all business, but you can usually gauge a person's personality somewhat quickly (they might be fun and personable or they might be more serious and "corporate"). Once you both get to a point where you start talking about topics that aren't related to work, you may begin to gain some perspective into their personality and very possibly some of their likes and dislikes. With this information, you can get a better idea of the type of design they might like to see. But don't worry if you aren't a good people reader because the fact that you'll concept more than one design should relieve any pressure that you might feel about missing the "personality target" on the first shot.

Another benefit to knowing your client on a somewhat personal level is trust; the better they know you, the more comfortable they are with you, and the more comfortable they are with you, the more they'll trust you and your decisions. The trust will continue to build the longer you work with them, but in the beginning you're probably going to have to earn it. After all, they are paying you good money to make sure their products and services sell well, right?

It Takes All Types (of Clients)

A great art director I know once told me that you can generally classify clients into three high-level groups and that you should quickly figure out which one a client falls under when talking to them about your work. Those three groups (for which I've made up my own names) are as follows, in no particular order.

The first type of client is the "tech-yes" type. These clients know about technology, they know that online is in the natural progression of advertising, and they embrace it with open arms. When talking to a tech-yes client, you can usually speak in industry and technology terms. If they don't understand what a certain word (or acronym) means, they aren't often shy or embarrassed about asking. However, you may still want to take the terminology down a notch by lightly explaining some of the things you feel people outside of the advertising and technology fields may not fully understand. They may know a thing or two, but you're the expert and there's a reason they hired you instead of doing it by themselves.

The second type of client is the "tech-maybe" type. Like the tech-yes type, the tech-maybes know that online advertising is something they need to do and they are willing to do it. The difference is that they are not quite as sure in their knowledge of the technologies. Their instinct is to give you any information you need or ask for and then trust you to be in charge of their project. Depending on your team, this can be either a very good thing or a very bad thing. For example, if you have developers on your team who are overly enthusiastic and loyal to a particular technology (Flash, HTML5, whatever), those developers may take the project down the wrong path with their blindness to other options. In that case, the project may fail, the campaign may suffer, and the client's trust will be lost. On the other side of that coin, if your team is smart and knows the right tools for the job, then the project, campaign, and client all have a much better chance of success due to well-placed trust in you, your team, and your work. When you're talking to a tech-maybe type, remember to try to keep the industry terminology down a little and explain what you are talking about.

The third type is the "tech-no" type. Tech-nos are your biggest challenge simply because they don't seem interested in the technology realm at all. Either they are intimidated by it or they just don't have the time to learn about it, and they don't seem to care too much for it. A tech-no client will actually create reasons to avoid moving their advertising dollars online and you may hear something along the lines of, "The results of offline advertising are always measured the same way, so I think we'll just stick with that for now." Even though this type of client is a challenge, don't give up on them right away. Remember, there was a time when even you didn't understand advertising or technology.

TIP

Whether you are talking to a tech-savvy client or a client who isn't sure how to attach a file to an e-mail, you should always explain everything and explain it in a step-by-step fashion. Use simple terms that are easy for anyone to understand while being very careful to avoid sounding patronizing. The last thing you want is for your client to feel like you're talking down to them because you feel like you're smarter than they are. Judge their knowledge level of the subject carefully and decide if you should act like you're explaining it to your grandmother or a coworker who is well practiced in technology.

Know the Brand

Knowing your client is not necessarily the same as knowing their brand because, as I mentioned earlier, you'll want to know your client on a bit of a personal level. However, their individual personality may very likely differ from that of the brand itself. Although your client may be a very relaxed, fun-loving, easygoing person who likes participating in activities like skydiving and snowboarding, the brand may be more refined and formal (or vice versa).

Knowing the brand will help you determine how you will design everything from where the logo will be placed to what will happen when users roll their mouse over the banner. If you're dealing with the refined brand, you'll probably want to have a nice, clean design with crisp lines and nice fonts. If you were dealing with an edgy brand, you would want the design to reflect that as well.

Although the ideas for your banner concepts can come from many different places, a good place to start is the site that the banners will drive users to visit. From that destination, you should be able to get plenty of ideas based on the look and feel, the motion, and if at all possible, you may even want to use some of the actual graphic elements from the site itself. The design of the site combined with the brand standards will give you items like colors, fonts, logo treatments, and so on. And while you need to stay within the confines of the brand standards, you may want to push the limits when you can. Obviously, some of your clients' brand standards will be stricter than others and that could, in turn, affect just how far you can push the limits. However, some brand standards are very loose and forgiving. Pushing the limits on these relaxed standards could lead to more projects (such as microsites), and who knows, you may even influence your client to come up with a new look and feel for their entire brand.

Know the Audience

Much like your clients, there are different types of people at whom you will target your design. These groups of people are called your target audience and they will be another determining factor in the look and feel of your design. The specifics of the target audience, such as age, income, influence, and other demographics, will most likely be found within the creative brief put together by the planner. Using those specifics, you can decide the direction your design will take. For an audience that is regarded as the elite, rich, upper-class decision makers, you might have a very clean, slick, simple design that gets straight to the point of the message. However, you may want to design something more edgy if you will be going after a younger audience that may be more into things like gaming, "extreme" sports, and screaming guitars.

Know the Placements

Hand in hand with knowing your audience is to know where your ads will be running. There's a lot to be said for knowing your surroundings and coming up with designs for banner ads is no exception to that. If you are aware of how many sites (and precisely which sites) your ads will be shown on, you can take some time to surf around to them for a little inspiration. This is not to say that you should go to those sites and copy their designs into your banners, but that you should look them over to better decide how you can make your ad stand out without doing so in an obnoxious way.

The number of placements in which your ad will be seen can greatly affect this approach. If there are a large number of sites that will be running the ad, it may be harder to find a design that fits within all of them at the same time. However, you may be dealing with a small or very specifically targeted account that only has the banners running on a single site. Either way, you want your ad to be seen and knowing the look and feel of the surrounding area can help make that happen. Before leaving this section, I would like to reiterate one important note: Avoid making your banners stand out in the wrong way on a site. The last thing you want to do is to annoy and distract people from the content they are actually there to read or view. The real goal should be to gently attract their eye to your design and make them want to interact with your client's brand. After all, they are your client's potential customers and you want them to have a good experience.

Campaign Goal

The goal of the campaign will be another on the list of items that will dictate how a banner should look and feel. You may have a different design for a banner that is being created to sell a service against one being created to sell a tangible product. You may have another completely separate design for a banner with the purpose of raising brand awareness against a banner being created solely to drive traffic to your client's microsite.

TIP

It's important to step back during each step of a project and try to view what you're working on from a user's point of view. Try to imagine how a person is going to experience the work the very first time they see it. Try to determine if they will be compelled to take the actions you are trying to get them to take and if the paths to those actions are immediately apparent. Remember that a user won't have the benefit of a creative brief or meetings about the project to fully understand the work in question. The work has to do that on its own.

The overall goal of a campaign will typically fall into one of two areas: brand awareness or direct marketing. The purpose of brand awareness is exactly what you would think it is: to raise awareness of the brand itself. You aren't necessarily advertising a particular product or service, but you are trying to drive customers to at least consider the brand more closely the next time they see it in the store. On the other side of that coin is direct marketing. When you use direct marketing, you want them to actually purchase the service or product that is being advertised in that ad.

Branding and Selling

As I said previously, your banners will generally be designed to accomplish one of two main goals: selling goods or raising awareness of the brand. That said, a banner whose purpose is to sell will still have branding in it, but a banner built for brand awareness will not necessarily contain any form of sales messaging. To explain exactly what I mean by that, let's look just a little deeper at each of these goals.

▌ALERT!

Because branding is such an extremely large subject that requires much more in-depth explanation than I could fit into this book, I have only given a very high overview on the subject.

Brand It

Raising the public's awareness to your client's brand makes them feel comfortable with it. It gives them something to identify with and at the same time it says, "Hey, I'm here. Remember me. Remember me when you see these images. Remember me when you see these fonts and these colors. Remember me when you think about _____." In addition to asking people to remember the brand, raising awareness also means that you're trying to evoke or solidify an emotion or feeling within them. As I mentioned before, that feeling may be comfort. However, the emotion/feeling that you actually want to call upon could also be something much different like excitement or curiosity. The simplest explanation of branding is that it consists of beautiful imagery, your client's logo, and some short but sweet message that appeals to the targeted emotions (possibly your client's tagline).

Designing for brand awareness can take on different levels of difficulty depending on the consumers' current view of the brand itself. If the public already has good thoughts and feelings about the brand, then the efforts that are currently in place are doing their job, and you'll simply need to stay within those design standards. However, a client may have sought you out to change the public's thoughts of their brand. Although there may be questions as to what caused the brand to develop an undesired image, the design process for a new brand direction can be a fun and challenging one. When a brand needs a new image, it needs to shine. This means that the brand design standards are usually very loose or even completely out of the window in favor of the new direction.

For both of these scenarios, there can be challenges. In the case of continuing successful brand awareness, it can be a challenge for some to stick within the strict (but again, successful) design standards. And when it comes to changing the public's view on a brand, some may find it difficult to have such an open design field to play in.

Sell It

Selling your client's product through online banner ads requires a different approach than raising brand awareness. For starters, your viewers are (hopefully) already familiar and comfortable with the brand. This works in your favor because they may only catch a glimpse of your ad from the corner of their eye as they are reading an article. Because the brand awareness campaigns for this particular client were successful, the viewer remembers the brand and takes a look at the banner. With this banner having the purpose of selling, users will no doubt see different elements and one of them is the message. The banner itself will be more offer-oriented, and the message within will get directly to the point it's trying to get across: "Buy this product!" or "Look at this incredible price! Now buy this product!"

Something to remember is that while sales-driven banners are definitely harder hitting with less fluff, they should still borrow some techniques from branding ads. Although they are highlighting an offer or a price on the surface, they should still have an underlying feeling of comfort and emotion that has come to be associated with the brand.

Designing to Move

Standard Flash banners are usually constrained to an animation time of 30–40 seconds. Rich-media banners, however, are most often only limited on animation time up until a user interacts with them. Either way, animation is one of the key benefits to using Flash for online advertising and the design of that animation is just as important as the design of the ad itself. The wrong movement can make an otherwise beautiful banner look amateurish and unplanned while the right movement can actually improve upon the look and feel. Even the most beautiful car in the world turns a little less appealing to some people if it doesn't run well.

Visualize While You Work

A good practice to get into is to go ahead and try to visualize your animations while you're creating your design. If you come across an asset that you feel would make a good moving part of the design, you should also take care to consider if it will be possible to make that piece move in the way it should. The only time you want something to look like it has unnatural, clunky movement is when the design actually calls for unnatural, clunky movement. In most designs, however, you'll want to try to create smooth, organic-style movement to keep the work from looking like it's trying too hard (and just to make it look good, in general).

Some things to keep an eye out for when you're planning animation in advance are moving parts, visual angles of photographs, transparent areas, backgrounds, and several other similar properties of the piece in question. When you're dealing with moving parts of a larger object, are those parts cut in such a way that they can each be animated as needed? In other words, can the object bend at its joints and rotate its gears? If there's a background, do you already have the image cut away from it and do you already have the background filled back in? It can get quite frustrating for a Flash developer to get a request to make a car drive across a background image, when the car is actually a part of that background image.

Animation Assets

You can plan an animation all day and night, but when it comes down to it, you can't actually create that animation if you don't have the proper assets. For example, you're working on a banner for your client and they want you to build an interactive 360° view of their product. However, you only have two images of the product: one from the front and one from the side. It goes without saying that you can't build much of a 360° view with only those images so you're left with some options. You can go back to your client and ask for the extra images of the product (which they may or may not have available), you can inform your client that extra money will need to be spent to do a photo shoot of the product, or you can spend your personal time doing your own photo shoot. There are other options as well, but you get the point here.

Turn Over a Little Control

If you're the person who designed the banner, there comes a time when it's good to let someone else take a little control and animations may be one of those times. Bringing an idea of movement to a Flash developer in the form of words (or even storyboards) may not always get the message across in exactly the way you wanted it to. Most times, when you explain something to someone (anyone, not just Flash developers), they are going to visualize it differently than you do. Because that's the case, the end result of the animation will most likely differ from what you originally intended. Step back, let go of your thoughts for a minute, and take a look at what the Flash developer has created. Although there is a chance that you could shoot down this new idea, there's also the chance that you may like it better than your own.

Another approach on this topic is to sit with the Flash developer while you both work together to get the major mechanics ironed out. For example, you know that you want object A to move from point B to point C. What you don't know quite yet is the detail of its trip between the two points. Did it bounce to get there? Did it ease into or out of the animation? Did it bounce after it got to its final destination? As the designer, try not to let those details bother you right now and let the Flash developer take care of those questions. There are a couple of advantages to taking this approach with your designs. First, the Flash developer can actually sit there trying different animations from directly within the Flash authoring environment. Once he or she finds the one that suits best, you can both decide together if it's the right animation for the project. The other advantage to this is pride of ownership. Turning over this control to the Flash developer will make the Flash developer feel more inspired to do a better job on the project due to the fact that he will feel more like the project is his instead of feeling like he's just another part of an assembly line.

Know the Strengths and Limitations

Because the design of each round of banners will differ, they will each have different strengths and limitations when it comes time to animate or program, and you'll need to be able to recognize them ahead of time in the design process. For example, moving objects over a large area at a very slow rate of speed can end up looking choppy if it's not done correctly. Another example, which I'll talk about in Chapter 5, is the format chosen for images used within a banner. Sometimes moving an object across the stage will require it to have a transparent area. This can be both a strength and a limitation at the same time: a strength because of the ability to support the transparent area of the image, but a limitation because of the extra amount of file size that can be taken by that image (as opposed to an image without transparency). Knowing the strengths and limitations of Flash is something that comes with time. After some experimenting, some trial and error, and needing to rework a few projects, more and more of these strengths and limitations will become apparent.

Just as it's important for designers to know the strengths and limitations of the developers and their tools, it's also important for the developers to know the same about the designers and their tools. With that being the case, I would like to make a suggestion that the two disciplines meet on a regular basis to discuss those things. You can call it whatever you like, but I call it a capabilities meeting and I believe it's good to hold them at least once a month if not every 2 weeks. Developers can use this time to showcase new features of Flash or new "tricks" they've learned since the last meeting. Another thing that may take place in these meetings might be for the designers to show other inspirational Flash sites that contain certain elements the designer particularly likes or has questions about. For example, a designer might show a site and ask if the developers on the team have the skill set to do something similar to feature X. Each time the designers and developers walk out of these meetings, both disciplines have a better understanding of the capabilities of each other … which is why I like to call them capabilities meetings.

Back to Step One

Don't forget, just because you completed that first concept, you aren't actually finished yet. As I stated earlier in this chapter, you'll need more choices to offer to the client. In addition to giving the client more options, you can also take this opportunity to do a little mix-and-match exercise. After you've come up with your two or three concepts, take a look back over each of them together and see if you can find pieces to pull out of one design to put into another. You may be able to find ways to enhance your designs and you may even find enough from each concept to develop a fourth piece that could possibly end up outshining all of the others!

Conclusion

Designing banners isn't as straightforward and simple as some might think. The amount of thinking and planning that goes on before, and behind the scenes of, the actual artwork can get very extensive in some cases. Knowing your client's brand and knowing your client's business is a must when you're designing their banners, but knowing your client at a somewhat personal level can give you an inside track on their likes and dislikes. On top of knowing your client, you should also know who your audiences are and the sites on which they'll be viewing your work.

The goal of the campaign will also be a determining factor in your designs. If you're working on a brand awareness campaign, you're going to treat it differently than you will a sales/marketing campaign. With a brand awareness campaign, you'll generally want to make users feel good about the brand and remember it the next time they see it. With a sales campaign, your overall goal is to drive users to buy a product by highlighting its price and value. At the same time you're asking them to buy, you'll also want to inject a little brand awareness into the design; something that says, "Buy me now, remember me later."

An important factor to think about in designing banners is how they will animate and how they will make transitions from one frame or section to the next. It's a good idea to think about these movements beforehand because once in development, it can sometimes be difficult to retrofit an animation of a particular object. In addition to thinking ahead, you'll also want to make sure that the assets you're working with can actually animate in the fashion you have pictured in your mind. In Chapter 3, I'll start getting into the steps involved in bringing your designs to life, from planning out how it will be built to using code as a time saver to sending your work through quality control.

3

PREPARING AND BUILDING ADS

So it's time to start building a round of ads, huh? That's good because that's just what we'll be discussing in this chapter. But you shouldn't just jump right in to animating and coding because you have to make sure that you have everything prepared and that you have all the information you need. You'll need to know who is involved with the project and what role they each take, so you'll know who to turn to for any particular question or needs. Speaking of questions, think of as many as you can up front. For example, have you thought ahead to how your ad will work? Is there artwork created for default images in case a user doesn't have Flash

Flash Advertising. DOI: 10.1016/B978-0-240-81345-5.00003-7

(or JavaScript) enabled? Do you have any class files already written that may work with this project? There are more questions to come, so let's get to it by looking at the following topics:

- Planning
- Setting Up Your File(s)
- Cutting Art
- clickTags and Links
- Creating Time with Code
- Conventions and Best Practices
- The Bandwidth Profiler
- HTML and JavaScript
- Default Images
- Quality Control

Planning

Before you start to build your ad, you'll need to do some planning. How will your images be cut? Will your animations be tweened on the timeline, will they be scripted, or will you use a combination of both? How many landing page URLs will you link to? Which areas will users click to get to those landing pages? These and several other questions will need to be answered during the life of the project, so you should try to answer as many of them as you can ahead of time, and you might even consider making a checklist that you can refer back to on each project.

If you are working with an art department, you will need to keep in very close communication with the designer who laid out your ad. He or she will most likely have a vision of the animation in his or her head, and you want the end product to match that vision as closely as possible. Since most of us can't actually read minds, you should get printouts (or Photoshop layer comps) of the main frames of the ad and have the designer sit with you to explain how he or she imagines the art coming to life. Once you have the designer's description, you will have a better idea as to the important pieces of the puzzle. Pieces like how your images need to be cut, which parts of the animation can be scripted, and at what speed they need to animate.

In addition to all the information that pertains to the creative aspect of your ad, you will want to know the details of the more technical side. For example, if there is a form in your ad that submits to a client's processing page, do you have all the correct variable names and possible values the processing page will be expecting? Also, for any ActionScript you may use, don't forget to check to see if you have snippets or classes you can pull from existing libraries that would meet this project's needs.

Specs

Another side to consider when planning is the specs that you are given by the hosting site or third-party ad-serving company. These specs will include the items that were covered back in Chapter 1, such as stage dimensions, maximum file sizes, amount of time and/or loops the animation can play, the highest version of the Flash Player you can target, and sometimes the highest frame rate that will be accepted. It is very hard to say which aspect of the ad is most important, and you would probably get a different answer from each person you asked. However, if you fail to stay within all the specs, your ad will most likely get kicked back to you from the sites, and they probably won't run it until it is revised.

A good tool to help plan time spent on your project is a lowest common denominator (LCD) sheet. An LCD sheet is exactly what it sounds like – a sheet listing the lowest specs accepted on each banner size by all sites. Let me explain a little further. You have a 300 × 250 banner that is going to run on five different sites. Of those five sites, two will accept a maximum file size of 40k, one will accept a file size of 35k, and the last two will only accept up to 30k. You obviously wouldn't want to create the same banner five times (once for each site), so the next thought might be to create one banner for each maximum file size giving you a smaller total of three banners. Well, as we all know, time is money, and you should strive to spend the time you need to create the banner one time and one time only. Since the 30k version fits within the specs of all sites involved, that's the file size you'll want to keep your 300 × 250 banner below.

Setting Up Your File(s)

Okay, so you've received the layouts from the art department, you've been given direction on the animation and interactivity, and you have your plan of attack ready to execute. Let's get started on the fun stuff by getting a file set up. You can use one of the advertising templates we discussed in Chapter 1, or you can set up your own. For this exercise, let's go ahead and set up our own 300 × 250 banner.

1. Create a folder to hold your Flash files. Let's name this folder "myAd."
2. Create a subfolder within the "myAd" folder and name it "cut_art" (this folder will hold all the images used in your ad).
3. Create a new Flash Document from the File menu or the Flash Welcome Screen (Fig. 3.1).

Figure 3.1 The Flash Welcome Screen.

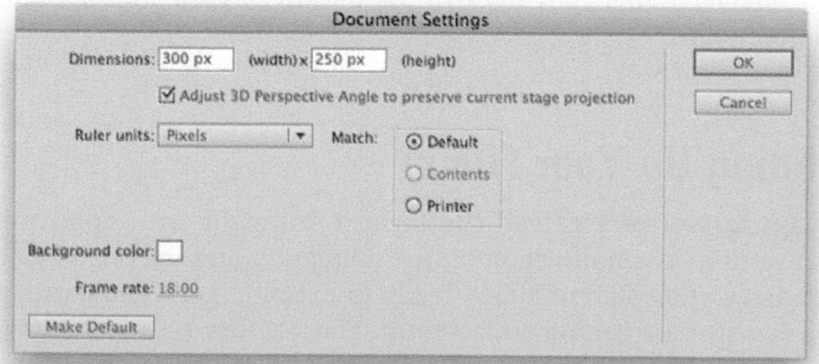

Figure 3.2 The Document Settings window.

4. Open the Document Settings window (Fig. 3.2) by clicking on the Edit button in the Properties section of the Properties window for the document.
5. Set the width to 300 pixels and the height to 250 pixels. While we're in here, let's go ahead and set the frame rate to

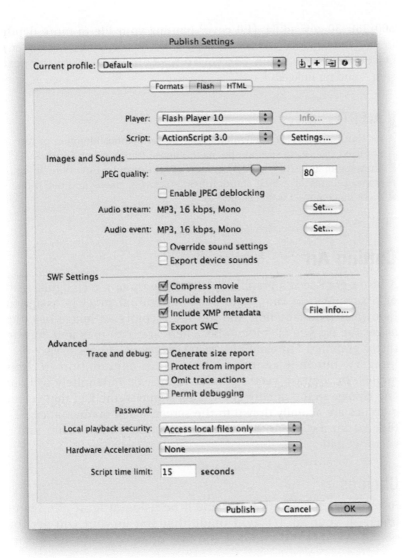

Figure 3.3 The Publish Settings window.

18 frames per second as well (IAB standard). After you've done that, click OK.

6. Open the Publish Settings window (Fig. 3.3) by clicking the Edit button next to "Profile:" in the Publish section of the Properties window.

7. Set the version according to the specs you received from the site.

8. Click OK and save your new file to the "myAd" folder.

When you save your file, you'll want to be descriptive in your naming convention. For this banner, we'll use a name such as

300x250_30_my_ad.fla. (I'll cover naming your file in more depth in the "Conventions and Best Practices" section later in this chapter.) Once you've saved your file, you're ready to move on to the next step – cutting images.

ALERT!

Version control is extremely important, but sometimes forgotten or just not used. There are several options to choose from such as SourceSafe, Subversion, and Git. I highly recommend you spend a little time doing some research on which solution best suits your needs and use it on every single project without fail.

Cutting Art

A raster graphic is a graphic that is made up of a rectangular grid of pixels. Within that grid, each individual pixel is assigned its own individual color, and the more colors an image has, the larger the file size is going to be. There are both pros and cons to raster graphics. For example, raster graphics can show very nice imagery, but they cannot scale without degradation in their quality. In contrast, vector graphics can scale indefinitely without any change in the quality at all. This is due to the fact that vector graphics are actually drawn to the screen using mathematics. See Fig. 3.4 for a comparison of zooming in on both a raster and a vector graphic.

Choices

In 9.827527 times out of 10, you'll be using at least one raster image in your ad. (Okay, I made that stat up, but you get the point.) Whether it's a photograph of a product, scene, or person,

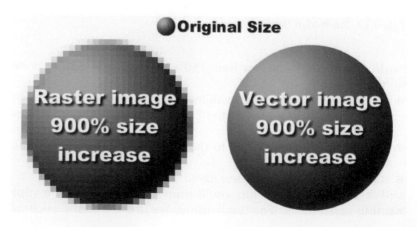

Figure 3.4 Zooming in on raster and vector graphics.

you'll need to figure out the best way to cut those images out of the Photoshop file and get them into your Flash ad. Most of the time, the choice of image format is extremely obvious. A few general rules of thumb that I like to follow are (1) if you will need to use transparency in the image, save it out as png-24; (2) if it's a photographic-type image and you do not need transparency, the best option is most likely .jpg; and (3) if it's a drawing or line art of any kind, try using vector art first, and if you can't, go with the .gif format. Whichever format you use, take care not to overcompress when exporting from Photoshop. Save the images at a high enough quality that they are very clear and you don't see any pixilation or fuzziness, and let Flash do some of the compression when it has its turn with the images. Now, for just a moment, let's step back a few sentences to my rules of thumb on .pngs and .jpgs. In the past, best practices for Flash have indicated that the best bitmap format to import into Flash is .png. However, while .pngs are very crisp and clear images, the file size for a .png image is typically larger than a .jpg, and one of your major goals is to fit your banner within a certain file size. Again, I'll cover more on image compression later in Chapter 5.

Cut Away

On to the actual cutting of the images. Since you spent a little time planning out your ad, you should be well aware of which elements from your Photoshop file will be static, which ones will be animated, and which ones will be interactive. When cutting out the images that will animate, you want to crop the Photoshop file down to the size of the object you need, hide all the layers you don't need, and export the image to the appropriate format. As you set the size to which you are going to crop, keep in mind that you should not cut exactly at the edge of the object you are cutting out. If at all possible, you should give yourself (and the Flash Player) a bit of room all the way around the image. I usually give about a three-pixel buffer, and that works out pretty well. The reason I allow this extra space is because of an old bug in the Flash Player that would sometimes cut off the edge of an image or shift the image data over by a few pixels. To the best of my knowledge, Adobe has fixed that issue, but I prefer to err on the side of caution in cases like this.

As for the static elements, try to include as many of them as you can in one image that can be used as the background of your banner. A lot of times you can treat interactive elements the same as static elements and include them in your background image as well. For example, if you have a logo that will remain in the top-left corner of the ad and that will link out to the client's home page, why make it its own image? Unless there is another element that needs to animate behind that logo, include it as part of the static background image and place an invisible button on top of it. Just in case you aren't sure what I mean by "invisible button," simply follow these steps to create one:

1. Draw a shape on the stage by using one of the shape drawing tools (Fig. 3.5).
2. Once the shape is drawn, select it and choose Modify > Convert to Symbol (or press F8) to convert it to a Button symbol.
3. Give the Button symbol a name, and press OK in the Convert to Symbol dialog box (Fig. 3.6).
4. After you've created the button, double-click it to edit it.
5. Move the shape from the "Up" frame to the "Hit" frame (Fig. 3.7).
6. Go back to the main timeline of your movie, and there you have your invisible button.

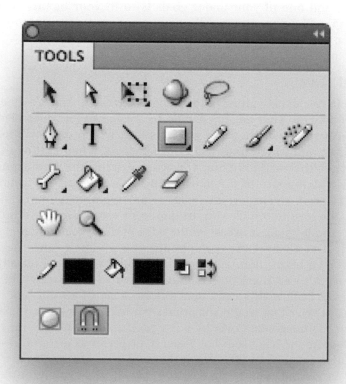

Figure 3.5 The Tools panel with the drawing tools.

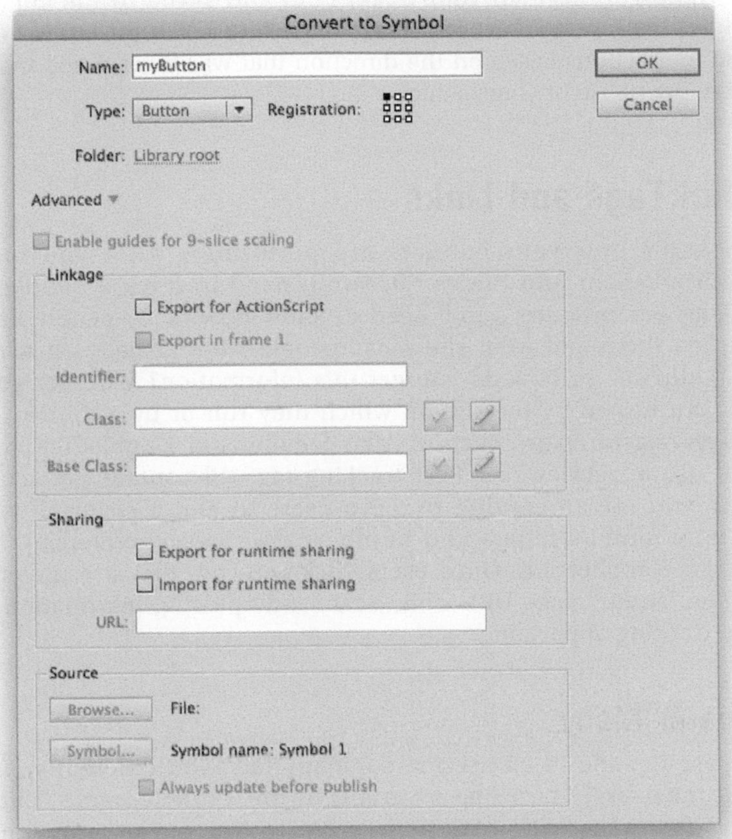

Figure 3.6 Convert to Symbol dialog box.

Figure 3.7 Move the shape to the "Hit" frame.

Once you have all your images cut and saved to the cut_art folder, it's time to start importing them into Flash for animations and interactions based on the direction that was determined in the planning phase of your banner.

clickTags and Links

To know how your banners are performing after you have released them into the world, you'll need to track a couple of things. For instance, you'll need to know how many people have clicked them and what site those people were actually on when they did so. So how do you get this information? Whether your ads are hosted by the site on which they run or by a third-party ad-serving company, such as Atlas Solutions or DoubleClick, you will use a tracking tag. That tracking tag will contain the actual URL you are attempting to drive users to and a string of seemingly random letters and numbers that are generated by the tracking application. Once users click your ad, they are directed to the landing page URL while seamlessly passing information to the tracking application.

One or Many

Unless the site or ad-serving company tells you differently, you will most likely be using a variant of the variable name "clickTag" (ClickTag, clickTAG, and so on) to link out of your units. Check with your site or ad server on the actual name you should use if you will be linking to a single landing page URL as some will ask that you add the number "1" to the end. For example, ad-serving company A might ask you to use "clickTag1," whereas ad-serving company B might ask you to use "clickTag" (without the "1"). When linking out to multiple URLs, most ad servers handle it the same way: clickTag1, clickTag2, clickTag3, and so on.

Prior to ActionScript 3, you didn't really need to worry about case sensitivity for the actual name of the clickTag variable. However, that has changed now, and since the ad-serving companies haven't agreed on a standard yet, some of them will use clickTag, whereas others use clickTAG or ClickTag or even ClickTAG. This can pose a serious problem when you are creating your ads because if you test with "clickTag" and then launch only to find out that the ad-serving company is using "clickTAG," those ads aren't going to work, and they will most definitely be removed from the sites on which they were running. So how do we handle this? Do we have to keep track of which variant of clickTag each ad-serving company is using? I suppose you could do that, but it's just another thing to keep track of, and what if they change it for some reason?

While I'm sure that there are plenty of solutions out there to work around this case-sensitive issue, I went ahead and created a class called ClickTagger to add to that list. You can download ClickTagger on the Web site for this book, and you can also find the code and a detailed breakdown in Chapter 12. For now though, a general description is that upon instantiation, it pulls in all your clickTags, converts their names to lowercase lettering, and arranges them in the correct order (clickTag1, clickTag2, and so on) for your use. After you've created a new instance of ClickTagger, you can assign a value to the `targetWindow` property, so the clickTags will launch in the correct window (_blank, _top, and so on). The `targetWindow` property has a default value of "_blank," the most commonly used target for ads. The last thing to do with ClickTagger is to use the `assignClickTag` method to assign listeners to your clickable objects. This method has three parameters: `element`, `failSafeUrl`, and `tagNumber`. While `tagNumber` is optional and has a default value of 1 (used if you only have one clickTag), `element` and `failSafeUrl` are required as the object to apply the listener to and the URL to use in the event that the click-Tag didn't load for some reason. In addition, the `failSafeUrl` not only makes it possible to do local testing from the Flash IDE where there isn't any HTML or JavaScript passing your clickTags in, but also works well as a safety net in case your clickTags don't load correctly after your banners are launched. The click may not get tracked, but at least the user will make it to the intended landing page, and after all, that is the purpose of the banner. So with all that said, let's assume that you have a banner that has two clickable elements called button1 and button2. Likewise, you have 2 clickTags being passed in from the ad server. Example 3.1 shows all the code needed in your .fla to make both buttons click out to their respective target URLs regardless of the variant of clickTag that was used. You'll also notice the two fallback URLs (`fallBack1` and `fallBack2`) being passed in to their respective places as well.

EXAMPLE 3.1

Using the ClickTagger tag to solve for clickTag case sensitivity

```
import com.flashadbook.utils.ClickTagger;
var fallBack1:String = "http://www.flashadbook.com";
var fallBack2:String = "http://www.jasonfincanon.com";
var clickTagger:ClickTagger = new
ClickTagger(stage.loaderInfo);
clickTagger.assignClickTag(button1,fallBack1,1);
clickTagger.assignClickTag(button2,fallBack2,2);
```

> **TIP**
>
> The majority of sites and ad-serving companies will ask that you use "_blank" as the target window. There are a few, however, that require you to target "_self," while still others require a target of "_top." It is best to check with your site or ad server for individual specifications.

The Value of a clickTag

Now that we have discussed linking out to a target URL via a clickTag, let's discuss how to get a value assigned to it. In most cases of running your units with an ad-serving company, you won't need to worry too much about getting the value of your clickTag inside the unit itself. This is because most of the ad-serving companies have their own HTML templates that are already set up to pass the value in. However, you will still need to test your banner before it goes live. While there are many ways to pass a variable value into Flash, I'll just show a quick one here that uses SWFObject to assign the value of two clickTags and then pass them in to your .swf as a part of the `flashvars` object. Keep in mind that I've left out a good amount of the code in Example 3.2, so we could put more focus on the clickTags. Note the different variants of clickTag. We will discuss more on SWFObject in the "HTML and JavaScript" section.

EXAMPLE 3.2

Assigning clickTag values with SWFObject

```
<script type="text/javascript">
    var flashvars =
{clickTag1:"http://www.flashadbook.com",clickTAG2:"http://
www.jasonfincanon.com"};
    swfobject.embedSWF("300x350_30_my_ad.swf",
"banner", "300", "250", "10.0.0",
"expressInstall.swf",flashvars);
    </script>
```

Creating Time with Code

As you spend more and more time building ad units, you will begin to find commonalities between them. Some of these will pertain to different ads for a single client, while others will spread across clients. When you start to notice these reusable pieces of code and assets, set them aside, so you can pull from them when you need them in another project. After all, that wheel has already been invented, right? For example, a large amount of your banners will have a single landing page and therefore will contain a single clickTag. In the typical case of having the entire banner clickable, why not utilize the graphics property of a Sprite to create an invisible button that covers the stage as in Example 3.3. Note that I also included the ClickTagger class we discussed earlier and that this is an example of timeline code.

EXAMPLE 3.3

Creating an invisible button

```
import flash.display.Sprite;
import com.flashadbook.utils.ClickTagger;

var fallBackUrl:String = "http://www.flashadbook.com";
var clickTagger:ClickTagger = new
ClickTagger(stage.loaderInfo);
var myBtn:Sprite = new Sprite();
var lineThickness:int = 1;

myBtn.graphics.lineStyle(lineThickness, 0x000000);
myBtn.graphics.beginFill(0x000000, 0);
myBtn.graphics.drawRect(0, 0, stage.stageWidth-
lineThickness, stage.stageHeight-lineThickness);
clickTagger.assignClickTag(myBtn,fallBackUrl,1);
addChild(myBtn);
```

In Example 3.3, the first few things we do are to create a new instance of ClickTagger, a Sprite named `myBtn`, and an int called `lineThickness`. Next, we use the graphics property of the Sprite to draw a rectangle that has a black outline and a transparent fill. This is done with `lineStyle`, `beginFill`, and `drawRect`. When we use the `drawRect` method here, the first two parameters represent the x and y coordinates of the upper-left corner of our button, whereas the second two parameters represent their width and height. The reason for subtracting `lineThickness` from the `stageWidth` and `stageHeight` is because the button will actually be drawn exactly to the edge of the stage and that ends up putting the right and bottom of the border outside of the visible area. So that's it. There's not a lot to it, and you can easily move this chunk of code from banner to banner. You could carry this a little further and create a BorderButton class as in Example 3.4.

EXAMPLE 3.4

The BorderButton class

```
package com.flashadbook.display {
    import flash.display.DisplayObjectContainer;
    import flash.display.Sprite;
    import flash.events.MouseEvent;
    import flash.net.URLRequest;
    import flash.net.navigateToURL;
    import flash.external.ExternalInterface;
    import flash.system.Capabilities;
```

```actionscript
public final class BorderButton extends Sprite{
    private var _bbParent:DisplayObjectContainer;
//the parent of the BorderButton
    private var _halfThick:Number; //half the
thickness of the border line
    private var _w:Number; //the width to draw the
BorderButton
    private var _h:Number; //the height to draw
the BorderButton
    private var _targetWindow:String; //the window
in which the targetURL will open
    private var _destination:String; //the target
url
    private var _playerType:String =
Capabilities.playerType.toLowerCase(); //check for local
testing
    private var _extInterfaceAvailable:Boolean =
false; //true if in browser AND ExternalInterface.available
    public function BorderButton(){
        super();
    }
    public function
draw(parent:DisplayObjectContainer, outline:Boolean =
false, lineColor:uint = 0x000000, lineThickness:int =
1):void {
        _bbParent = parent;
        _bbParent.addChild(this);
        _halfThick = lineThickness / 2;
        _w = _bbParent.stage.stageWidth -
_halfThick;
        _h = _bbParent.stage.stageHeight -
_halfThick;
        graphics.lineStyle(lineThickness,
lineColor);
        graphics.beginFill(0, 0);
        graphics.drawRect(0, 0, _w, _h);
    }
    public function activate(targetUrl:String,
targetWindow:String = "_blank"):void {
        buttonMode = true;
        _destination = targetUrl;
        _targetWindow = targetWindow;
        if(!hasEventListener(MouseEvent.CLICK)){
            addEventListener(MouseEvent.CLICK,
clickOut, false, 0, true);
        }
    }
    public function erase():void{
        if(_bbParent != null){
            deactivate();
```

```
                    _bbParent.removeChild(this);
            }
        }

        public function deactivate():void{
            if(hasEventListener(MouseEvent.CLICK)){
                buttonMode = false;
removeEventListener(MouseEvent.CLICK,clickOut);
            }
        }
        private function clickOut(e:MouseEvent):void {
            if(_playerType=="activex" ||
_playerType=="plugin"){
                _extInterfaceAvailable =
ExternalInterface.available;
            }
            if (_extInterfaceAvailable) {
ExternalInterface.call('window.open',_destination,_target
Window);
            }else{
                navigateToURL(new
URLRequest(_destination),_targetWindow);
            }
        }
    }
}
```

This BorderButton class is covered in detail in Chapter 12, but I thought it was worth a quick look here as well. Table 3.1 outlines the BorderButton's draw method parameters.

Table 3.1 BorderButton Draw Method Parameters

Variable	Purpose
_bbParent (DisplayObjectContainer)	The parent object of the BorderButton
_halfThick (Number)	Half the thickness of the border line
_w (Number)	Width to draw the BorderButton
_h (Number)	Height to draw the BorderButton
_targetWindow (String)	Window where targeted URL will open
_destination (String)	The target URL
_playerType (String)	The type of Flash Player currently being used (plugIn, external, and so on)
_extInterfaceAvailable (Boolean)	Set to true if content is being played in the browser AND ExternalInterface is available; default is false

Now let's take a very high-level look at what's actually happening inside the class. Once an instance of BorderButton is created, you'll call the `draw` method that uses its parameters to draw the button. The next thing you'll want to do is call the `activate` method and pass in the target URL to make the instance of BorderButton clickable. Other methods in the BorderButton class include `erase` and `deactivate`, which do exactly what their names imply: remove the instance and make it nonclickable. One implementation of BorderButton might be as seen in Example 3.5. You could alternatively use BorderButton in conjunction with the ClickTagger class as in Example 3.6.

EXAMPLE 3.5

Using the ButtonBorder class alone

```
import com.flashadbook.display.BorderButton;
var borderButton:BorderButton = new BorderButton();
var targetUrl:String = "http://www.flashadbook.com";
borderButton.draw(this);
borderButton.activate(targetUrl);
```

EXAMPLE 3.6

Using the ButtonBorder class in conjunction with the ClickTagger class

```
import com.flashadbook.utils.ClickTagger;
import com.flashadbook.display.BorderButton;
var fallBackUrl:String = "http://www.flashadbook.com";
var clickTagger:ClickTagger = new
ClickTagger(stage.loaderInfo);
var borderButton:BorderButton = new BorderButton();
borderButton.draw(this);
clickTagger.assignClickTag(borderButton,fallBackUrl,1);
```

Forms

Another good example of a reusable asset is a form. Forms will be covered in more depth in Chapter 4, but for now, let's assume that we've already created one, and let's simply call it "Our Form." Our Form was created to be used from within a banner that we've built for client X, and its purpose is to search client X's inventory for a user's desired product. Once we have Our Form built and functioning properly, we should set it aside in its own .fla so that each time we need to use it in another banner we can just grab it, place it in a new banner, and resize it or move elements around as needed.

TIP

In addition to reusable code, you should also keep an eye out for reusable graphics such as logos, products, and backgrounds.

Conventions and Best Practices

I think it's pretty obvious that the more everyone on a team is on the same page thinking as much like one another as they possibly can when it comes to writing their code, the more time they can save when they have to work together on individual projects. I also feel that standardizing that team's code design, naming conventions, folder structures, and so on is a huge step in the right direction of getting everyone on that same page. At some point, you will be sick or on vacation and a coworker will need to open your files to make some changes. Or maybe, the coworkers are out and you're the one who has to make the changes to their files. Wouldn't it be nice to open their code and, within a matter of seconds, know exactly what they were thinking as they wrote each line?

At the time of writing this, there's a page on the Adobe Open Source site titled "Flex SDK coding conventions and best practices." The very first thing on that page is a note letting you know that the page is a work in progress but that there is plenty of information there to get you started (which there most certainly is). Even if you're working in Flash and not with the Flex SDK, these conventions and best practices are still very much worth following since it's all ActionScript and it's all in the Flash Platform. Think about writing an ActionScript class. Now think about that class being used in both a Flash project and a Flex project. Wouldn't it be great for all the conventions to carry over between the two? (The correct answer here is, "Why yes, Jason. That would be great!")

With the topic of conventions and best practices being somewhat large in its details, I'm going to highly suggest that you go to the Adobe Open Source site and take an in-depth look at them there. However, there are a few I would like to cover here before we move on.

Naming Objects

When naming your objects, you want to be descriptive, so you will know exactly which item your ActionScript is communicating with and what kind of object it actually is. Obviously, you can name them however you and your team like, but Table 3.2 shows a few example names following the convention of using the object's type as the last part of the name.

Along with standardizing the names of your objects, you should also try to come up with a standard structure of folders for your library. My personal favorite library setup uses folders named by type, where the "MovieClips" folder contains MovieClips, the "bitmaps" folder contains imported images, the "graphics" folder contains graphic symbols, the "sounds" folder contains audio files,

Table 3.2 Naming Convention Examples

MovieClip containing a form	formMovieClip
TextInput for user's e-mail address	emailTextInput
Button to submit a form	submitButton
Sound object for background music	musicSound

and so on. You get the gist of it. Again, all these names are just suggestions, and if you haven't already, try to set up a time to talk about these conventions with your coworkers to make sure you are all on the same page.

Naming Banners

Another thing that should be consistent throughout your projects is the naming of your banners. Your banner names should be descriptive and easy to understand at a glance because you may need to revisit one of them later. An example of this would be if a particular ad performed very well and your client wanted to use the same creative, but to change the message within it. There are many naming conventions you could choose to go with, but I would like to recommend one here. If you refer back to the section "Setting Up Your File(s)," you'll notice we named that file 300x250_30_my_ad.fla. This is a pretty self-explanatory name because it contains all the information you need, and each part of that information is separated by an underscore. The first part of the name is obviously the size of the banner (300 × 250). After that is the maximum file size, in kilobytes, allowed for this particular ad (30). Next in line, we used the word "my"; this is where you would place either an abbreviation or the full name of the client for which the banner is being built. Finally, at the end of the file name, you'll want to use another abbreviation to describe the creative being used. For example, if the creative is that of water being poured into a glass, use the word "pour." Another good standard to practice is limiting your file names to a certain number of characters (including the file extension); somewhere around 30 is usually a good number to go with.

Code

Another in the many items to be agreed on in this area is code-related standards. This ranges from frameworks and design patterns to naming your classes, methods, and variables. And as much as some of you may not like it, there will even be times when you need to standardize when to put code directly on the timeline and what that code should look like. Since we're discussing banners in this section, we're not going to spend any time on frameworks because they are, quite honestly, complete overkill for something as small as banners. However, something that we can very easily discuss here is naming conventions and class package structures.

In general, your class packages should be in a reverse domain format for your company (or your client in some cases). For example, the base of your packages might be com.yourcompany and a package for utility classes might be com.yourcompany.utils. Once your package structure is in place, the team should discuss and agree on the criteria to decide which package a given class will go in. Some will be very obvious, whereas some others may technically be able to fit okay in more than one package (though they never should go in more than one). As for naming conventions of classes, methods, and variables, be as descriptive as possible. When you saw the name of the ClickTagger class, it was pretty obvious what its purpose was, and even more obvious was the `assignClickTag` method and the `targetWindow` variable. The point is to make it as easy as possible for someone else to step in and use the code with as little ramp-up/learning time as possible. The quicker standards are agreed upon within your team, and the quicker other developers can jump in and use the code, the better.

The Bandwidth Profiler

While Flash's Bandwidth Profiler can be very helpful in the development of microsites, it can also be invaluable when you are creating banners. The most useful part of the Bandwidth Profiler during banner development is going to the left side, which contains all the information about the banner (Figs. 3.8 and 3.9).

What You See

A quick rundown on the left side of the Bandwidth Profiler (see Fig. 3.9) gives us the following information under the "Movie" heading: "Dim" signifies the dimensions of your stage; "Fr rate" shows the frames per second at which the banner will play; "Size" is one of the more important ones here because it shows the file size of your published banner; "Duration" lets you know how many frames long your banner's main timeline is and then goes on to do the math and show you the actual number of seconds it will take for your banner's main timeline to get to the end (this is very useful when you are dealing with time constraints in your specs); and finally, "Preload" will tell you how long it will take your banner to download to a user's computer.

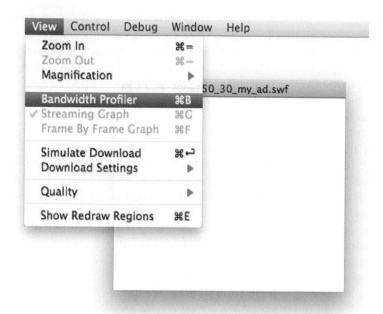

Figure 3.8 Opening the Bandwidth Profiler.

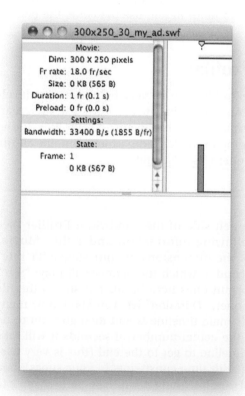

Figure 3.9 The Bandwidth Profiler.

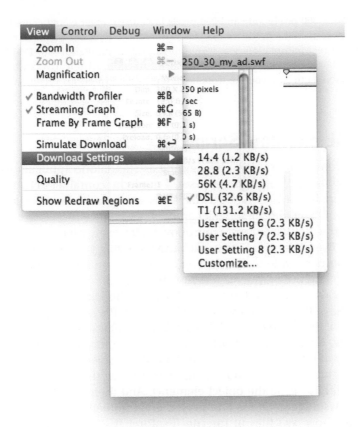

Figure 3.10 Select an option to change the bandwidth setting.

Next is the "Settings" heading, which has only one item under it – "Bandwidth." This is where you see the bandwidth that the Flash movie is being tested against. You can change this setting by choosing one of the options in Download Settings under the View menu of your tested movie (Fig. 3.10).

The last section of information you see on the left side of the Bandwidth Profiler is "State." Like the Settings heading, the State heading only contains a single item – "Frame" – which shows both the current frame of the movie that the Flash playhead is on at any given time and the amount that particular frame is contributing to the overall file size of the banner.

TIP

In previous versions of Flash, if you were using any code that was dependent on the height of the stage and you ran your file in the test player, the Bandwidth Profiler would cause the player to read the wrong value for the height of the stage. For example, if you were working on a banner

> that was 300 pixels wide and 250 pixels high, the Profiler would cause the player to read the height as 150 pixels. In order to force the player to read the correct information, you would need to hide the Bandwidth Profiler and then retest your file. This has been fixed, but I felt it was worth mentioning in case you are working in one of those previous versions.

HTML and JavaScript

Since your banners won't be running as standalone applications or even by themselves in the browser, I think the container HTML and JavaScript is worth discussing. Like I was saying earlier in this chapter, pretty much all the ad-serving companies will have their own HTML that you won't have direct control over. However, what you do have control over is the HTML that you'll use for testing your banners before sending them on to the ad-serving companies, and there's no reason you shouldn't stick with standards-compliant code. Also, let's not forget that we'll need to have some kind of fallback in case the users don't have the required version of the Flash Player or – prepare for shock – if they have the Flash Player disabled, blocked, or not installed.

Now, if you've been working in Flash for more than a couple of years, you'll likely remember the days of the object and embed elements and the "twice-cooked" method (where the embed element was actually inside the object element). And then one day a certain little lawsuit came along and played great influence on the way we had to show .swf files in Internet Explorer if we wanted a smooth user experience. I have no scientific data to prove it, but I believe that lawsuit also helped boost the popularity of a couple of excellent JavaScript solutions by the names of SWFObject and Unobtrusive Flash Objects (UFO). Since then, the authors of the two solutions – Geoff Stearns and Bobby van der Sluis – decided to combine their efforts and eventually released SWFObject 2 as a project on Google Code. If you'd like to learn more about the history of SWFObject, check out the project at http://code.google.com/p/swfobject/. Now let's discuss what SWFObject is and how to use it.

SWFObject

SWFObject is a nice, clean, simple way to not only get your Flash content into the page but have plenty of control over it as well. As I'm writing this, it is at version 2.2, and when you download the swfobject_2_2 zip file, you'll find several files including sample HTML files to show you the two different implementations (static and dynamic), files for running an express install of the Flash Player, and the swfobject.js file itself. First, let's discuss the two publishing methods and a few words about them from the project site.

According to the documentation, both methods have their own set of advantages, and you should choose which one to use based on the needs of the project at hand. In the following code examples, I won't include all the code needed to make SWFObject run. Instead, I'll only be showing the one JavaScript tag where SWFObject is implemented and the div tag where your .swf would be shown. So let's take a look at the static method first in Example 3.7.

EXAMPLE 3.7

Using SWFObject's static method

```
...
<script type="text/javascript" src="swfobject.js"></script>
<script type="text/javascript">
    swfobject.registerObject("myBanner", "10.0.0",
"expressInstall.swf");
</script>
...
<div>
    <object id="myBanner" classid="clsid:D27CDB6E-AE6D-
11cf-96B8-444553540000" width="300" height="250">
        <param name="movie" value="300x250_30_my_ad.swf" />
            <object type="application/x-shockwave-flash"
data="300x250_30_my_ad.swf" width="300" height="250">
                <p>Alternative content</p>
            </object>
    </object>
</div>
...
```

Since the full breakdown of what the code is doing is available on the Google Code project page, we'll just cover some of the basics here. The call to the swfobject.registerObject method shows three parameters in the example. The first parameter is required and is expecting a String representing the ID of the object element further down in the code named "myBanner" in this instance. The second parameter (also required) expects another String representing the minimum version of the Flash Player in which your content can reliably be viewed and interacted with. The version number should be in the form of major.minor.release such as 9.0.260. However, if you are only testing for the major version number, you can leave out the other two. To show this, the number in Example 3.7 could have been input as just "10" instead of "10.0.0." The third parameter in this example is an optional String in the form of a URL pointing to your express install .swf file, and the fourth parameter (not shown here and also optional) expects the name of a JavaScript function that will fire off both when your .swf loads and when it fails to load.

Further down the code is the div tag that contains the object element in which your .swf content will be seen. Obviously, your .swf is taken care of in the param tag named "movie," but what's up with the other object inside the object? Simply put, that's the fail-safe for your ad. If the users don't have Flash installed or simply have it blocked, they'll end up seeing whatever content you put in this element, and that's where the alternate content or default image comes in. Another cool thing about that particular object element is that in addition to being able to show a default image for banners, you can also use it to make your sites more readily available to search engines. But let's wait until Chapter 9 to get into that.

Before we move on, we still need to take a look at the dynamic method of SWFObject. A quick quote from the documentation states that "SWFObject's dynamic embed method follows the principle of progressive enhancement and replaces alternative HTML content for Flash content when enough JavaScript and Flash plug-in support is available." Again, there are pros and cons to using either method, but if you like less HTML, this one's for you. Just check out Example 3.8.

EXAMPLE 3.8

Using SWFObject's dynamic method

```
...
<script type="text/javascript" src="swfobject.js"></script>
<script type="text/javascript">
    swfobject.embedSWF("300x250_30_my_ad.swf", "myBanner",
"300", "250", "10.0.0");
</script>
...
<div id="myBanner">
    <p>Alternative content</p>
</div>
...
```

As you can see, the explanation of this one is going to be much shorter. For this dynamic method, we don't use swfobject.register Object. Instead, we use the swfobject.embedSWF method, which requires a few more parameters. While there are other optional parameters that can be used with the embedSWF method (such as flashvars and attributes), let's just look at the five required parameters listed in the example. All five of them are expecting Strings, and the first one is the URL of your .swf. The second parameter is the name of the div in which to show your .swf content, and the third and fourth parameters are for the width and height, respectively. Finally, the last one is the Flash Player version to test for. This one is exactly like the static method in that it is in the form of major.minor.release or just major. For a ton more information on SWFObject, please pay a visit to the Google Code page at http://code.google.com/p/swfobject/.

Default Images

Now, I know this is going to sound really crazy, but what if an end user doesn't have Flash installed? Or what if he or she doesn't have JavaScript turned on? Or what if he or she is using a Flash blocker? Sure, you could just say it's his or her loss, but it's really your client's loss (and thereby your loss). In the interest of driving all possible users to your client and to keep your client happy with you, you'll really want to serve up a default image in place of the Flash banner to these unfortunate few people. Note the spots that say "Alternative content" in Example 3.7 and Example 3.8. Basically your default .gif or .jpg is either a still frame or animation (.gif) that can get the same branding and messaging across that your Flash file does. While designing and saving your default images for the Web, keep file size in mind because the sites that will be showing them generally give you even less than they do for your Flash files.

Quality Control

Once you have built your ads, it is best to have someone other than yourself test them. This is simply because you are too close to the project and you know exactly what to do and when to do it. Quality control's job is not only to make sure your work is within the specs it should be, but also to basically try to break your work by doing nearly anything it takes to do so. While in this step of the process, your ads should be hammered as if an end user wants to prove that he or she can render your ad useless (yes, there are people out there who will do it just to show that they can). In addition, your ads should be tested on different operating systems, in different browsers, with different versions of the Flash Player, with and without the Flash Player or JavaScript, and with pretty much anything else that may cause them to either perform in an unexpected manner or not perform at all. The end goal of all of this is obviously to make sure that your ad shows, plays, and is as interactive as it should be to as many end users as possible. As I mentioned in Chapter 1, you should expect to receive fixes and revisions from your quality control person or team. You'll also remember from that chapter that I discussed doing the best you can to test and catch bugs even before your work is sent to them in order to make everyone's job just a little easier.

> **TIP**
>
> Bug/issue tracking software is an invaluable tool when it comes to working on a team. While I can recommend a couple that I've worked with in the past (OnTime by Axosoft and Mantis Bug Tracker), a quick search online will produce plenty of results to figure out which one is right for your team.

Sign-off Sheet

Because it can be a little frustrating for several people if there are changes to be made after the work has been tested for bugs and fixed and is ready to ship out, you'll want to complete another quick task before sending it to quality control: a sign-off sheet. The sign-off sheet should contain a checklist with items that are common to all banners that you create. Some of those items might be that the final .swf is within the maximum file size, the width and height of the final .swf match the specs, you have a backup image for users without the Flash Player, and the banner matches the original creative layout. Of course, there should be several other items on the list, but you get the idea. Once you have checked that all the items in the list are complete, you'll need to get the sign-off sheet from the designer and the person in charge of the client account. By getting these sign-off sheets, you're minimizing the chance of things like creative changes after the banners have already been tested and fixed and are ready to go out the door.

Prioritize

I have found that when I do receive my changes, it is best to read through them before jumping right into making them. By doing this, not only can you prioritize but you can also determine which changes may affect other changes. As I'm sure you're well aware, making changes to one piece of code can sometimes cause other code to react in unanticipated ways. On the other hand, fixing one problem can also sometimes cascade into correcting other errors at the same time. When it comes to prioritizing the changes, there are some things to consider. If the ad is acting differently in a very, very minor way in a very particular version of a particular browser on a particular operating system, the change that's causing that issue may be put lower on the list. On the other hand, if the ad opens up and doesn't play or link out to anywhere, that problem needs to go closer to the top. Now, to take it a step further, prioritize by how long each task will take you to complete or by how involved it is. To be perfectly honest, I switch this one around depending on how I'm feeling on a given day. What I mean by that is that sometimes I do the tasks that are more involved and take longer first and sometimes I knock out the quick ones first. It's really a personal preference, and you should figure out which way of prioritizing works best for you today and then again tomorrow and again the day after that.

Conclusion

Let's take a quick look back over this chapter that started off with planning. With a good plan, your work can move much faster than it would without one. Think of how you want to build your ads before you actually start building them. In your head, picture how you are going to get from a blank white stage to an interactive work of art in a banner. From there, I discussed setting up your file, and we started a new file for a 300 × 250 Flash banner ad. After that, I discussed cutting images to work in just such a file. In the next section, I went on to explain how to link out of an ad with clickTags. While clickTags are the industry standard for linking out of your ads, the ClickTagger class also requires a fallback URL for both local testing and a failure to load the intended URLs from the ad servers. Another topic that I discussed was scripting to save time, which basically means using any class files or code snippets over and over again as opposed to rewriting them every time. Don't reinvent the wheel. Next up, I discussed standardizing your naming and coding conventions within your team or organization. Sticking to the standard conventions and best practices can dramatically improve production time and make your work easier for you and others to decipher at a later date. I also discussed HTML and JavaScript for your ads and covered a bit about SWFObject. After the HTML and JavaScript came a little information about default images, and we wrapped it all up by sending our ads through a round of quality control.

If you remember back in the "Creating Time with Code" section, I briefly mentioned forms in your banners. In Chapter 4, I'll be going more in depth on setting them up, using them, and what they mean for your ads.

4

FORMS AND DATA

In some ads, you'll need to gather information from your users to improve their experience. You may want to give them the opportunity to select options on a new car as in the Typical Motors example earlier in this book, or you may want to let them fill out information for something else altogether. Another good example of an ad in which to use a form might be one for a travel company. Again, for the sake of an example, let's choose a fictional name for our travel company – how about "Orbitocities."

Orbitocities comes to you and says that they want to let people know about discount prices for flights and hotels that people need to reserve for the upcoming holiday (and there's *always* an upcoming holiday). You or your creative team sit down, design some layouts, and show them to your new client. After choosing one of the designs, Orbitocities lets you know that they would like to include a form to let users choose the city they are leaving from, the city they are traveling to, their departure date, and their return date (the length of stay in the hotel can be determined from these dates). Once the information is filled in, users can press a submit button to not only go to the Orbitocities site but be taken to a specific page showing the results of the information they entered in the form.

So what do users experience with this setup? Well, let's assume that they are reading an article about upcoming holiday events in the city they plan on visiting. While reading, they come across your Orbitocities banner and decide to go ahead and fill out the form to see what kind of prices Orbitocities had to offer. Since they are

Flash Advertising. DOI: 10.1016/B978-0-240-81345-5.00004-9

taken directly to a results page upon submitting their data, they can choose the flight and hotel they like and book them right away. There's no need to search around the Orbitocities site to find what they are looking for because you seamlessly took them directly where they wanted to go. So now let's go back behind the scenes again and discuss what it took to get them there by going through the following sections:

- Where Are You Going?
- File Size Consumption
- Collecting and Passing Data

Where Are You Going?

The biggest piece of information you'll need when using forms in your banner ads is exactly where you need to send your users. In some cases, you'll send them to a page where the information from the form only partially completes all the information needed for the results. Our Typical Motors example would be a good example of this because there usually isn't enough room on the stage in a banner to include a form that would ask for all the information needed about selecting a new car. There are trim packages, engine sizes, custom wheels, leather or cloth interior, and so on. So you use a couple of options such as the trim package and paint color and then leave the rest for users to fill out on the site. While this doesn't instantly return the results a user was looking for on a new car, it does get him or her one step closer to that end goal. On the other hand, our travel company, Orbitocities, only needs to know the dates and cities that a user will travel to and from. With only four pieces of information to gather, this can easily fit within our banner dimensions, and the user can be taken to a page with full results.

Required Variables

You can probably guess that knowing where you need to send your users is really only a part of the information you need to complete your task. You'll also need to know name and value pairs for the form you're asking them to complete. You can get this information in a couple of ways: you can ask your client to get it for you, or you can get it directly from the forms on their site. I often choose the latter simply for the sake of speed and efficiency. The reason I say speed and efficiency is because your contact at your client's offices is not very often one of the people who wrote the code on their site. Knowing that, you may have to ask your contact for the information and expect some delay. The delay is simply because your contact may need to get your requested information from their site developers before they can relay it back to you. Depending on how large of a company your client is, it could possibly be a day or more before you get your answer. So let's go back to the quicker option of getting the information directly from the forms on their site. For that, I'm going to recommend one of two courses of action. The first is to simply view the source of their forms, and the second is to use a tool like Firebug or ServiceCapture. Just in case you are unfamiliar with viewing the source of a Web site, follow these steps:

1. Open your Web browser and navigate to the Web site from which you need information.
2. Right-click and choose the option in the menu to view the source of the page.
3. Search for a word or phrase that you know is next to a field in the form from which you want to gather information.
4. Once you find the form in the code, you should see the name and value pairs you need.

TIP

There are several different tools available that will allow you to monitor a site's CSS, JavaScript, DOM, and a number of other things. One of the many things you can use these tools for is to discover the name and value pairs of a form on a Web site. Just open up your monitoring tool of choice, fill out and submit the form, and watch the tool report everything back to you. As I mentioned in the main text, a couple of tools you may want to check out are Firebug and ServiceCapture. I personally use and switch back and forth between both.

Now that you have the name and value pairs, you can build out your form and test it to make sure it works. "But Jason," you say, "when I build the forms into my banners, my file size goes way up, and I have to crunch the quality of my images so much that the client will never approve them!" Ah yes, the file size consumption of Flash components.

File Size Consumption

A key factor to keep in mind from the very beginning of a banner that will contain a form is the amount of the file size that is taken up by the Flash components you may need to use. Don't get me wrong, I think the built-in Flash components are just fine. I just wish they were less of a strain on file size. As a matter of fact, unless you're using the ComboBox from way back in Flash 6 or 7, you can pretty much plan on it being too much file bloat to fit in a standard banner. Back in those versions, you could plan on the ComboBox taking up about 15k, but now you would be looking at more than triple that amount and that's going to automatically push you over the size limit on most ads. Another component you may find yourself considering in a form is the TextInput. While the TextInput component doesn't add as much to the file size as the ComboBox, it does still add to it, and you may want to look into simply using the Text Tool to draw a text field on the stage instead.

TIP

Rather than a using a TextInput component in a form that requires users to type in their information, try using the Text Tool to draw a text field on the stage and set its text type property to "Input Text." The file size consumption for the TextInput component is approximately 16k, whereas the file size consumption of a text field placed on the stage with the Text Tool is much lower, approximately 2k (Fig. 4.1).

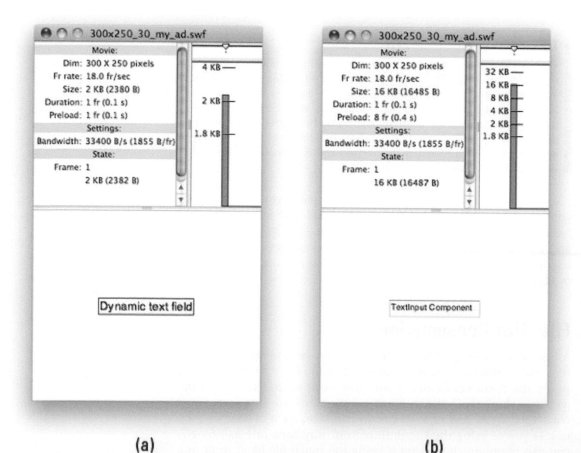

(a)
(b)

Figure 4.1 A text field drawn on the stage (a) eats up much less file size than a TextInput component (b).

The Bulk Is Up Front

If you plan on using the TextInput, you'll also need to plan on it using about 16k right up front. So if 16k is already taken out of the 30k you're allowed in your specs, what happens when you need more than one TextInput? This is where you can relax at least a little and know that the initial hit was the hardest because each additional TextInput after the first one adds a minuscule amount of file size.

The reason for all the bulk up front is because components are generally made up of several different pieces, which all get placed in your library and built into your .swf. For example, when you place one TextInput on the stage and then check your library, you'll notice a folder filled with assets for that component. However, when you add the second TextInput, those assets are already in the file, and they don't need to be added again. Since the amount of added file size by the subsequent TextInput is so small, it would be safe to say that one TextInput is equal to three TextInputs and that's also equal to five TextInputs as far as that file size is concerned.

So now that you know how much of your file size is going to be used up by components, you'll quickly realize that you don't have much left to use toward the design. This leads me back to the design process of the banner; if you know ahead of time that you're going to need to use any components, you can't plan too much animation involving the raster images of the layout. One way to combat this issue is to build your banners to be served by a rich-media company, which will be discussed in Chapter 6. Since running your ads from these companies gives you more file size and the option of loading child movies, you obviously won't have to worry as much about going over the size listed in your specs. On the other hand, you may not have the option of using a rich-media company. In that case, there's the option of building your own custom components, which may actually be your only option in the case of the ComboBox (Fig. 4.2).

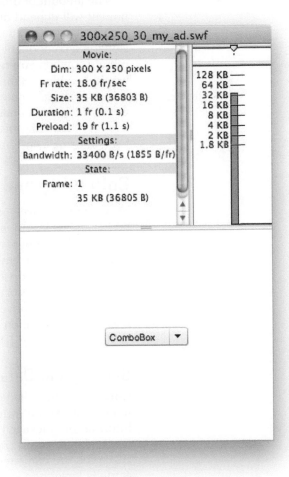

Figure 4.2 Because of the size it ads to your .swf, Flash's ComboBox may not be an option.

Custom Components

As I mentioned earlier, a Flash component brings its assets into your file when you place it on the stage and that increases your file size by a relatively large amount. If you are able to take the time to build your own component, you can save a large amount of that file size, and you'll be able to customize and reuse it elsewhere.

> **ALERT!**
>
> Component creation is a large enough subject that entire books could be (and have been) written on that subject alone, so I won't go into the actual process myself.

The amount of time it takes you to create your own custom component will depend on the component itself. Some may take under an hour to build, and others may take days to perfect. The good news is that if a component is built correctly, you won't have to go back to rebuild it when you need it on another future project. Instead, you would be able to simply place your component on the stage, assign values to its parameters (if it requires any), and move on with your work. Much like a built-in Flash component is heavy with the first use and less thereafter, the bulk of the amount of time involved in creating and using a custom component is up front as well.

Collecting and Passing Data

Now that you have your form put together and you know where it's taking users, you need to pass their input to the target location. The details of how you collect the information might vary from form to form, but how you pass it will generally remain the same in most cases. The vast majority of the time you won't be storing the information directly from the banner itself, but it may be captured and stored once it reaches the destination site. On the other hand, the information may only be used to display the correct page or data once a user has made it to the destination.

Sending the Data

Once a user has filled out the form and hit the submit button, you'll need to do some quick processing behind the scenes to get the information packaged up and sent over to the correct destination. Granted, you could create a string that is made of the landing page URL plus the concatenated values of the text fields (and you may actually have to in some cases), but it would be better practice and easier to work with if you separated the target URL from the name and value pairs that you're sending. This is where the combination of the URLRequest and URLVariables classes comes in quite handy.

While the URLRequest class holds the target URL and will be used with the `navigateToURL` method, the URLVariables class is used as an object to pass variables between a Flash file and a server. Once you've created an instance of URLVariables, you can then assign it to the data property of your URLRequest object and also start assigning those name and value pairs as well. In Example 4.1, you can see a simple function that uses the URLRequest and URL-Variables classes to pass the information gathered in a form containing a few text fields. This function assumes that your form has text fields named `firstNameInput`, `lastNameInput`, and `zipCodeInput`. It also assumes that it is being triggered by a MouseEvent listener.

EXAMPLE 4.1

Using URLRequest with URLVariables

```
function submitForm(e:MouseEvent):void{
    var urlRequest:URLRequest = new
URLRequest("http://www.flashadbook.com/urlVariablesPost.php"
);
    var urlVariables:URLVariables = new URLVariables();
    urlRequest.method = URLRequestMethod.POST;
    urlRequest.data = urlVariables;
    urlVariables.userFirst = firstNameInput.text;
    urlVariables.userLast = lastNameInput.text;
    urlVariables.userZip = zipCodeInput.text;
    navigateToURL(urlRequest, "_self");
}
```

In this example function, the first thing we do is create a variable named `urlRequest`, which is of course a URLRequest object. Also, since we know the URL we're going to be pointing to, we'll go ahead and put it in the url parameter for the URLRequest:

```
var urlRequest:URLRequest = new
URLRequest("http://www.flashadbook.com/urlVariablesPost.php"
);
```

Next, we create an instance of URLVariables, name it `urlVariables`, and assign the name and value pairs (remember that these variable names must match the corresponding variable names on the landing page URL). Using the variable names from the server in conjunction with the text fields in our form, we have the values we need to pass to the server:

```
var urlVariables:URLVariables = new URLVariables();
urlRequest.method = URLRequestMethod.POST;
urlRequest.data = urlVariables;
```

```
urlVariables.userFirst = firstNameInput.text;
urlVariables.userLast = lastNameInput.text;
urlVariables.userZip = zipCodeInput.text;
```

Now that we have the variables packed up and organized all nice and neat, it's time to send the user and his or her package of variables on over to his or her destination. The parameters for the `navigateToURL` method are expecting the following (in this order): the URLRequest containing the target URL and the target window or frame. The parameter for the target window is null by default, and if no value is given, a new empty window is created.

```
navigateToURL(urlRequest, "_self");
```

The target URL used in this example has been set up to receive the variables used in this example. If you would like to test this function, you can either set up your own Flash file that uses it (leave the variable names and target URL as they are) or go to http://www.flashadbook.com/urlVariablesForm.php to see my working version. Remember that if you set up your own Flash file, you may need to run it in an HTML wrapper as opposed to the external player that's used when you test movies from within the Flash IDE (Integrated Development Environment).

Conclusion

When you're working in advertising, your end goal is to get users to do something. You want them to complete some sort of task, and exactly what that task is depends completely on the client and the product or service being advertised. If you work on enough online advertising projects (and it doesn't take many), you'll inevitably be involved with one that is asking users to complete the task of filling out a form of some kind.

Whether you're asking users to fill out a form with information pertaining to the color, trim level, and engine size of your client's new car or you're asking them to fill in the dates that they would like to book a flight and hotel for their vacation, you'll need to know where to send that information. On top of that, you'll need to know what variable names and possible values the processing page will expect when users are sent to it. There are many ways to get this information including asking your client for it or even visiting and viewing the source of their version of the same form on their Web site.

Something to keep in mind when you're building banners with forms in them is file size. If your forms contain a TextInput component, you can plan on it eating up most of your permitted file size, and if you plan on using Flash's ComboBox, you can also plan on going over your file size limit. In order to avoid this issue, you can either run your ads as rich-media banners or do a little research into building custom components.

After your form is all laid out and ready to program, you'll want to use the URLRequest and URLVariables classes. As I said in the "Sending the Data" section, the URLVariables class organizes all your variables into a nice little package. Once your variables are all packed up like a suitcase, you can send users on their trip to the destination Web site. Once there, they'll unpack all the variables and receive the information they were after when they started filling out your form.

5

FILE OPTIMIZATION

Whether you're building banner ads, microsites, games, applications, or anything else, it's always a good practice to do your best to keep your file sizes as low as you can while still achieving your design and animation goals. Although microsites and games are going to be bigger than banners, you don't want them to be too big because you may risk the loss of potential users. Those potential users are, in turn, potential customers for your client. Banners need to be kept down in file size for a different reason: specs. When you go over the file size allowed in the banner's specs, the site(s) on which it is running will most likely reject your banner.

Enter file optimization. Optimizing your Flash files can consist of anything from changing the compression settings on your images to slimming down your code or using vector drawing instead of imported images. There are several ways to reduce your file size and knowing some of them can not only help your sanity, but also help you in building your projects without the need to remove any key features or images.

Flash Advertising. DOI: 10.1016/B978-0-240-81345-5.00005-0

There are generally two major areas in which you can optimize your files: graphics and code. Within those two areas, there are smaller areas of discussion that I've split into the following sections:

- Image Types
- Image Compression
- Vectors and Fonts
- Optimizing Code

Image Types

Different images call for different formats. If you have a picture of a person, you'll generally want to use a .jpg (.png is definitely an option, but the .jpg's file size is most likely going to be smaller). If you have a line drawing or any other image that isn't photographic, you'll probably want to use a .gif and for the most part, you'll probably want to save the .png format for images that contain transparency.

.jpg

As mentioned earlier, .jpg files are best used for photographs or images with smooth variations of tone and color. They use what is called a "lossy" data compression method, which basically means that the data is compressed in such a way that it is actually different from the original data but still close enough to be used. As the compression levels increase, the resulting file size reduces. However, with that higher compression and lower file size, you start to see image artifacts that give less quality to the pictures. Figures 5.1–5.4 illustrate the same image with four different quality settings: 100%, 80%, 60%, and 0% (higher quality setting = lower compression). For each of these examples, I've zoomed in on the same area to better show the image artifacts.

The image in Fig. 5.1 has a quality setting of 100% and is hard to distinguish from the original photograph even though the original can take up to six times more file size. If you are using Photoshop's "Save for Web & Devices…" function, you'll notice that 100% is also called "Maximum" quality under the .jpg settings.

With a quality setting of 80%, Fig. 5.2 is less than half the file size of the uncompressed original image in this case. At 80%, the image still looks great, but we can still go lower for the Web. Photoshop's "Save for Web & Devices…" function labels 80% as "Very High" quality.

Figure 5.3 shows the quality that you'll most likely want to use for your Flash projects (or almost any project on the Web). This is because at 60% quality, the image artifacts that start to appear because of compression are extremely small and mostly unnoticeable at the 72 dots per inch (dpi) that computer monitors display. The final file size of a .jpg saved at 60% quality can be up to 20 times

Figure 5.1 Image quality: 100%; file size: 328k.

Figure 5.2 Image quality: 80%; file size: 193k.

smaller than the original image. In Photoshop's "Save for Web & Devices…" function, 60% is also called "High" quality and can be found as a preset.

The only real use for including Fig. 5.4 at 0% quality is to illustrate what is happening at a much higher level than the previous figures. With the quality set this low, you can really notice the

Figure 5.3 Image quality: 60%; file size: 127k.

Figure 5.4 Image quality: 0%; file size: 37k.

image artifacts. With such a poor visual quality, you should never use an image compressed by this much.

TIP

Image artifacts are basically blocks of color that become larger and more visible as the compression rate of an image gets higher.

.gif

Due to the cost of graphics cards that rendered more than 256 colors at the time the .gif format was first introduced, .gif files themselves were limited to a palette of 256 colors. Because of this limitation, .gifs are most useful for graphics with fewer colors than you would find in a photographic image; graphics such as diagrams, cartoon-style drawings or any other imagery that is intended to use a limited color palette. .gifs use a different compression method from .jpgs called "lossless." Lossless data compression differs from lossy data compression in that it allows the exact original data to be reconstructed from the compressed data and this exact reconstruction is very important when image details must be seen clearly.

Unlike .jpgs, .gifs support image transparency. However, it's important to remember that when you create a .gif with transparent areas, you'll get a single pixel of solid color around the nontransparent area. This works fine if the background of your animation is the same solid color, but not so well if your background is multicolored or gradient. See Figs. 5.5 and 5.6 for examples of the same .gif on different backgrounds.

TIP

It should be noted that .gifs support frame-based animations and that these .gif animations may be a great choice for your non-Flash backup image.

Figure 5.5 A .gif with transparency on a solid white background.

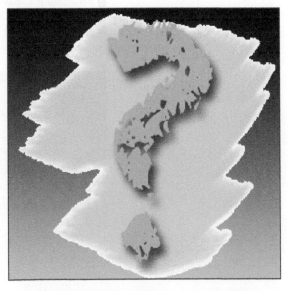

Figure 5.6 A .gif with transparency on a gradient background.

.png

The .png format was specifically created to replace the .gif format. Although the file size of a .png graphic may generally be larger than that of a .gif, remember that .pngs support true-color imaging. Like .gifs, .png files use lossless data compression and support transparency. Unlike .gifs, .pngs don't include a pixel border around the nontransparent area of your images. Because of the true-color imaging and better alpha transparency, .pngs are ideal when you have photographic-style images that need to animate across a multicolor or gradient background. Figure 5.7 illustrates the same image from Figs. 5.5 and 5.6 on the same background. However, Fig. 5.7(a) is a .gif and Fig. 5.7(b) is a .png. Note the lack of a white border around the nontransparent areas of the .png.

TIP

Both .gif and .png formats support transparency. However, .gif files will give you a border that appears as an outline around the opaque area of the image. In addition to the absence of the pixel border, .png files usually have a better image quality than .gif files. The cost of that better image quality is, of course, file size.

TIP

When you're working with .pngs and you're saving your files through Photoshop's "Save for Web & Devices," you'll usually want to go with png-24. However, if the color palette contains fewer colors, then you may want to use png-8.

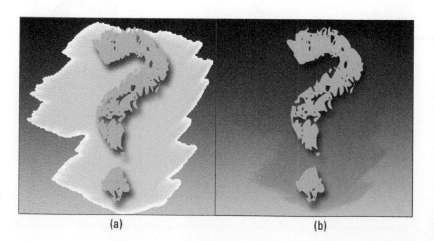

Figure 5.7 A .gif (a) and a .png (b) on the same gradient background.

(a)   (b)

Image Compression

When it comes to optimizing images for use in Flash, I've heard advice stating that compressing your images before importing them is better and I've also heard that letting Flash do the compressing is better. I'd like to offer the following "middle of the road" advice: Compress a little before importing and let Flash do the rest. By that, I mean you should save your images at a high-quality compression setting and then adjust as needed within Flash.

High-Quality Images

Because you are most likely creating work to be viewed on a computer monitor, you don't need to worry about your images having high resolutions as you would for another medium such as print. The fact that computer monitors show everything at 72 dpi also helps with your file size. One mistake I've seen made by various people is to save an image from Photoshop with the "Save As..." command as opposed to using the "Save for Web & Devices..." option in Photoshop's File menu (Fig. 5.8). The reason I consider this to be a mistake is due to file/image control and resulting file size. Although the difference in the resulting file sizes may not be huge in some cases, there is still a difference that could end up pushing your work just over the constraints set by your project specs. The "Save for Web & Devices..." option is a very easy process that I've outlined in the following steps:

1. With your image already open in Photoshop, choose "Save for Web & Devices..." from the File menu (Fig. 5.8).
2. In the resulting window, choose "JPEG High" (or any other available choice) from the Preset menu on the right and press the Save button (Fig. 5.9).
3. When the Save Optimized As window opens, navigate to the correct folder where your image will live and name your file accordingly (Fig. 5.10).
4. Use your saved image in your banner or microsite.

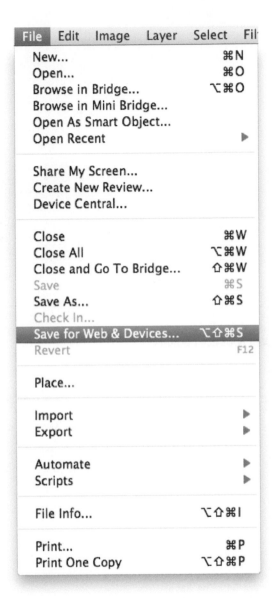

Figure 5.8 The Photoshop File menu.

Figure 5.9 The Save for Web & Devices window.

Figure 5.10 The Save Optimized As window.

Manage Compression in Flash

Once your images are saved, it's time to bring them into Flash and fine-tune some compression settings. In some cases, you'll only have a couple of images and a large file size to work within. So, before you do any compressing, build and test your Flash movie to make sure that you absolutely need to tweak the settings. If you find that you need to lower the file size of the resulting .swf, then it's time to start modifying some compression settings.

TIP

If the images you'll be using are going to be "pulled in" as external files, then you'll want to manage their compression from your image-editing software such as Photoshop.

It's tempting for some to use the JPEG quality slider in the Publish Settings dialog box (Fig. 5.11), but this will result in changing the compression for every image in your file. One reason to avoid this is because, sometimes, you can get away with applying a lot of compression to one image like a blurry background image, but not on another image like the picture of the main item of focus within your project.

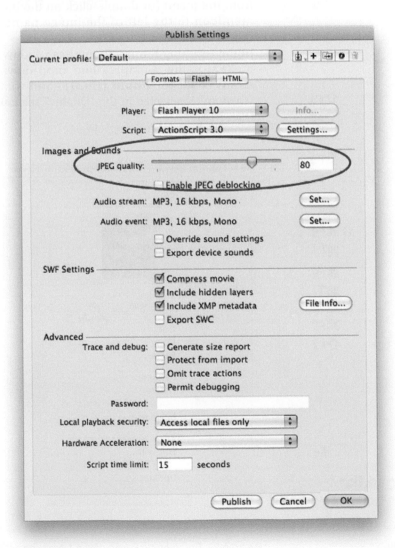

Figure 5.11 The JPEG quality slider in the Publish Settings dialog box.

Window	Help	
Duplicate Window		⌥⌘K
Toolbars		▶
Timeline		⌥⌘T
Motion Editor		
✓ Tools		⌘F2
Properties		⌘F3
✓ Library		⌘L
Common Libraries		▶
Motion Presets		
✓ Actions		⌥F9
Code Snippets		
Behaviors		⇧F3
Compiler Errors		⌥F2
Debug Panels		▶
Movie Explorer		⌥F3
Output		F2
Align		⌘K
Color		⇧⌘F9
Info		⌘I
Swatches		⌘F9
Transform		⌘T
Components		⌘F7
Component Inspector		⇧F7
Other Panels		▶
Extensions		▶
Workspace		▶
Hide Panels		F4
✓ 1 300x250_30_my_ad.fla*		

Figure 5.12 The Flash Window menu.

If you need to lower your file size, you'll want to optimize each image on an individual basis by adjusting the bitmap properties of the images in your library. The following steps and Figs. 5.12–5.15 explain the process with the assumption that you already have a Flash file open that contains images in the library.

1. With your Flash file open, choose "Library" from the Window menu (Fig. 5.12).
2. In the Library window, right-click on the image for which you'd like to alter the compression settings and choose "Properties" from the menu (or double-click on the bitmap icon to the left of the image name) (Fig. 5.13).
3. In the resulting Bitmap Properties window, make sure the "Compression" drop-down menu is set to "Photo (JPEG)" and that "Custom" is selected in the "Quality" section (Fig. 5.14).

Figure 5.13 The right-click menu for a Library item.

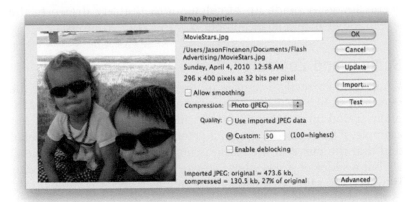

Figure 5.14 The Bitmap Properties window.

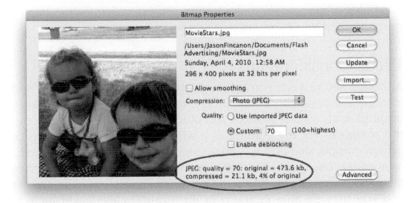

Figure 5.15 Original and compressed file sizes of the modified image.

4. Again, with "Custom" selected, change the number in the input box and press the "Test" button to see the original file size, the compressed file size, and a preview of your image with the current setting (Fig. 5.15).
5. Once you're happy with the compressed size, press OK and your image is ready to go.

Vectors and Fonts

There are times when a simple image can be re-created as a vector graphic instead of using a raster (bitmap) graphic. Due to processor usage, the simplicity of the image itself should play a key role in your decision to use vector or raster. Keep an eye out for images that can be redrawn with a small number of lines, as well as flat colors instead of gradients. If you find that you have come across one of these images in your work, take the time to redraw it as a vector graphic, and you'll generally save some file size because the vector image is made up of calculations that are drawn to the screen rather than a large number of static, colored pixels.

Scaling and Zooming

When used correctly, vector graphics will not only lower your file size, but, unlike raster images, they offer the ability to be indefinitely scaled up or zoomed in on without any loss in quality. For example, if you scaled a .jpg of a green sphere to 900%, you would find that the curve of the circle is not actually a smooth curve at all, but a series of pixels whose square shape creates a jagged edge. However, the same green sphere created as a vector graphic proves to have nice smooth curves no matter how much you increase its scale. In Fig. 5.16, I've created a drawing of the sphere and saved it as both a raster and a vector graphic. I then zoomed in on the same area of each to show the results. The smoother vector graphic is on the right while the raster image is on the left.

Vector Considerations

Although using vector graphics correctly can save file size and increase the scalability of the image, there are some things to keep in mind such as the number of colors, the use of gradients, and the complexity of the graphic as a whole. If your artwork starts to get too complicated and has lines numbering in the high hundreds, or even reaches more than 1000, you may want to reconsider using a raster image instead. While the vector re-creation may be prettier and you may be able to zoom in on it much closer, you have to remember that the Flash Player on the end user's computer will have to recalculate every line contained within your drawing every time that drawing moves even a single pixel. On its own, a very complicated vector line drawing can end up considerably slowing

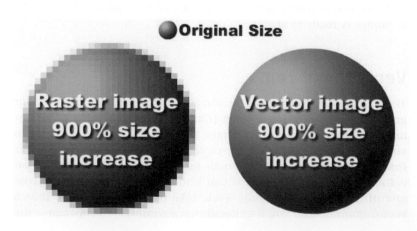

Figure 5.16 Vector versus raster zooming and scaling.

the frame rate of your movie. When you start adding other factors like user interaction, other animations happening at the same time, and functions running their code when they're called, you can imagine the potential consequences.

The colors you use in your vector art should be just as much of a consideration as the complexity of the lines. As you might imagine, gradients are more complicated than solids and they contain a good deal more data for the Flash Player to process. Obviously gradients can't be avoided 100% of the time, but you should try to limit how often you use them and how many you have on the screen at any given time (especially if they will be animated).

Text and Fonts

Something else to consider in the optimization of your work is text and fonts. I'm including them in this chapter because they can sometimes bloat your file size by great amounts without you even realizing that it's happening. They can also be treated in the wrong way and end up looking like a big blurry, unreadable mess. When you're working with a specific font that is used by your client, don't embed the entire font if the text is going to be static. Instead, embed only the letters, numbers, and punctuation that will actually be used. Another option for static areas of text is to use an image. It might sound a little antiproductive in the sense of optimization, but if you only have one or two words in a particular font, sometimes an image produces a smaller file size than embedding any of the font at all. If you do end up using such an image, be aware that changes to the wording will mean more work. Instead of just opening up your Flash file and typing in the change, you'll have to open up another tool like Photoshop to make the change, save the new image, and update it in your .fla. With the number of changes that can very easily be coming your way, it can get a little tedious.

Another option that you may want to experiment with but generally avoid is breaking apart the text. In some cases, this may save you a small bit of file size and it may be just enough to squeak that banner in under the required size. However, you should also remember that when you break that text apart, it is converted into vector shapes and lines. Jumping back just a bit, you'll recall that I suggested avoiding complicated vectors and there are some fonts out there that can have extremely complicated outlines. In addition to the complicated vectors, there's also the issue of editing the text after it's broken apart. Imagine if you were working on a project where you were creating 30 banners and all of them had the same tagline in them. Now imagine you break apart the text for the taglines in all of them. Next, imagine that you have finished creating all of the banners and you're told that one of the words is misspelled. Just like making edits to text in an image, this one could get very tedious as well.

Optimizing Code

Optimizing your code can be just as important as optimizing your images in terms of both file size and processor usage. As with most steps in your projects, it is always best to keep code optimization in mind from the very start before you have written a single line. However, we all know that there are times when we just need to make it work as quickly as we can, no matter what it takes. The trick to those hurried times is to remember that we need to set time aside so that we can later go back and optimize, or "clean up," our code. In the rest of this section, I'll be passing on a few suggestions that have either been passed on to me or that I have found in my own projects over time.

Don't Repeat Yourself

I often find that I remind myself not to reinvent the wheel while I'm working on projects. An example of what I mean would be that if I find myself writing a function that does something very similar to another function I've already written within the same project, I can usually modify the first one to serve the needs of both. I remember a particular microsite I was working on at the same time I was working on a large round of banners. Although it's not unusual to work on more than one project at a time or for those projects to have tight deadlines, this site had grown in size and scope as it progressed. While the project was in midswing, new sections and functionality were being added that affected the way the site was being programmed. The deadline, however, could not be adjusted due to critical timing on a product launch.

In order to get the new sections built into the site, I had to work fast. And because those sections were added after all planning had been completed, I had to get a little "creative" in my programming. The end result, I'm a little embarrassed to say, was a fairly tangled web of messy code in which I had multiple functions completing the same tasks on the same objects and variables. If you've ever run into this situation, you know how confusing it can be to go back in and make changes or fixes to that kind of "spaghetti code." You quickly discover that you're asking questions like, "Did I call function A from there or was it function C?" or, "Well, I had to fix function A and function B does the same thing ... do I need to fix it as well? Am I even calling function B from anywhere?" Once you hit that point, you have no choice but to take the time to go back and optimize your code.

Allow the Flash Player to Relax

Computers have come a long way since I first sat down in front of my dad's Apple II with a beginner's game programming book for children (how's that for dating myself?). They've come a long way in graphics, hard disk space, physical size, memory, and speed (as well as many other aspects). As computers advanced in all of these ways, software developers wrote their programs to utilize the changes, and we, as Flash Platform developers, have done so as well. However, as fast and efficient as a computer may be, it can still be "bogged down" without too much effort. And, like the computer itself, the Flash Player in which your work is viewed can be bogged down or even stop responding if the correct preventative care is not taken.

The Flash authoring environment will let you know about a few problems in this area such as an infinite loop. What it won't tell you is how to optimize and/or speed up your working processes. The following are just a few tips that will help the Flash Player run more smoothly.

If you're looping through several objects and you're calling a simple function that affects each of those objects individually, move the contents of that function inside the loop. In other words, don't make the Flash Player start a loop, find the object to be affected, go outside the loop to find the function you're calling, run the function contents on the object, and then return to the loop only to do it all again with another object. Instead, let the Flash Player start the loop, find the object, affect it, and move on to the next one.

When you give your objects data types, avoid overusing the ambiguous Object type. Instead, figure out which type is better suited for the needs of the object, such as String, Number, or Array. While those three types are very different, there may be times when more than one type will suit your immediate needs. The Object type should only be used when there is no other option, and if you're unsure which type to use, the Help section of the Flash authoring environment should be able to answer your question.

> **TIP**
>
> If you're able to target Flash Player 10, you may want to look into the Vector class for some of your Array needs. A Vector is very much like a typed Array that is typically more efficient than an actual Array. Also, if you are used to working with Arrays, then working with Vectors will be very easy because they contain many (but not all) of the same methods. You can find an example of the Vector being used in Chapter 12.

If you're writing a "for loop" that is running the length of an Array, avoid actually using Array.length in the for statement itself.

Instead, assign the value of the Array's length to a variable that you can then reference. Example 5.1 shows the two different techniques.

EXAMPLE 5.1

```
//Assign the value of myArr.length to a variable before using
it in a for loop:
var myArr:Array = new Array
("item1","item2","item3","item4");
var myArrLen:Number = myArray.length;
for(var i:Number = 0; i < myArrLen; i++){
    trace("Array item at position " + i + " is: " + myArr[i];
}
//Instead of accessing it directly:
var myArr:Array = new Array
("item1","item2","item3","item4");
for(var i:Number = 0; i < myArray.length; i++){
    trace("Array item at position " + i + " is: " + myArr[i];
}
```

Conclusion

As I've covered in this chapter, optimizing your files can be achieved on several levels. When it comes to file size, you should always optimize as much as you can without making heavily noticeable sacrifices to image quality or functionality. When you prepare your images for your Flash files, remember to choose the best file type for the individual image and to save that image at a high enough quality so that it's clear on your monitor. If you see obvious image artifacts, raise the quality of the image before you use it in Flash. Once inside Flash, manage the compression of your images on an individual basis from the Library window instead of globally from the Publish Settings window.

Use vector images when you can, but remember to use them wisely. If you've got a visually complicated image, go ahead and use the raster version. However, if that image can be re-created with a minimal number of lines and colors, you may benefit from drawing it in vector format in order to achieve a possibly smoother representation that can be scaled without worry of quality loss. In addition to keeping the number of lines and colors to a minimum, do the same with gradients, as they require the Flash Player to work just a little harder. As for fonts, try to embed only what you need to embed and only if you need to embed them at all. If you need to use a specific font for only one or two words, try using a raster image of those words, and try to avoid breaking the text apart into complicated vector shapes.

Your code should be optimized not only for performance, but also for readability and maintenance. As you are writing your ActionScript, pay attention to what your different functions are doing. If you have two functions that are doing very nearly the same thing, consolidate them into one function that can handle both of your objectives. Another thing I like to suggest is to look back through your code at certain intervals to make sure you aren't repeating yourself or that you haven't left any code that you aren't using anymore. In other words, refactoring is good and you should do it. Remember that making your code base smaller optimizes your file and your time now and later.

In Chapter 6, I'll be talking about some third-party rich-media companies like Eyeblaster and PointRoll. As you read about them, you'll learn that one of the benefits in utilizing their technologies is that you are allowed more file size for your banners. However, that fact should never keep you from optimizing your work because one of the overall goals of any project should be an end product with a file size that's as small as it can reasonably be.

6

THIRD-PARTY RICH-MEDIA TECHNOLOGIES

Third-party rich-media technologies are a powerful tool when it comes to advertising. As I mentioned previously, these technologies are available through companies who specialize in opening new, more captivating channels for advertisers' usage. Without these technologies in place, Flash banners would most likely be limited to the regular old standard ads and constrained to 30–40k in file size. However, since they are available and ready to be used, we can create banners that are capable of everything from playing video to expanding out to a larger size to working like tiny Web sites (mini-microsites, if you will). All of these options offered by rich-media companies afford us the room to give users more information than we could fit in a standard Flash banner. And did I mention that the file sizes allowed are usually much larger than standard ads, or that unlike standard ads, you can load external files such as child .swfs, .xml files, and .jpgs? There are even options out there for streaming full-screen video. So let's get to the following sections in this chapter:

- When to Utilize Rich-Media Technology
- Rich-Media Companies

When to Utilize Rich-Media Technology

One question that is often asked is, "How do I know when to choose between a rich-media technology and a standard Flash ad?" As I mentioned at the beginning of this book, a key factor in this

Flash Advertising. DOI: 10.1016/B978-0-240-81345-5.00006-2

decision can be cost. However, because there are so many extra features and advantages gained through using a rich-media technology, your clients may decide that it's well worth the extra money, and it's up to you to inform them when they should and shouldn't utilize the technology.

Audio/Video

For those that have done any work with audio and/or video, it's pretty obvious that you'd be safe betting against much (if any) of it fitting in a Flash file that's constrained to 40k. Those banner ads that will use audio or video are prime candidates for use of a rich-media technology. With companies like Eyeblaster, EyeWonder, and PointRoll, your media can actually be streamed into the ad.

The only usual requirement is that you can't start the audio until a user interacts with the banner. While it may seem that it would be beneficial to start playing your audio as soon as the banner appears on a user's screen, this requirement can actually work in your favor. If a user went to a Web site that was running your ad and your ad immediately started playing sounds, then that user could very easily get annoyed with your banner and thereby annoyed with your client. Imagine a user at work in a quiet office who doesn't realize his/her speakers are turned on and all of the sudden, your ad starts blaring out the audio from one of your client's commercials. Another bad situation would be the potential consumer who is using a dial-up connection (yes, they are still out there in fairly large numbers). These users are the reason I would even suggest that you refrain from playing a video in a muted state. Instead, give them instruction on how to start viewing the video. Although the key word is "streaming," you still don't want to be a bandwidth hog unless users want you to be one. If any of these users run into your banner again, they may start to build a worse opinion about your client than they would have otherwise. However, if you put users in control, the opposite may happen. They may watch the video and be entertained by it or they may pay more attention and learn something about your client that they didn't know before. The key, again, is putting users in control rather than forcing it on them and eating up their bandwidth without their consent. Another good thing about waiting for user interaction is that you generally start the video over when they click. By doing this, you can be sure that users viewed the entire video (or at least that they didn't miss the beginning of it). And finally, at the end of the video, you can give them an opportunity to click through to the site where they can learn more information from watching more videos or a longer version of the one in the ad. Again, more interaction and time spent with the brand.

> **TIP**
>
> When you're working with video in a rich-media banner, check with the rich-media company to see if they have a Flash video player already built for use in their system. They may have special code to work with their streaming servers, and you'll just need to skin their player to match your design.

Dynamic Content In Your Ads

I was once approached to answer a question about feeding dynamic content into a banner. The reason, in this particular case, was because we had just launched a microsite that was entirely driven by user-generated content. In the site, a user could fill out a form to submit two different sides on any topic. If the topic was approved by the microsite's administrator, then other users could go on to debate which of the two sides of the topic was better. For example, one topic might be sports and one discussion in that topic might be about football versus fútbol. Users would go to the microsite to use text, audio, or video to weigh in on the side they liked better. In addition, users could simply click a button to vote on their favorite side without saying anything at all.

> **TIP**
>
> Remember that if you want the capability to load external files such as XML or images, you're going to need to use a rich-media company to serve your ads.

Getting back to the banner ads with the dynamic content; with such a site running off of user-generated content, the topics of discussion are always current and up-to-date with real-world events. Because the microsite always had current information, the banners needed to have current information as well. The answer was to build a single round of banners that could be updated "on the fly." Because regular 40k standard Flash banners don't allow the luxury of loading external files or content, rich media was the option available.

Once the banners were built, they would pull their content from an external XML file that could be changed at any time deemed necessary. And because all of the content within the banner was dynamic, only one banner had to be built for each size. In other words, even though there were 10 different sites running the 160 × 600 ad with different content on each banner, there was only one 160 × 600 banner built. The readers on site A might be interested in different topics of discussion than the readers on site B, and using the rich-media technologies allowed us to give them each the dynamic content that they were interested in.

Extra Loads

If you have clients who refuse to show anything less than their entire line of products in a single banner, they're going to need to understand what that means in terms of file size. Once you find yourself having to use a certain amount of photographs in a banner, it doesn't matter how much you compress your images, they simply won't fit inside a file size constraint of 40k or less. Enter the rich-media technologies with their increased file size limitations and ability to load external files (such as .jpg or .swf).

This is one of the easy ones to explain to clients who are having difficulty in understanding why they need to incur the extra cost involved in utilizing rich-media technology. If you run into any issues in this area, you can simply show your clients the file size of a Flash movie with all of the required images. They will appreciate that you have actually taken the time to both explain and show them why their banners would be turned away from any site on which they are supposed to be shown. If they still insist on having the same number of images in the banner, they will feel better about spending the extra money.

More Interactivity

Another thing to consider when choosing between a rich-media technology and a standard Flash banner ad is the level of interactivity available with each. Regular ads basically give you a defined area in which to show your content and a set file size in which to do so. However, rich-media technologies offer not only the previously mentioned option to load external files and content, but also the ability to literally take your creation outside of the box. With floating ads, expandable ads, interactive video ads, and many more options, there isn't much that you can't accomplish in terms of communicating your message to your clients' potential customers.

Floating Ads

Floating ads are ads that actually appear over the content of the page on which they are played. Because they are played on a transparent layer above the page, they can take on any shape you like within a certain defined area. An example might be if you created a floating ad for an auto manufacturer, and you actually built the ad to take on the shape of their newest car.

Expandable Ads

Expandable banners are a great place to pack a large amount of information into a small space. These ads are where the mini-microsites, which I mentioned at the start of this chapter, would fit.

Inside Advertising

While I only list a couple of the rich-media ad formats here, there are many more available for your use. To learn more about all of the formats, visit the Web sites of companies like Eyeblaster (http:\\www.eyeblaster. com), EyeWonder (http:\\ www.eyewonder.com), and PointRoll (http:\\ www.pointroll.com).

In a nutshell, your expandable banners will be made of more than one Flash movie: the main movie, which might be put together like a regular 160 × 600 (or one of several other sizes), and the child movies or "panels." The number of panels your ad has depends on how much information there is and exactly how it will be presented. When a user interacts with the main banner, a panel movie is loaded and the overall size of the advertisement is expanded. From there, the user might be able to open more panels or simply click the (usually required) close button if he or she has finished.

Rich-Media Companies

There are many choices out there when it comes to rich-media companies, and while several of them started out specialized in one or two products (such as expandable units, floating ads, or video ads), most of them have come to offer a wide range of options in recent years. Some, like PointRoll (http:\\www.pointroll.com) and EyeWonder (http:\\www.eyewonder.com), offer a downloadable file that integrates directly into the Flash authoring environment to help speed up and streamline your work. Some other companies, like Eyeblaster (http:\\www.eyeblaster.com), offer an online tool for setting up your ads. Once you log into their tool, you simply upload your files, change a few settings accordingly, and assign the ad to the correct placement. With a seemingly endless amount of other options available out there, it's definitely worth doing your research because you'll find some great companies that are working very hard to provide some great tools for us to work with.

> **TIP**
>
> The different rich-media companies offer several of the same ad formats, but at the same time, each of them may also offer something a little different than the rest. I won't try to sway you one way or the other, but it's not an entirely bad idea to utilize one more than the others. The reason being is that the processes involved in running ads with each company are different, and it's good to use the same process as much as possible. If you need to run an ad format that isn't available with your primary rich-media company, simply move it over to the company that has that format.

They're All Different In the Same Ways

Because the majority of the rich-media companies you'll work with have come to offer a lot of the same options when it comes to ad formats, you may want to research their costs and get a feel for their levels of service. Just like with any product or service, you're going to find different rates and you're going to be happier with how you are treated as a customer by one company as compared with how you are treated by another company. Keep in mind that levels of service shouldn't only be measured on how you were treated as a person and customer, but how much help and support the company is able to provide when you need them.

Conclusion

As online advertisers, rich-media companies and their technologies offer us the means to create advertising experiences that might otherwise be unavailable. Although those options are nice to have at our disposal, it's important to know when to use them and when to stick with a standard Flash banner. A major aspect of any campaign that will come into play when you're making the decision is cost; because you're getting more out of the advertising and technology, the price is going to be higher.

As I mentioned in this chapter, the options you have with a rich-media advertising technology will allow you to create banners that incorporate more engaging content such as audio and video. You're also afforded the luxury of loading external child files, which you wouldn't be able to fit within certain file size constraints, and the ability to load dynamic content from something like an XML file.

When it comes to the companies that house these technologies, you'll want to spend a little time doing some research to see which one you should go with. Although there are those that offer options not available by any others, a majority of them offer many of the same ad formats. The main differences you'll find between them may come down to the cost of their products and their customer service levels.

7

TRAFFICKING AND TRACKING YOUR ADS

Trafficking your ads is when you actually load them into an ad-server system or onto the hosting site. This is the step in the process when your work is actually made "live" on the Internet. This is very obviously an important step in the life of a project, because without it, no one would ever see the ads and no one would ever make it to the site that is being promoted within those ads (at least not by way of the ads themselves).

Flash Advertising. DOI: 10.1016/B978-0-240-81345-5.00007-4

Once the banners are live, you will be able to track aspects like impressions, interactions, and clicks (I'll explain these later in this chapter), as well as determine the cost of these metrics. You can then use the gathered information to optimize the campaign. Before any of this is possible, and even before the banners are built and programmed, there are other steps that take place, such as the media buy. If you have a media team, they are no doubt involved from the very beginning of a campaign all the way through to the end (and even beyond). It's the steps they take that I'll be discussing in this chapter, and I'll lay those steps out in the following sections:

- The Media Buy
- Ad-Server Tools
- Tracking Your Ads
- Rich-Media Ads
- Site-Served Ads

The Media Buy

Aside from actually gaining a new client or having an existing client let you know they'd like to run a new campaign, the media buy is one of the very first steps that take place in the life of a banner project. Much like trafficking your ads at the end of the project, the media buy is a very important step that could very well decide the fate of the campaign itself. If done properly, the ads will be seen by the correct target audience and they will perform very well. However, if the wrong placements are purchased and the ads end up running on sites that have absolutely nothing to do with your target audience, they will perform poorly and large amounts of money can be lost in the process.

Target Audience

There are certain people who you want to respond to your campaign, and as harsh as it may sound, there are also certain people whose response is less important (on a particular campaign). Those people who you are trying to reach are called your "target audience," and they will vary from client to client and sometimes even from campaign to campaign. They are groups of people who fit into predefined categories involving their lifestyles, behaviors, and other key factors.

The audience can generally be narrowed down using different levels of targeting such as demographics. Demographics are essentially the characteristics of a given population and include variables like race, age, gender, income, employment, and location (as well as others). With the information gained by demographic studies, you can gain information like what type of person is visiting a given Web site. For example, upon doing a study for Web site A, you may find that the vast majority of its visitors are married, middle-class females in the 25–54 age range.

Another part of the study of your audience might be the psychographics. Similar to the demographics, the psychographics offer insight to different aspects of the given population. The difference is that with psychographics, you gain a little deeper information than with demographics. The information gained here would be attributes related to users' personalities, attitudes, interests, and several other "under the surface" factors. You may also hear these factors called "IAO variables," which is short for interests, attitudes, and opinions. By combining your demographics with your psychographics, you can further narrow your audience to make sure your ads are being seen by the correct people. To carry the demographic example a step further, we may now have targeted married, middle-class females who are 25–54 years old, and are interested in entertainment and have purchased items online in the past 6 months. With that kind of information sitting directly in front of you, it's hard not to hit your intended audience.

The target audience for a given campaign will most likely be given to you by your client, and it will not always be the audience you thought it would be. For example, you may have a client whose product or service is typically associated with senior citizens. When your client tells you that they want to target men who are 25 years of age and older, you may be surprised. However, when you stop to think about the fact that your client's product is already associated with senior citizens, you'll find out that they most likely already have a hold on them. Therefore, it would make more sense to spend the advertising dollars targeting a new group that is not currently using the product/service to its full potential.

So now that you know who your target audience is, the next challenge is how to find them. There are several ways of doing so right at your fingertips. If you do a search online for something along the lines of "Internet market research," you'll get results pointing to many Web sites and companies where you'll find both free and fee-based information. As you might guess, the fee-based information is going to be much more in depth and probably more reliable as well. A couple of the industry leaders in market research are Nielsen NetRatings, which can be found within the main Nielsen site at http:\\www.nielsen.com, and Quantcast (http:\\www.quantcast.com). The extensive audience research and solutions from companies like these offer advertising agencies an easy way to find their target audience for any given campaign. By utilizing the information found in their research, you'll know that your ads are being shown to the intended viewers thereby maximizing your client's advertising dollars.

Placement Availability

As I've said about most of the topics in this book, placing your ads on a Web site takes forethought. Although there are some sites that may be able to run your ad the very day you first call them, they are getting to be few and far between. Most Web sites' policies and procedures require advance notice before running any ads on their pages, and exactly how far in advance can depend on several factors. Some of the factors involved can include things like what dates you plan on running your banners or how many other advertisers are running ads at the same time in the same place.

> **TIP**
>
> Available placements can indeed sell out on any given Web site, and it happens more and more every year. Although it makes complete sense that this can happen, it's not something that everyone thinks about every day. One way to look at it is like a time-share condo; in any given week, there are only a certain number of hours that can be split between the renters. Once those hours are all taken, you have to move to the next week if you want to spend your vacation there.

It is a good idea to plan on purchasing your placements about 3 months in advance. However, there are special dates where you may be better off getting your order in 6 months or more in advance. The Super Bowl is a good example. We all know and love the television commercials that air during the Super Bowl, and with more and more of those commercials directing viewers to Web sites, the traffic to those sites is increased by leaps and bounds during (and after) the game. In addition to that online traffic is the increased number of visitors to sports-related sites leading up to, during, and after the Super Bowl. Because the traffic to all of these sites grows so much during these times, they have become prime spots for online advertising and as with anything in high demand, this leads to placements selling out more quickly.

Ad Rotation

Because I've used the analogy of a time-share condo to explain placements selling out, I'll go ahead and use it again for ad rotation. If the placement itself is the condo, then your ad is a renter. There are other renters (ads) out there that are sharing the condo (placement) with yours, but they all get it at individual times. However, the placement isn't normally purchased by the day or week; it is instead purchased in blocks of 1000 impressions (each time your ad is viewed, it's called an impression).

A common misunderstanding about ad rotation is how the time is split up among banners. If you maintain your own Web site, you may have seen ad rotation scripts that other developers have so kindly distributed free of charge. Most of them (that I've seen) display different ads, which have been predetermined by you, based on percentages. For example, you may tell the script to show banner A 75% of the time and banner B the other 25% of the time. However, running banners with ad servers doesn't work quite exactly the same way due to the fact that percentages vary greatly from site to site. Where two million impressions may be equal to 1% on a very popular and busy site, that same two million may be equal to 50% on a less popular site. So instead, the percentage is set across the entire ad campaign. Using the same banners from the previous example, you can look at it like this: If banner A is set to run 75% of the time across an entire campaign then banner A will be shown three times before banner B is displayed regardless of the site that each ad is running on.

Ad-Server Tools

A huge plus to using an ad-serving company to host your banners is not only the level of control you keep on your work, but the set of tools they have available to help you achieve that control. The ad-server tools allow you to set up your entire campaign, upload your work, enter every piece of important information that pertains to the campaign, and have the ability to actually look back at that information to track how the campaign is performing. I'll go into more detail on tracking later in this chapter.

Each ad server is different, but they all have pretty much the same capabilities when it comes to the workflow for getting your banners up and running. Here's a very general breakdown of the steps involved.

1. Enter your media plan.
2. Load your banner files and landing page URL.
3. Test your banners.
4. Assign each banner to its placement to get the "tag."
5. Send the "tag" to the site that is running your ad.

Enter Your Media Plan

The first step involved in getting your banners running on an ad server is to enter the media plan into the ad-server tool. The media plan will consist of items such as the placements for your banners, the number of impressions that have been purchased for the campaign, all of the costs involved with running the banners (such as the cost of the impression), and the dates your banners will actually be running. This information will be extremely important in tracking the performance of your ads.

Inside Advertising

When purchasing the banner placements on Web sites, the placements are bought in blocks of 1000 impressions. The price of those blocks, which can range anywhere from $2 all the way up to $100–$200 for standard Flash banners and an additional cost from around 80 cents to around $5 for rich-media banners, is known as the cost per thousand (CPM, where the M is the roman numeral for one thousand). The actual percentage that your purchase works out to will vary from site to site and that percentage is called the share of voice.

Load Your Banner Files and Landing Page URL

This step in the process is pretty self-explanatory. Each ad-server tool has an interface that allows you to upload your files to their servers. For each file you upload, you enter the URL (usually referred to as the landing page URL) that users will be directed to when they click on the banner. The URL that is entered here is the URL that is passed in to the variable you may know as "clickTag" (see Chapter 4).

Test Your Banners

Test, test, and test. While writing this book, I've come to notice just how much testing we do on each and every banner that gets created. I've also come to notice that the testing itself becomes such second nature in the work that some of us may not even realize just how often we're doing it, and that's not a bad thing by any stretch of the imagination. As noted by this step, testing should continue all the way through the life of a project, and testing the banners at this point is very important because they are only a few clicks away from being visible to the rest of the world.

Get the "Tag"

Once the banners have been uploaded and tested, it's time to generate the "tag" for the banner. The tag is basically a reference back to the code that will house the banner. That code may be for something like an iFrame or the JavaScript that will place the banner on the page in which it will be shown. Different ad servers may have slightly different steps for tag generation so you'll want to check with yours for the exact process.

Send the "Tag"

After the tag has been generated and everyone has approved the banner, it's time to take the final step in releasing your banner to the world by sending the tag to the site from which you have purchased your impressions. As I mentioned before, the tag is a reference to a piece of code that will house your banner, and by sending a tag to the site, you are not sending your actual files.

Tracking Your Ads

After your ads have been set up in the ad-server tools, the next thing to do after a predetermined amount of time has passed is track their performance. Tracking the performance of your banners can give you a wealth of information that can be used, in part, on future projects. You will receive information relating to how many times the ad was viewed, how many viewers clicked on it, and whether or not the ad ended up helping your client make a profit on their advertising dollars. All of this information is available in the same ad-server tools that were used to launch your banners. It's the reason you entered all of the details about the media plan in step one of the previous section, and because of the tracking, you will be able to show your client their return on investment (ROI) in regards to a particular campaign.

> **TIP**
>
> When you sit down to figure out the ROI for a direct marketing campaign, keep in mind that the number of sales for the particular product or service may be skewed. This is due to a gray area that lies in between the direct marketing approach and the brand awareness approach. The most likely course of customer action that would fall into this gray area would be if they viewed your ad for a product and then later drove to the store to purchase (as opposed to buying online). Because the in-store purchase cannot be directly tied to the banner view, the sale cannot be figured in with the ROI.

Impressions, Interactions, Clicks, and More

People often get the terms impressions, interactions, and clicks confused with one another the first few times they hear them. I'll go ahead and admit now that when I first came into the advertising field, I wasn't 100% sure if I was using each term correctly when I spoke of them. However, I'm happy to say that I quickly caught on and can now confidently pass the information on.

When the tag that was explained in the previous section is called, your banner is shown and an impression is counted. Also mentioned earlier in this chapter is the fact that the number of times your ad will be shown is predetermined by the amount of impressions that have been purchased in the media plan.

Interactions and clicks can be very easily mixed up just by looking at the words themselves. The difference between the two is that when an interaction is counted, it means that someone interacted with something in the banner, but didn't actually visit the landing page. Interactions can be anything from rolling over a certain item in the banner to scrolling through images in the banner. A click is different because when a click is tracked, it means someone literally clicked on the banner and was taken to the promoted Web site.

Because you now have the numbers on hand for how many times your ad was shown (impressions) and the number of times someone clicked on the ad to visit the landing page (clicks), you can find out what the click-through rate (CTR) is. The CTR is the rate at which users click on your ad based on how many times it was shown. In most cases, the math will be done for you by the ad-server tool, but just in case, the formula is simply clicks divided by impressions times one hundred ((clicks ÷ impressions) × 100). So if you have 1000 impressions and 100 users clicked on the ad, your CTR would be as follows: (100 ÷ 1000) × 100 = 10%.

Finally, a conversion is counted when a user has clicked on your banner, been directed to the landing page, and performed the action that you intended for him or her to perform. For example, your banner may have directed a user to a page with an e-mail sign-up form. If he or she fills out the form and submits it, a conversion is counted. Likewise, you may have directed him or her to a page where he or she could instantly purchase your client's product. Again, if he or she makes the purchase, a conversion is counted.

Determining the "Cost per Everything"

Now comes the part where you find out how well the banners are working for their money. If you aren't already working in the online advertising world, you may have never heard several of the terms I'm about to talk about. Then again, you may be working in online advertising but never paid much attention to what these terms mean. Either way, I'm about to explain a few costs that are determined by the information gained from tracking your banners' performance.

In regard to figuring out how well an ad was performing on a cost basis, I was once jokingly told, "We have a cost per everything." There's a cost per click, a cost per interaction, a cost per conversion, and so on. There are formulas for figuring out each of these costs but they will most likely be done for you in the ad-server tool. In short, the ads that are performing better will have lower costs associated with them, and the ones that are performing worse will have higher costs. The importance of knowing how much each aspect of your ad is costing comes into play on several occasions and one of those is when it's time to optimize the campaign.

Optimize Your Campaign

At some point, enough time will have passed that you can use the numbers from your tracking and costs to optimize your campaign. When you optimize your campaign, you're making the banners work more efficiently for the money spent, which in turn means that your client is getting a better return on their advertising dollars. Figuring out how exactly your campaign should be optimized is pretty straightforward. The first step is to study the performance of each banner on each site. After comparing them all against each other to find which ones are doing better, you'll know which ones to remove and which ones to keep. However, removing some and keeping some is only part of the optimization. After you remove the ads that are performing poorly, you need to increase the number of times the better performing ads are shown. If an ad is performing well, increasing the number of times it's shown will mean even more clicks, and, as I mentioned earlier, more clicks equals lower costs and lower costs equals happy clients.

Rich-Media Ads

There was a time when the tracking and reporting from rich-media companies (see Chapter 6) was far less robust than the reporting you get from a general ad-serving company. However, in the past few years, they have expanded their capabilities to match. With that said, trafficking and tracking rich-media ads remain a little bit different because there is a necessary third party involved in the process. Additionally, the final piece of reference code that you send to your client will be different as well.

Trafficking Rich Media

When trafficking a rich-media banner, the steps taken may differ a little from one rich-media company to another. One quick example would be the process you might experience when trafficking your ads through a company such as Eyeblaster, which has an online interface (or tool) that allows you to log in to complete every step involved in getting your ads live on the Web. Once you have logged in to the tool, the steps are pretty straightforward and not all that different from setting up your standard banners.

1. Enter your media plan.
2. Upload your files and enter the landing page URL.
3. Preview your banner.
4. Assign each banner to its flight.
5. Send the Eyeblaster reference to the site.

Enter Your Media Plan

Just as with the standard banners, the first thing you should do when running your ads through Eyeblaster is enter the information about the media plan. Again, this information includes things like the number of impressions purchased, the costs involved, and the placements where the ads will show.

Upload Your Files and Enter the Landing Page URL

When it comes to uploading your files, Eyeblaster has made it nice and easy with a piece of their interface that will allow you to add a file using a simple form. But what if you're setting up a campaign that is running 30 different banners? Uploading all of those Flash files and backup images could be very tedious and time consuming, so Eyeblaster went ahead and included the ability to upload multiple files at the same time, which helps streamline your day a little.

Preview Your Banner

After your files are uploaded, the Eyeblaster tool has an ad-preview feature that allows you to see a fully functional version of your ad. You can either preview it by itself on a blank background or you have the option to see how it looks laying on top of any Web site of your choice. Once you're happy with it, you can e-mail a link to the preview to yourself, your quality control team, and anyone else who may need to approve the ad before it goes live.

Assign Each Banner to Its Flight

In the Eyeblaster tool, placements are called "flights," and once your ad is approved by all of the appropriate people, you can start assigning them. When you do start assigning your ads to their flights, remember that each individual ad can be assigned to multiple flights at the same time. In other words, if you had 10 flights that were running a 728 × 90 ad, you wouldn't actually need to create 10 different 728 × 90 ads unless they were visually different from one another.

Send the Eyeblaster Reference to the Site

Sending the ads to the sites on which they will be running is a little different when you're using Eyeblaster as opposed to setting up a standard banner. With Eyeblaster, you'll use their interface to send an e-mail to the sites (and anyone else you specify) notifying them that the ads are ready for their review. Within the e-mail are any notes you've included, as well as instructions for the recipients to view the ads. Once they have looked over the ads, they can then use the Eyeblaster tool to respond by approving or declining them. If they have chosen to decline, they will write their reasons in the response. Based on those reasons, you can make the needed revisions and resubmit the ads until they are correct.

Tracking Rich Media

Tracking rich-media ads is similar to tracking standard ads. In fact, the two are so similar that you can do the tracking for both with the same ad-serving company like Atlas or DoubleClick. That also means that all of your tracking can be in one place for a given campaign in which you have both standard and rich-media banners. Generally, this is possible with the use of a 1 × 1 transparent .gif file. The .gif is loaded from the ad server (Atlas, DoubleClick, and so on) into the rich-media placement. Each time the .gif is loaded, it gets counted as an impression of the banner.

On top of all of your tracking being in one central location, the reason it's a good idea to track your rich-media banners through a standard ad server is because the conversion reporting is far less robust with rich-media companies (if they offer it at all). That said, rich-media companies do report on actions like clicks, impressions, interactions, and so forth.

Site-Served Ads

Site-served ads are simply ads that are hosted by the site on which they are running instead of being hosted by an ad server. The more time that passes, the more rare site-served ads have become for several reasons. Although it may seem like less hassle and trouble to go ahead and send your files directly to the site, you end up with far less control, and the ability to track the performance of the ad is greatly reduced.

ALERT!

When a banner ad is site served, you will lose many valuable pieces of control over it, such as the ability to quickly make changes.

Loss of Control

If your banners are site served, you are going to lose a very considerable amount of control over them. For example, you'll be sending the site your actual files instead of the previously mentioned reference tag. This means that you'll need to depend on the person in charge of programming that site to get everything right. By turning over that control, you may find that your 728 × 90 banner was accidentally placed in a 300 × 250 spot ... without being tested. In addition to possibly using the wrong dimensions, the code that shows the default image in the case of a viewer not having the Flash Player installed may not be used. Another large loss is the assurance of knowing the ad was even placed on the site when it should have been. The only real way you have of knowing is to take the time to visit each individual site on which you're running a site-served ad (and you probably have more important things to do with that time).

Slow Changes

If you've ever had to change anything online, you know how nice it is to have direct access to the files you need to alter. But imagine for a minute if you didn't have access to those files. If you have any ads being site served, you'll run into this problem if your banner needs to be changed or replaced. There is a big difference between using an ad server or running site-served ads when it comes to easily making those changes, and that difference is time. Because of the channels you'll most likely have to go through to change a site-served banner, it could possibly take up to a week before the change is actually made. However, while hosting your banners on an ad server, the same changes could be done in an hour.

Less Tracking

Along with not knowing for sure if your ad has actually been placed when and where it should be, your ability to track how well your ad is performing is reduced. Of course that means less ability to look at costs, clicks, conversions, profitability, and anything else that falls under the tracking umbrella. With less tracking, you'll have a harder time knowing how well that particular banner contributed to the campaign or if you should even spend money in the future to run more ads in that same spot.

Conclusion

To wrap up this chapter, let's take a quick walk back through it. One of the very first steps in any banner project is the media buy, which, as I hope I've shown, involves much more than simply picking up the phone and placing an order. Making sure you're purchasing the correct placements for ads means not only knowing who your target audience are but also what they do, what sites they visit, what they're interested in, and much, much more. Once you have that information, you can better decide where, when, and how often to run your ads. That is, of course, dependent on those times and placements being available.

Also covered in this chapter were the general steps involved in setting up your banners in an ad-server tool. Just as a quick recap on those steps, they were to first enter your media plan, then load your banner files and landing page URL. The next step is to test your banners. Once tested, you assign each banner to its placement to get the tag and finally you send the tag to the site that is running your ad.

Once your banners are live online, you can track their performance and figure out how much each individual ad (and even detailed aspects of it) is ultimately costing your client. Based on the performance of your banners, you can then optimize the campaign by removing poor-performing ads and increasing the share of voice for ads that are doing better.

Another topic covered in this chapter was that of trafficking and tracking your rich-media ads. Although there are differences between these and trafficking/tracking standard banners, the general process is very similar. Once it gets down to the actual tracking, standard banners and rich-media banners are no different at all because you can track them altogether in one location.

Finally, I talked about site-served ads. Although having your ads hosted by the individual sites themselves is becoming an increasingly rare occurrence, there may still be times when you don't have much choice. It's generally a good idea to avoid site-served ads, but if you find yourself in the situation, keep in mind (and let your client know about) the downsides, such as slow changes, less tracking, and less control over the placement itself.

8

DESIGNING MICROSITES

As I mentioned in Chapter 2, there are similarities between designing microsites and designing banners. If you recall, I also mentioned that there are differences between the two as well, and this chapter concentrates on the microsite side of things. These differences can make designing a microsite a very exciting and fun experience due to many factors. Factors such as no file size constraints, more freedom of design, and the ability to load various types of external files at runtime all help open up the channels of creativity required to create a microsite that will be viewed and passed from person to person. As you read through the sections in this chapter, you'll notice several visual examples of microsites that have been provided by Click Here, Inc. (Fig. 8.1 through Fig. 8.13).

- Less Constraints
- Conception
- Know the Brand (and Learn It if You Don't)
- Navigation
- Designing to Move

Flash Advertising. DOI: 10.1016/B978-0-240-81345-5.00008-6

Figure 8.1 2006 Hyundai Azera – Produced by Click Here, Inc.

Less Constraints

Before getting into a discussion about the actual designing of microsites, I'd like to discuss a little more about some of the differences between microsite design and banner design. More specifically, I'd like to point out those differences that open up the avenues of creativity by removing the invisible box of constraints. As with just about anything else in life, when the constraints are lifted, more brilliance is possible. On the other hand, sometimes, when constraints are removed, more discipline is required.

No File Size Limit

When you transition from designing banner ads into designing microsites, you'll find that one of the most noticeable differences is the lack of file size limits. The main reason

Figure 8.2 Casio G'zOne – Produced by Click Here, Inc.

banner ads have file size constraints is because the banners themselves are not the main focus of the page on which they are displayed. However, when it comes to your microsite, people have navigated to your URL to see it and it alone. In other words, your microsite takes a back seat to no one at its own Web address.

With no file size limit, you are much freer to do nearly anything you like as far as images and other aspects of a file that raise the final size of a .swf output. Notice that I say nearly anything. I say that because even if you are informed that the sky is the limit on file constraints, even if you're told that your only target audience is in office buildings with the highest available Internet connection speeds, and even if you're told that your files will only be seen across an intranet, you should always aim for the lowest possible file size on your final output. This is where increased discipline comes into play, and it can be very important to the success of your microsite. Remember to shoot for the moon, but then reel it back in a bit until you feel comfortable with the final file size and subsequent load times.

Figure 8.3 GameStop/Left 4 Dead 2 – Produced by Click Here, Inc.

No Timing/Looping Limit

Your microsites obviously aren't going to just sit there and loop an animation over and over again, but you may have some element on your site that does. Perhaps it's a particle effect like sparks, fire, or smoke, and if you ran that same element inside a banner, you'd have to put a stop to it after a given amount of time. On the other hand, you don't have to worry about any of those timing or looping constraints within your site. The main reason I mention this in a chapter about designing is to let you know that you can feel free to run animations and effects for any given span of time that you feel necessary (even indefinitely if you like). You should, however, keep processor usage and distraction from the content in mind. If your user is too distracted from the content, then they aren't as likely to buy into your client's products or services. Also, if the site has so much going on in it that it causes the user's browser to bog down, they'll be less likely to come back.

Conception

While coming up with a design for a microsite can sometimes be very involved and challenging, the amount of fun that can go into it makes it worthwhile. If you compare designing a microsite to designing a full company Web site, you'll find that the biggest differences are usually structure and content weight. Since company Web sites are the online representation of the companies themselves, they usually want those to be nice, clean, corporately structured, and full of business-related content (depending on the client, of course). On the other hand, microsites offer companies a more interactive and immersive escape of sorts to show how fun and free flowing their product or service is when it's in your hands.

Lighten Up, Man

Like I said, microsites are typically a lot more fun than company sites. A comparison might be like saying that if the company Web site is equivalent to sitting in a meeting in the stuffy boardroom on the 50th floor of a corporate glass tower, the microsite should be like doing a base jump from the window of that same boardroom. Both scenarios involve the same company, but the experiences are quite different.

Figure 8.4 ArcLight Cinemas – Produced by Click Here, Inc.

Along with being more entertaining, the microsite is also usually a lot shorter on content than the company Web site. The simple reason for that is because people visit the company Web site to get information about the company itself, but people visit the microsite to experience a product. It's all dependent on what users are after. If they are looking for heavy amounts of corporate information, the company site is their target destination. If they are looking for something that gets right to the point of a product while being big on emotion and experience, then you'll want to direct them to the microsite.

Let the Product Guide You

What your client actually does is obviously very important to the design of a microsite. There are certain industries (and even specific products within an industry) that lend themselves to somewhat of a predefined look and feel. Some will scream for a

Figure 8.5 Kiwi – Produced by Click Here, Inc.

shiny, extravagant design with lots of bells, whistles, and extra features to amaze viewers and users, while others will call for more of a simple, elegant, slick design. On a more detailed level, the product itself should also influence the colors you choose. For example, if you were designing a site about rocket engines, you might use a combination of reds, oranges, and blues to add to the feel and signify the fire and sky associated with rockets.

Know the Brand (and Learn It if You Don't)

Being familiar with the brand for which you're building a microsite is worth mentioning again (I spoke to this topic in Chapter 2 as well). It should significantly sway your thoughts of design for the site just as much as the individual product if not more. But what happens when you get a project to design a microsite for a brand that has never been targeted at you, one that you're not familiar with, or one that you've simply never heard of? Well, it's time to hit the Internet and the stores to start studying up.

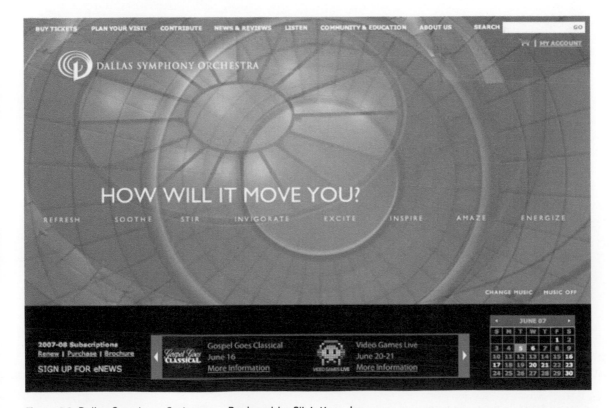

Figure 8.6 Dallas Symphony Orchestra – Produced by Click Here, Inc.

Find Information

If you're unfamiliar with your client's brand or product, don't hesitate to search around the Internet for it. In this day of free-flowing information, you can usually find what you're looking for extremely fast. First off, visit the client's current Web site to read about them, view their products, and experience their brand as it exists prior to your redesign. In addition to visiting their Web site, find out who their competitors are and take a look at how they are presenting themselves.

Another good place to look is to your friends and family. If you are female and the brand is targeted at males, talk to some men who might know something about the product in question. The same can be said for any of the demographics, such as age range. The people you're looking for are those who actually interact with the brand and might be able to tell you their take on it as a consumer. Once you've talked to the correct people, try to put yourself in their shoes and see the brand the way they do.

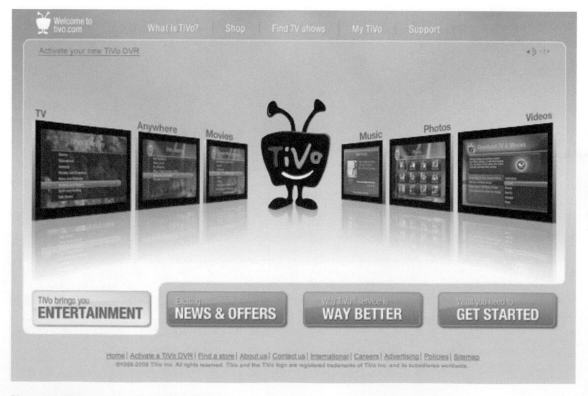

Figure 8.7 TiVo – Produced by Click Here, Inc.

TIP

In addition to a company's Web site and your friends and family, social tools like Facebook and Twitter are an excellent source for gathering opinions and experiences with products. You're almost guaranteed to get plenty of replies if you put a question out there asking people if they've used product X and what they thought about it.

Finally, look to the world around you. Everywhere you look, something is being advertised, and there are brands being shown around every corner. Take a look at billboards as you drive to work, pay attention to advertising on the side of buses you pass, don't be so quick to skip over the ads in a magazine you're reading, and watch the commercials that interrupt your favorite television shows. While you're noticing all of this advertising that surrounds you day in and day out, pay attention to those that are similar to the brand you're currently working with. What is most important here is that you don't look at the ads in terms of copying any designs, but rather look to them for inspiration. One last thing to pay attention to is life. Ideas can come out of any strange little happening that you may miss. They can spur from a single sentence that someone says to you on the elevator or from a lunch conversation that has absolutely nothing to do with the topic. I even have to wonder how many great advertisements were born from some silly little thing a child said while doing nothing more than playing with his or her toys and imagination. The point here is to keep your eyes and ears open because you may just catch onto something that fits perfectly with the brand.

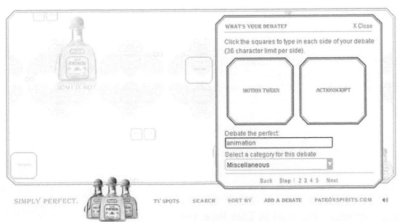

Figure 8.8 Patrón, Simply Perfect (create a debate) — Produced by Click Here, Inc.

Navigation

Navigation is an extremely important element when it comes to designing a microsite. Not only should the navigation menu be easy to find, but it should also be easy to understand and use. The most typical placement for a site's menu is going down the left side of the page or across the top. If there are subsections under any menu items, they typically drop down under the top navigation or show up beside the left menu when a user places his or her mouse over that item. However, this is Flash, and Flash affords us the luxury of things like interactive animation.

What Can't You Do?

Since we are now in the world of Flash, the question changes from, "What else can I do with navigation?" to "What *can't* I do with navigation?" Well, there isn't a whole lot that you can't do, but there are a number of things that you shouldn't do. A quick browsing session of Flash sites on the Internet can usually give

Figure 8.9 Patrón, Simply Perfect (join a debate) – Produced by Click Here, Inc.

you some ideas of both good and bad navigation. Putting the actual look of the menu aside, you should think about aspects like movement, interaction, readability, and the submenu (if there is one).

Plain or Pretty

While you're figuring out how you want the navigation to look and move, don't forget to consider the number one factor in the project: your client. The menu design of some sites will have to be plain, while others get to be more decorative and pretty. It may go without saying, but if you're working on a microsite for cancer research, you're probably not going to design the same menu as you might for a fun-and-games site for kids. One will be more straightforward and simple, while the other has a crazier, outside-the-box look to it. However, both menus should be very easy to understand and navigate. If you find that you have to include any kind of directions telling users how to use the menu, it may be time to rethink the design.

Figure 8.10 Patrón, Simply Perfect (watch the commercials) – Produced by Click Here, Inc.

Designing to Move

A couple of details that some people tend to let slip their minds when designing are transitions and animation. When a page or section of a Flash microsite is designed, you should always think about what happens between the times that users click on a button and when they arrive at the resulting destination. Will the page simply do a "hard cut" type of change as it would with an old-school, pre-AJAX HTML page, or will there be some movement to get them from point A to point B?

Plan to Move Users

Since we are working with a toolset that will allow us to literally "move" users from one section of a site to another, we should take advantage of that when the situation calls for it. Sometimes, the best thing to do is the hard cut, but there will be plenty of other times when a nice quick animation will actually strengthen what the design is attempting to portray or just make the site a

Figure 8.11 Hoovers Hoov Lane – Produced by Click Here, Inc.

little more interesting to navigate. If you stop and think about some of the sites where transitions caught your eye, there's an extremely high chance that those animations didn't just happen by accident. Instead, they were very well thought out, planned, and designed in advance of the site actually being built and programmed in Flash.

Just as I stated in Chapter 2, it's a good idea to plan your major animations while you are laying out the design (and even sooner than that when you're only visualizing the design in your head). A very big part of that planning is making sure that you have the assets you need to make the animation happen. Without the correct images (or video), the person that will be animating and programming the site can't create the correct movement. I am reiterating the importance of this again in this chapter because it does happen that animations are planned without thought to how they will be (or if they even can be) executed with the available assets.

Squash, Stretch, and Anticipation

While the major movements of the transitions and animations should absolutely be planned in the design phase of the project, you would be okay to wait on the details of those movements. When the design is handed over to the Flash developer, do your best to let go a little while still staying involved. First, explain the major movements that you have designed to the Flash developer. After working with him or her to get the overall mechanics of the animation created, ask him or her to tweak the movement accordingly. In other words, let him or her work out and create the details to making the animation feel as it should rather than just suddenly moving from one point to the next. For example, you may have a ball in your design that you want to get from one side of the screen to the other, and the major movement you've decided on is bouncing (as opposed to rolling or being thrown). Let the Flash developer know your thoughts and work with him or her on getting the general bounce animated. Then, walk away and let him or her apply the details such as the general animation rules of squash, stretch, and anticipation. During all this tweaking, remember that there could be a couple of projects where timelines/deadlines may not allow for all the tweaks you'd like to see. If you find yourself in that situation, try to think of which animations and tweaks are the most important and which ones will be okay with simply moving an object from point A to point B. The bottom line is to trust the Flash developers with the work. After all, it's what they do for a living, right?

Figure 8.12 Pork Recipes – Produced by Click Here, Inc.

Know When to Say When

Knowing when to stop animating is just as important as knowing what to animate and when to animate it. Knowing when to stop animating also means more than one thing: it means not overanimating the microsite (unless the brand calls for it), it means animating at the right speeds and intervals, and it means knowing when to stop making changes to the animations.

Overanimation of a microsite can get very annoying to a visitor very quickly. That is unless the overanimation enhances the experience of the brand. As with several other design and animation rules, this one will apply differently to different projects. The main thing is to pay attention to how much animation you have happening within the site that doesn't serve much of a purpose, like getting a user from one section to the next. Again, you'll have to make a judgment call on this from project to project.

The speed and frequency at which an animation happens is also something that can either keep users coming back to

Figure 8.13 Mix & Match Pork – Produced by Click Here, Inc.

your site or drive them away after the first visit. How many Flash-based sites have you visited where every little move you made played an animation before you could get where you wanted to go? And how many sites have you been to where you find yourself waiting longer than you feel you should for those animations to finish? How about sites where you spend more time watching things animate than you spend actually reading the content? Your visitors have most likely experienced the same thing at other sites as well. That's why it's important to use animations and transitions quickly and only where they help add to the experience of the site.

A final list of all the major animations should be decided on prior to animating and programming the site. Any new animations that are thought of after the site is in full swing of production could possibly set the timeline back depending on the complexity of the new movements. While changes to the site are definitely going to be inevitable in some cases, try your hardest to avoid adding new animations or even changing the existing ones too drastically. Depending on exactly how the site in question is built, retrofitting it for a new animation may even mean having to scrap and rebuild parts that could have taken hours to complete the first time.

Conclusion

Designing for microsites has a few different steps and several of the same steps as designing for banner ads. Going back over some of those steps in this chapter, you'll see that one big difference between the two is the fact that you aren't constrained by final file size or time limits when you're working on a microsite. However, while more and more people are moving to some form of broadband Internet connection, you should still try to keep your files and your site from getting too bloated. If you make people wait too long to see your microsite, they may give up and leave.

Coming up with a concept for microsites is similar to coming up with a concept for banners, but more detailed and on a larger scale. Your clients want their product (and brand) to be remembered, and your design will help them accomplish that goal. Remember that this isn't your client's corporate Web site, so depending on the product and where it takes you, keep your concepts from being too stuffy and strict. In other words, try to design for users to have a memorable experience rather than forcing them to read a bunch of legal copy.

Part of being able to create concepts for a new microsite is to know something about the product and the brand. If it's a brand that you're already familiar with, then ideas should start generating in your head right away based on your past experiences with it. On the other hand, it may not be anything that you've ever come in contact with and that means you'll need to do a little research to get a feel for the brand. One way to find your answer is talking to people you know who fall into the target audience of the product.

Menu design is very important on a microsite. It's how users will find their way to new areas of the experience, and they should be able to do so very easily. Just like the overall design itself, the layout of the menu is going to be dependent on the client or product involved. For some, you'll need to stick with the classic left or top menu bar, while others will call for something more creative and fun. The most important thing to remember in designing the menu is to make it easy and intuitive. Otherwise, you may end up with users who leave too soon simply because they got confused on how to navigate the site.

Finally, think about how your design will live and breathe. You're designing a microsite that will be built in Flash, so go ahead and design some animation and transitions while you're at it. However, remember to actually plan those movements while you work. Make sure you have all the assets that will be needed in order to create those animations in advance of handing the design over to the Flash developer. Once you do hand it over, work with the developer to get the major motions and mechanics of the animation created. After that, let go and turn over some creative control to let the developer flesh out the small details in the movement. Once everyone is happy with all the animations, and aside from changes that absolutely must be made, try to keep from making big modifications or additions in terms of the animations themselves. Afterthoughts and retrofitting animation could possibly push a project over its deadline.

9

PREPARING AND BUILDING MICROSITES

As I've mentioned before, a microsite is exactly what it claims to be: a site that is smaller than a regular, full-size site. You could probably also guess that building a microsite is a good deal different than building a banner. For starters, there's going to be a lot more information and interactivity available for your audience on a microsite than on a banner. Despite the differences, there will also be similarities between the two projects. As with building a round of banners, you'll need to plan out how you're going to work on the microsite. You'll also need to make sure you have assets in order and a backup plan for users who have disabled the Flash Player and/or JavaScript. If you've already read Chapter 3, you'll notice some of the similarities and differences in preparing and building microsites as you read through this chapter, which is broken into the following sections:

- Choosing Your Tools
- Planning Your Work
- Collecting Assets
- Building to Standards

Flash Advertising. DOI: 10.1016/B978-0-240-81345-5.00009-8

- HTML and JavaScript
- No-Flash Backup
- Deep Linking
- Collecting User Data
- Quality Control

Choosing Your Tools

When you're tasked with building a Flash Web site, it doesn't necessarily mean that you'll be working in the Flash IDE. It really just means that you'll be using one (or more) of several choices of tools to compile .swf files for users to view and interact with in the Flash Player. The tools you use will depend on several factors ranging from the project requirements to your personal experience level to budgets. Oh, and let's not forget a few more important factors like the capabilities of a given tool or the ease of execution of a given task. For example, a project with a lot of animation is probably going to call for Flash Professional CS5 over Flash Builder 4. On the other side of that example and in my own personal experience, Flash Builder is probably going to be a better choice for a project that's more about data (HTTPService, WebService, and so on) and less about animation. Of course when it comes to making things look pretty, both options are outstanding and you're only bound by your creativity.

Flash

As I was saying, one option you have when you're creating a Flash Web site is to do so with Flash itself and this is the most likely option when you're talking about microsites in the realm of advertising. For this book, I'm using Flash Professional CS5 (Fig. 9.1) but CS4 and CS3 are obviously still extremely valid options. If you're

Figure 9.1 Flash Professional CS5.

reading this book, I have to assume that you're at least somewhat familiar with Flash so I won't spend a huge amount of time describing it in depth. However, I'll go ahead with a very quick background and talk about it at a bit of a high level for anyone who happens to be reading this who isn't a Flash developer or designer (i.e., project managers, and so on).

Although Flash has been around since 1996, most people didn't know about it until a little later as it started showing up in more and more places on the Internet. At that time, it was primarily used and known for Web sites with large amounts of animations and glitzy little spinning and blinking effects. Due to the fact that most of those sites were way bigger in file size than they really had any business being in a primarily dial-up connection world, Flash also started being known as a way to show an "intro" for your site while it loaded. Fast forward to today since I said I'd keep it high level and the Flash experience has matured by leaps and bounds in terms of user experience and interaction design. Today, it's very easy to find that Flash is used to create everything from banners and full-blown Web sites to games and applications.

When you're looking at Flash as a possible candidate for a given project, or even just a task within a project, one of the main things you'll want to consider is animation. If you're dealing with animated assets like characters with walk/run cycles, your life will be much easier if you create those animations on the timeline as opposed to trying to write code to accomplish the same thing. Another thing that would make Flash the ideal choice is if the design is very image heavy and there are a lot of cut images to work with. Finally, the final .swf size is typically smaller when published from Flash as opposed to Flex/Flash Builder because it doesn't need to compile the Flex framework in with your project. Speaking of Flash Builder, let's look at that option next.

Flash Builder (Flex)

So another option that you may find yourself considering is Flex. There are a number of ways to work with Flex including (but not limited to) using the text editor of your choice in conjunction with the free SDK (Software Development Kit) or working in Flash Builder 4 (Fig. 9.2), which was previously named Flex Builder. If you've downloaded and installed Flash Builder, then you've also installed the Flex SDK and you're ready to go.

Although Flash is going to be the choice more often in advertising, there will still be times when you'll want to use Flex because of its feature set or because of the project requirements. A few things that might make you lean toward Flex for a microsite would be data collection, charting/data visualization, or certain classes that are included in the Flex framework but aren't available in Flash.

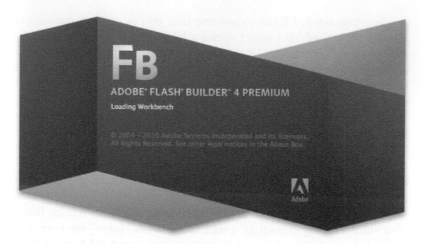

Figure 9.2 Flash Builder 4 Premium.

For example, you may have a contest microsite where you've built several forms for collecting information from the user. With the validators that are available in Flex (EmailValidator, PhoneNumberValidator, and so on), you can validate the information a lot easier than you would be able to while working in Flash. A broad, general rule of thumb that I like to use if I'm considering Flex/Flash Builder for a project is this: If it performs more like a data-centric application than an "experience," Flex may very well be the answer. That thinking also ties in with how heavy the project is on graphical assets, movement, transitional animations, and so on.

TIP

Even if you're using the various validators in Flex, you should still perform server-side validation of any data sent across.

Other Tools

In addition to Flash Professional CS5 and Flash Builder 4, there are many other tools available for you to work with when it comes to writing the code for your project. Depending on what you're looking for and what operating system you're working on, your choices range from free to a small fee to hundreds of dollars. Some of the options are much more robust than others in that they include features like code hinting, formatting, debugging, and even launching a test movie from the editor (through Flash). With all of that said, I'd like to suggest you do a bit of research into what tools work best for you. To get you started in that direction, do a quick search and take a look at tools like FDT, FlashDevelop, and TextMate.

Planning Your Work

Having a good plan in place before working on any project is priceless. If you get into a project and find out that things weren't planned out quite well enough after spending a good amount of hours on it, you just may find yourself in a very troublesome position. You may find that you have to change so much in the site to accommodate for the lack of planning that you end up reverting back by half of the time already spent.

So where do you start to plan for your build? Discuss with the artist on the project, of course. Before the artist designed and laid out the site, there was already some planning in place. Planning of what the client wanted to accomplish, a wireframe of the site, possible paths that users might take to navigate the site, and so on. That planning should have played a major role in how the site was designed from a creative standpoint and that artist has a vision of how it should all tie together.

Inside Advertising

A site wireframe is a diagrammed skeleton of the site itself. It contains all of the navigation items and how each one ties into or connects with the others. By looking at the wireframe, you can see possible paths of navigation and how many pages deep a given section of the site may go. On some pages, you can see processes that may occur and a general outline of the content, as well as the importance of a given piece of content. Figure 9.3 is an example of a single page from a site wireframe.

Page: Video/Audio file administration and moderation

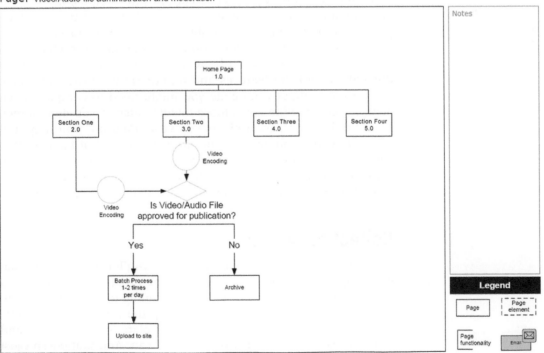

Not intended to show design, only to inventory page contents and relationships.

2

Figure 9.3 Example page from a site wireframe.

ALERT!

When you're creating and working with information architecture documents, such as site maps and wireframes, it is very important to let your clients know that those items are intended to show site organization and content hierarchy/importance, not design. On top of verbally informing them of this, you may also consider including it on the documents themselves. Simply place a sentence like, "These documents are not intended to show design, only to inventory page contents and relationships" in a place where they will be seen on each page.

While you are talking to the artist, get as many details as you can and take plenty of notes on his answers. Don't be scared to ask about anything no matter how small it may seem because you will often find out that not everything was thought of beforehand. If there are multiple pages in the site, how will you transit between them? Do the buttons have rollover states and are menu items animated or do they just cut from the up state to the over state? What if a user clicks that button right there? And that button? Where does this button take the user? You get the idea. The point to this line of questioning is multifaceted: on one side, you need to know how the site will live and breathe; on another side, you need to know how the site will react to certain interactions; and on yet another side, you and the artist can (and should) try to detach yourselves from the project and think like an outside user.

Another thing to do while you are in the planning phase is to think about the code you'll be writing. When you're talking with the artist about the features and functionality of the site, make mental notes about what code you might need to complete each item. Better yet, write down those mental notes so you don't forget. Also, think about past projects you've worked on. You may find that you worked on another site or even a round of banners that have code you can use in the form of classes or snippets. If you do happen to think of such a project, you'll know that you can already plan on saving a little development time by reusing that code.

Collecting Assets

Before you can actually build a microsite, you'll need to know what it's going to look like, right? Okay, so the artist on your team has designed the layout of the site and hopefully given that layout to you in at least the form of a Photoshop file (and possibly printouts). That layout is your guide and template for this project and your goal is to mimic it as closely as you can. And that doesn't just mean images either. You'll also need to pay attention to aspects like the typography. There's an art to everything you see in the layout and the text is no exception. Kerning, tracking, leading, ragging – every bit of it is as intentional as the location of the client logo or the menu item names, and you can't forget to build it into the site the same as it appears in the design.

Speaking of typography, another asset to collect is fonts, and you'll need to get your hands on any that the artist used in the layout. If you don't have a place on your servers where you store fonts, ask the artist to get you the fonts you need to build the site. Because the artist used the fonts in the design, he or she should be able to get them for you. Be sure to get exactly the right fonts too. Most fonts have different sets even for the bold or italic versions. If you only get the "regular" version of a font and then try to add bold or italics inside Flash, you may end up with a font that appears slightly different than the one you should actually be using, and that could make enough of a difference in the end product that you may not get creative approval (or client approval for that matter).

Any imagery within the design will need to be exported from the layout for use in your site. A lot of times, there can be a mixture of both raster and vector art. Looking back at Chapter 3, you'll remember that raster images are defined as images that are a rectangular grid of pixels with individually defined colors. Although raster graphics are generally larger than vector graphics in file size, they will be required for many parts of your work such as photographs of client products. Again referring back to Chapter 3, when cutting raster images from Photoshop, you should give yourself about three pixels of cushion between the edge of the object in the image and the edge of the crop area if you can.

Vector graphics are different than raster graphics in that they are not based on a set grid of pixels. Instead, vector graphics use mathematics with primitive shapes like points, lines, and curves. Vector graphics also scale much more gracefully than raster graphics. As a matter of fact, you can scale a vector graphic indefinitely with no loss to the quality of the image it creates. Try that with a raster image and you'll end up with a poor-quality, pixilated picture that looks more like a piece of blurry mosaic art than the image you started with.

Any time you have a piece of the design that can be built with vector art, you should do your best to build it that way. If, however, the artist on the project has already built it as a vector graphic, you should be able to export it from Photoshop, Illustrator, and so forth and bring it directly into Flash. This will ensure that you are keeping exactly to the layout as it was originally designed.

Building to Standards

As I covered in Chapter 3, it's a good idea to find a naming convention and stick with it. Whether it's you developing the site on your own or a team that you're a part of, a good naming convention just

Table 9.1 Naming Convention Examples

MovieClip containing a form	formMovieClip
TextInput for user's e-mail address	emailTextInput
Button to submit a form	submitButton
Sound object for background music	musicSound

makes everything that much easier to find and work with. Table 9.1 contains the same examples I used in the "Conventions and Best Practices" section of Chapter 3, but I thought I'd include it again for people like myself who tend to flip around in books.

Separating your site into different files is another good practice to get into. You gain several benefits when you compartmentalize your work in this way. One of those benefits is the option to easily split the project among more than one developer where each person works on a set number of sections in the site. You also gain the benefit of quickly isolating and resolving issues and errors with the site. For example, a bug might be reported to you that only happens in the "About Us" section of a site you've just passed on to quality control. Because each section of your site is broken out to its own file(s), you're going to have a 99.9% chance that you know exactly which file to open to fix the bug. Additionally, since that file doesn't contain the entire site itself, you won't have to dig through any overly large libraries or classes to find the culprit of your problem.

Because we're talking about compartmentalizing your work, let's talk a bit about classes. I'll be completely honest here and admit that I didn't make any real use of classes until just before ActionScript 3 came out. During the days of ActionScript 2, I was big on putting the majority of my code on the timeline, and the most I strived for was to get as much of it on the first frame of the main timeline as I could. Now I find myself striving to have as little code on the timeline as I possibly can while reminding myself and understanding that sometimes it's necessary and it's definitely not any kind of a sin. Quickly for those who aren't familiar with classes, ActionScript classes are files with the .as extension and they can contain the code to do anything from completing a simple task like dispatching a custom event to building entire custom components. Something else worth noting is that while writing classes with ActionScript 2 was more forgiving in its rules, ActionScript 3 has changed that leniency. In the years since ActionScript 3 was released, there has been much debate in the development community about whether or not that strictness is a good thing or not. As a matter of fact, you can probably still find developers discussing if

Figure 9.4 The ActionScript Technology Center on the Adobe Web site.

it has made the language stronger or if it just made us have to write more code to accomplish the same tasks. My quick take on it is that it's a great thing because it seems to have done a lot to change the strength, speed, and quality of the code itself. For more detailed information on ActionScript, give a visit to the ActionScript Technology Center on the Adobe Web site at http://www.adobe. com/devnet/actionscript/ (Fig. 9.4). There they list plenty of learning resources, tutorials, and so on. At the time of writing this, you can also find a section for ActionScript 2 tutorials and one for migrating from ActionScript 2 to ActionScript 3.

HTML and JavaScript

Referring back to the "HTML and JavaScript" section of Chapter 3, you'll find some information and quick examples of SWFObject. Although that section of the book was covering banners, the same methods are used to implement SWFObject in the case of a microsite. As a matter of fact, the same methods are used to implement it with *any* .swf. The main difference between using it with a site versus a banner is the HTML you end up putting in the containing div and we'll talk more about that in the next section. If you haven't read it already, turn back to Chapter 3 and give a quick read to the section about SWFObject.

No-Flash Backup

It's probably because of being a Flash Platform developer, but I don't completely understand why some users choose to disable the Flash Player in their browsers. I hear their reasons, but I still think they're just missing out on so much of the truly rich, interactive Web. At any rate, it happens and we need to be prepared for it. There are several options to choose from when it comes to a no-Flash backup, so let's discuss some of them and you can decide which is best for your project.

One option is to present users with an image or some text that lets them know that they need the Flash Player to view your site. Although you may choose to take this route, there are some downsides that go along with it. If you limit your site to Flash only, you limit the potential reach of your client's information. Your clients are trying to sell their product and they are relying on you to help them do so. If you have any control over it, you should avoid this option and save it as a last resort.

Another option is to have a landing page that gives the user an option of a Flash site or a non-Flash site. This option at least lets the Flash-disabled person get to the content of the site. But who likes the old "choose your own adventure" landing page anymore, right? All the more reason to take advantage of SWFObject. If the user's Flash Player is disabled, they'll get to see the HTML you placed inside that div that we keep talking about. Well now, you've just saved your audience from an extra click and took care of it for them while also making sure they were able to get to the information they were trying to find in the first place. That's mighty thoughtful of you. So what about the fact that you've only built one page worth of information within that div? Build a menu into that page for access to other pages. In other words, build it as if it's the home page to a non-Flash site (because it really is).

With this site behind the site, you're allowing full access to all of the information that you are trying to get to the user. Also, by using the same information in the non-Flash site that you use in the Flash site, your information can be found by search engines and that's obviously another plus. In order to handle the links that will be indexed by the search engines, you'll want to include some form of deep linking into your Flash site. Let's jump in to another scenario real quick: Pretend for a moment that a user is searching for a product that your client sells. The user presses the search button and a link to the microsite you've built is within the results. This link could appear in many ways depending on which language you've chosen to write your non-Flash site. One example might be PHP where the link looks something like this: http://www.yoursite.com/pages.php?p=prod. The important part of that URL is the variable "p" on the end. We'll take the value of that variable, pass it in to the Flash site, and have the Flash site respond accordingly. In our scenario, the value of p is "prod" and we know that we want to see the products page.

I won't go any further into the non-Flash site itself because that's another book on another language all together. But let's go ahead and discuss a bit about deep linking.

TIP

While I use PHP as the example language in my non-Flash site scenario, remember that you can use your language of choice as long as you pass the correct variable(s) into the Flash site. I remember a particular project I worked on that used Ruby on Rails for the backend. The deep linking worked in such a way that the URL might read "http://www.yoursite.com/123" and the Flash movie would receive the "123" from the end and know where to go within the site.

Deep Linking

Deep linking in a Flash site is not as hard as you might first think it is, and as with most things, there is more than one way to accomplish it, so let's quickly run over them in no particular order of importance or preference. We'll get back to the PHP query string example in a minute, but first let's take a look at frame anchors. Frame anchors work much like HTML anchors because they mark frames on the timeline where the .swf will jump to in the event that the URL includes a reference to them. Also like an HTML anchor, the URL uses the pound sign (£) as the anchor identifier. Example 9.1 shows a possible URL pointing to the "About Us" section of yoursite.com.

EXAMPLE 9.1

Sample URL for use with frame anchors
```
http://www.yoursite.com/#about
```

Setting up a frame anchor is exactly like setting a frame label except that you'll set the label type to "Anchor" instead of "Name" (Fig. 9.5). And once you've given the frame anchor a name, you'll notice the anchor icon on the frame that you anchored to (Fig. 9.6).

After you have your anchors set up, you'll need to change the "Template" in the HTML Publish Settings to "Flash with Named Anchors" (Fig. 9.7). Changing that setting tells Flash that it needs to add a little extra to the HTML wrapper in order for the frame anchors to actually work. More specifically, you should notice

Figure 9.5 Select "Anchor" from the type selection for the frame label.

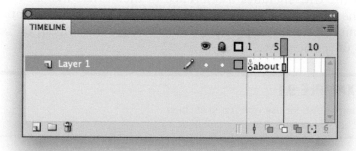

Figure 9.6 The frame anchor icon.

something similar to Example 9.2 added to your HTML. As you can imagine, if you're not using the default HTML that the Flash IDE pumps out, you'll need to extract these extra bits and put them in your HTML.

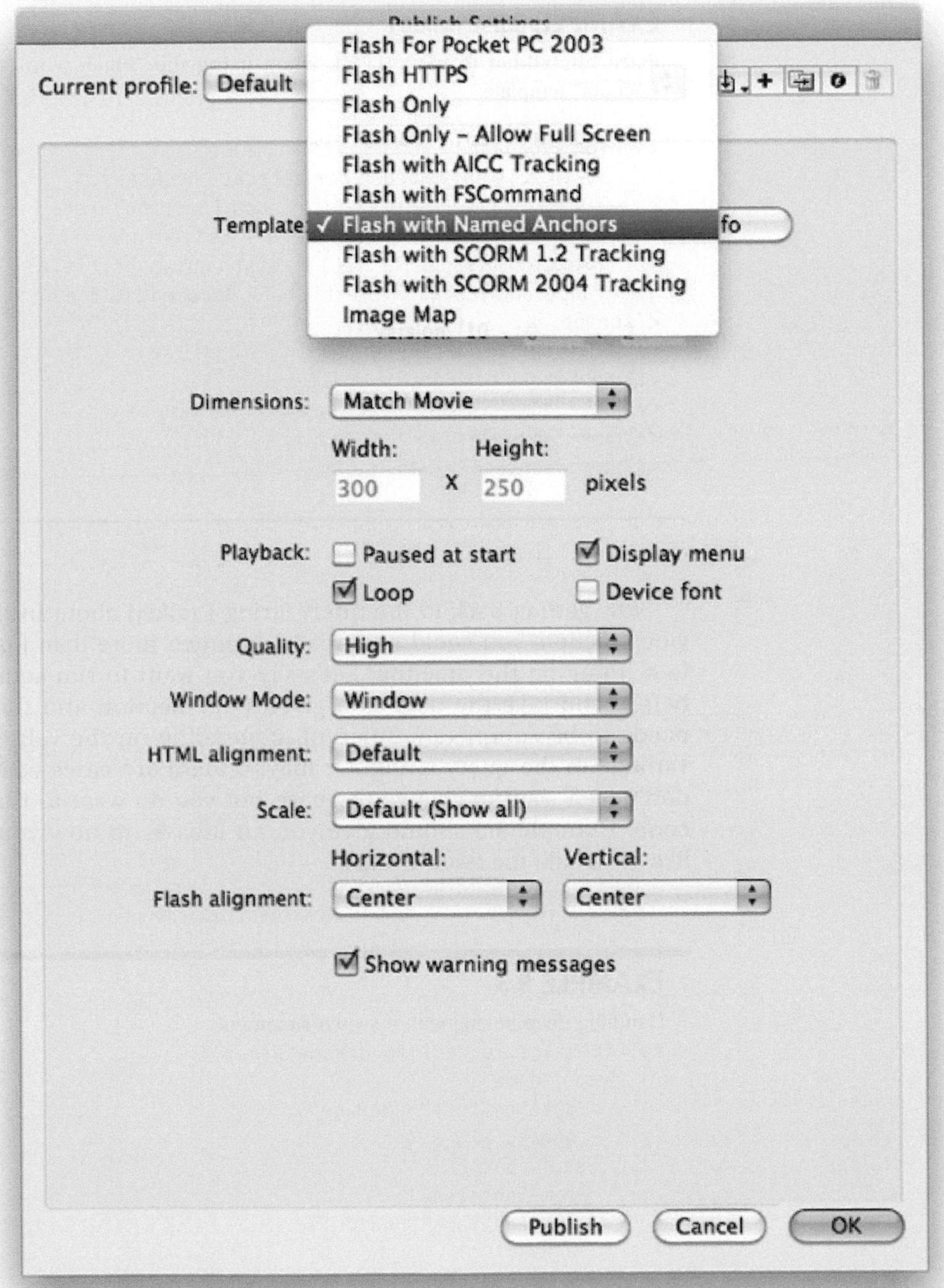

Figure 9.7 Changing the HTML Template to "Flash with Named Anchors."

EXAMPLE 9.2

Extra bits added to your HTML when using the "Flash with Named Anchors" template

...

```
<script language="JavaScript">
    // This is only needed for Netscape browsers.
    function flashGetHref() { return location.href; }
    function flashPutHref(href) { location.href = href; }
    function flashGetTitle() { return document.title; }
    function flashPutTitle(title) { document.title = title; }
</script>
...
<!--bookmarks used in the movie-->
<a name="home"></a>
<a name="about"></a>
<a name="contact"></a>
...
```

Now getting back to the query string I talked about in the previous section, you could potentially do much more than just jump to a frame on the timeline. Let's say you want to run some code before you take the user to a given page/section and that code needs to be completely different, depending on the value of the variable in the query string. Or maybe there are cases where you don't even want to change the page but you do want to run some code. Example 9.3 should give you an idea as to how you might like to handle the issue yourself.

EXAMPLE 9.3

Handling deep linking with a switch statement

```
switch(stage.loaderInfo.parameters.p){
    case "home":
        gotoAndStop("homePage");
        break;
    case "about":
        someFunction();
        gotoAndStop("aboutUs");
        break;
    case "contact":
        launchContactForm();
        break;
    default:
        break;
}
```

In this example, we're using a switch statement to determine where the user is trying to go. The value for the variable "p" has been passed into your movie through FlashVars, and we need to look at the parameters of the `loaderInfo` to find out exactly what that value is. Depending on which case evaluates to true, we handle things differently. Something to remember if you're going the route of frame anchors or query strings passed in through

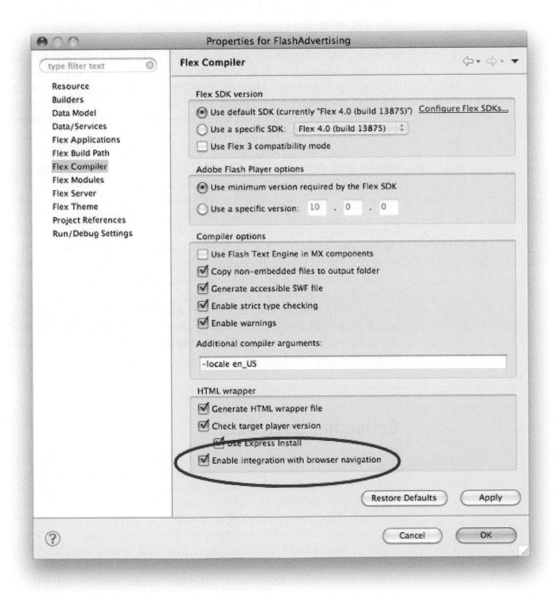

Figure 9.8 "Enable integration with browser navigation."

FlashVars is that once the user comes to the site, then that URL is going to stay as it was when they got there. That may be perfectly fine, but if you want the URL to update as they work their way through the site, you'll need to write up some code to handle it. However, if you're thinking about doing that, you may want to reconsider because someone else has already taken care of it for you.

Another option for deep linking is SWFAddress by Asual. SWFAddress works with SWFObject and not only does it provide you with deep linking in your Flash and Flex sites, but also enables use of the Back, Forward, and Refresh buttons in your browser. It does this by utilizing the ExternalInterface functionality introduced in Flash Player 8 and, at the time of this writing, supports the following browsers: Mozilla Firefox 1+, Camino 1+, Internet Explorer 6+, Safari 1.3+, Opera 9.5+, and Chrome 1+. To download SWFAddress and read much more information about it, visit http://www.asual.com/swfaddress/.

While we're talking about deep linking, I should also go ahead and mention the BrowserManager in Flex. Along with the URLUtil class, the BrowserManager class enables you to access the URL and more specifically, the portions (or "fragments") of the URL that are found after the pound sign. The pound sign works just like the question mark in a URL in that it marks the beginning of a query string or set of parameters. In order for this deep linking to work, your HTML wrapper needs a few extra files that Flash Builder should include for you. Those files are history.css, history.js, and historyFrame.html. To enable deep linking in your Flash Builder project, you need to make sure that the "Enable integration with browser navigation" option is selected in the Flex Compiler section of your project properties (Fig. 9.8).

Collecting User Data

Microsites are a prime location to collect information about your users. They are also a great place to give those users an opportunity to sign up for information about your client. Maybe your client has a monthly newsletter that they offer from their main site, but they want potential customers to have access to it from the microsite as well. Or maybe your client wants to know whether users have been to their physical storefronts and how they would rate their experience. In any case, you'll be collecting information from the users, and the forms you build will be determined by the end goal of what that information is going to be used for.

Going back to Chapter 4, remember that I talked about the amount of file size that is taken up by Flash components such as the ComboBox. Do you also remember how I went on to suggest building your own custom components to save that file size? Well, while file size is still important in your microsites, it's not quite as imperative that you stay under a given amount. If you're in any kind of situation where you might be running tight on your deadline and you still need to build out a form, you might stick with the Flash components. If you need them to match the color scheme of the site, you can still skin them. However, if you have the time to create your own components or if they already exist, you can make the choice of which component to use in your forms: Flash's components or yours.

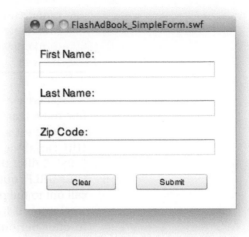

Figure 9.9 An example of a simple form in Flash.

Once you have the forms built, you'll need to process and store the information being given to you. To do this from within Flash, you'll need an outside processing page. The processing page can be the same as one you might use for a non-Flash site. As a matter of fact, you could even build a single processing page for your Flash site and your non-Flash backup site. The only thing you'll need to make sure you know is the name/value pairs for the fields in the form. As with the non-Flash backup site, your processing page can be in any one of many choices of programming languages such as PHP, .NET, Ruby on Rails, and so on. Once you pass the user's information to the processing page, it will most likely be stored in a database for later use. I'll get into some of those uses in just a bit, but first let's take a look at Example 9.4 and how to pass that information to the processing page using URLRequest and URLVariables. For the example, we'll assume your form has a "Submit" button and text fields labeled "First Name," "Last Name," and "Zip Code," as in Fig. 9.9.

EXAMPLE 9.4

Handling form information.

```
function submitForm (e:MouseEvent):void{
    var urlRequest:URLRequest = new
URLRequest("http://www.yoursite.com/processingpage.php");
    var urlVariables:URLVariables = new URLVariables();
    urlRequest.method = URLRequestMethod.POST;
    urlRequest.data = urlVariables;
    urlVariables.userFirst = firstNameInput.text;
```

```
urlVariables.userLast = lastNameInput.text;
urlVariables.userZip = zipCodeInput.text;
navigateToURL(urlRequest, "_self");
}
```

So here's a quick rundown of what's going on in Example 9.4. The first thing that happens in this `submitForm` function is that we set up a URLRequest and point it to our processing page. Next, we set up a URLVariables object and set the method of the URLRequest to "`POST`." After that we assign the URLVariables to the data property of your URLRequest and set up all of the name/value pairs. Finally, we call out to the processing page with `navigateToURL`.

Captured information about visitors can be used by your client to offer periodic e-mails such as updates, newsletters, or limited-time sale offers. Because the Federal Trade Commission (FTC) made the CAN-SPAM Act law effective in January 2004, there are a set of rules that must be followed. These rules are very important for you to know because if they are broken, there may be legal consequences such as sizeable fines. Some of the overall rules to follow are that you should not be misleading about who has sent the e-mail, don't be deceptive in the subject line, and give users the ability to "opt-out" of your e-mails.

ALERT!

When allowing users to sign up to receive any kind of e-mails from your client, you should be fully aware of the CAN-SPAM Act. If you are not familiar with this law, please take the time to learn about it on the FTC Web site at http://www.ftc.gov/spam/.

The opt-out feature gives a user the choice to stop receiving e-mails from your client, and there must be backend code in place to handle these requests for a certain amount of time after you send the e-mail. One thing you don't want to do is make your client's customers unhappy with them, and forcing unsolicited e-mails to their inboxes would most likely do just that.

Quality Control

You didn't think you were going to get out of this chapter without someone testing your work and trying to break it, did you? If so, think again. Everything you build should not only be continually tested by you but also by someone else and preferably by someone whose actual job description involves testing and quality control. You should send your banners through a quality control process, and you should definitely send your microsites through one as well. Although some microsites can be very small and live up to their namesake, some of them can be very deceivingly wide and involved. Generally, common sense tells us that the wider and more involved something is, the more potential it has to be problematic for us. You could carry that thought over to your microsites and say that the more pages, sections, and functionalities it has, the more chances there are that you'll come across some errors and bugs.

Because your microsite is most likely larger than your banners, it will require more time for the quality control person to test it. There are pages to click through, scenarios to enact, and generally much more for them to try to make it break. So I ask you this: Should they (a) wait until you are completely finished before they start testing, or (b) test while you are working on it? The best answer here is (b). For the best results on that answer, you'll need to keep in close contact with the quality control person the entire time you're working on the site. The general idea is that you do several builds in succession of one another. Your first build might consist of as little as the navigation menu. Have quality control make sure that they can't break the navigation and also let them know it's working by placing a dynamic text field on the stage to tell them what section they just clicked on. From there, you add more and more to the site until you have it entirely built out. The advantage here is that quality control can inform you of bugs before they become a part of a larger problem. Now, to avoid the fact that they can't really test something that you keep changing while you're working, you'll need to set up two environments: the development environment and the staging environment.

▎TIP

When working with gradual builds of a site for quality control, be sure to let them know of any issues you are already aware of and working on. Also let them know of parts of the site that are in progress and will probably break. This will keep quality control from spending time on nonbugs, and it will also keep you from having to sift them out.

Development Environment

The development (dev) environment is where you'll do most of your own testing and work on your microsites. The environment for each site will differ according to the site itself and the dev server should be set up exactly how the live server will be. If the final live site will be using Linux, Ruby on Rails, and a MySQL database, that's exactly what should be set up on the dev server. Because this is the first place you'll be able to tie your Flash work in with the backend, this area should be thought of as your development team's own private sandbox. Anyone looking at the site on this server should most likely expect bugs and glitches right up until the end of the project.

Although accessing data that resides on the dev server is completely possible from your local computer, you should also be sure to test your Flash movies from the server as well. Because the development environment is set up to mimic the live site, it's an excellent source for discovery and problem solving. You may find the occasional issues that arise only after you move your files to a server, and you'll be able to solve those problems before the site goes live.

Staging Environment

The staging environment should also be set up to mimic the live site. Because the backend languages, databases, server software, and anything else that may be specific to the site are all the same as the dev server, you can simply move your files over once they are ready to be tested by quality control and viewed for internal approval. You can think of the staging environment like a rehearsal of sorts where your site is practicing to perform for the world.

Conclusion

As you can see from this chapter, there are a few similarities between building a banner and building a microsite. However, there are also many differences like menus, pages, deep linking, and so on. A big part of either project is planning. Without a good plan, your site can very easily start to spin out of control and be hard to get back on track. Once you have a plan in place, you can start collecting assets you'll need to build the site (don't forget about the fonts your artist used in the layout). Something else I talked about in this chapter was standardizing your projects by means of naming conventions used for your files, objects in Flash, code, and so on. Having your files and code set up in such a way that it is completely understandable and reusable is very important because it makes projects run a lot more smoothly. After the standards, I went into the topic of the HTML page that houses your Flash files and the site behind the site that allows users without Flash to still access the information they are trying to reach. Additionally, I talked a bit about deep linking into your Flash movie, gave a couple of quick options on how to do so, and a little information on SWFAddress by Asual. Beyond those topics was discussion on collecting user data and then a look into quality control where I talked a bit about the different environments you should use while building a microsite. In Chapter 10, I'll give information about driving traffic (visitors) to your newly created microsite.

10

DRIVING TRAFFIC TO YOUR MICROSITE

The specific purpose of any given microsite may be as individual and unique as the site itself. The site's intention may be to educate and inform its visitors about a product or to simply entertain them with games and videos while exposing them to your client's brand. However, there is always an underlying objective of any microsite created within the advertising domain: brand and/or product awareness and interaction. When users come to your client's microsite, they should be able to later recall whose site it was when they think of it. If they do remember (and they remember for the right reasons), the site was a success. But before they can

Flash Advertising. DOI: 10.1016/B978-0-240-81345-5.00010-4

remember your client's microsite, they need to be told it exists, and they need some sort of vehicle to drive them there. The topic of this chapter deals with the step that takes place before the users' interaction with, or even knowledge of, the site.

There are several ways to get your client's potential customers to visit their site. Some of those ways cost a little money and some of them are completely free. In this chapter, I'll cover several options to drive traffic to your microsite and those options will be spread across the following sections:

- Paid Search
- Banner Ads
- From Main to Micro
- Viral Marketing and Social Networking
- User Interactions and Referrals

Paid Search

One of the most valuable ways to drive users to a Flash microsite is by way of a paid search. In a nutshell, you're actually purchasing words and terms in a search engine such as Yahoo! or Google. When people do a search for those words, your microsite is displayed in the results. While your site may also find its way into the results based on unpaid (or natural) search terms, this takes time. And because many microsites usually have a limited life span, time is something that may be against you here.

Another advantage that paid search has over natural search is guaranteed placement. By purchasing search terms, you are ensuring your client a spot in the search results that they may not get by means of natural placement. As for how high in the results your client's microsite is placed, each search engine determines its ranking differently. Although some search engines actually base the placement on who paid more for a given search term, others have formulas they use to determine the order of the results. One example is that a search engine may take into account how much was paid for the search term, but they also look at the click-through rate for each placement. By figuring in how many people were clicking on a placement after searching for a particular term, the results are more accurate and relevant to the term itself. That extra bit of sorting can make all the difference of where your client's site ends up on the list of results.

Small Costs, Big Results

With costs starting at mere pennies per click on the larger search engines, paid search consistently has the lowest cost per acquisition of any outbound marketing you can do for a microsite outside of

Inside Advertising

When you are choosing which search terms to purchase, be sure to keep the list relevant to the industry, client, and site. If your client is in the automobile industry, it wouldn't make much sense to purchase a term like "waterslide" or "baseball." Although those examples are very clear, there are terms that are less obvious but just as irrelevant. On top of being bad practice and a potential waste of advertising dollars, some search engines will check the relevancy of your terms to make sure they are in line with the advertised site.

viral marketing, which I'll cover later in this chapter. Although you can find some cases of the cost reaching up to $100 per click in certain industries, most terms will fall in a lower range under a couple of dollars.

When you talk about the actual price of a search term, there are a few factors that come into play. For example, if you're looking at buying a very broad term that is more likely to be searched more often by more people, you'll have to pay more money. However, a very specific search term is going to cost less money. Let's say you purchased the term "code." That term could apply to an extremely wide range of results, and the reason for the higher cost in this case is because your microsite will be included in the results of everything from "computer code" to "morse code" to "state code" (law). However, a more specific term like "Action-Script" is going to be searched by a smaller group of people and, therefore, your site will be included in fewer results. You may be wondering why it costs more for the broad term when you're going to end up in less relevant results. The reason for the higher rate is the popularity of the term itself and how many other companies have also purchased it. Although it would sometimes be smarter to spend less money to reach a more targeted search audience, there are times when the broad term will be worth the extra dollars. For instance, if within 1 month the targeted term yields 30 clicks that result in 5 conversions (the user purchased, signed up for e-mail, and so on) and the broad term yields 300 clicks resulting in 50 conversions, it was probably worth spending the extra money.

Targeting Your Search Terms

When you purchase your search terms, you'll have other options to choose from to further define your target audience. Some of the options will make the target more refined and narrow and some others will widen the target to reach even more people. How you choose between them will change from project to project and client to client.

Matching

When people do searches, they are less likely to search for a single word than they are for a phrase. For that reason, you will want to look at some of the matching options for your terms. One of those options is called *broad matching*, and it basically watches for your word to be used in any search that is performed. If you have purchased the word "car," then broad matching will return your site in the results of searching for everything from "car dealer" to "car wash" to "new car." The upside to broad matching is that you get exposure to thousands of search phrases, but you only had to set up one term. The downside is that your site may end up in irrelevant results. However, remember that more results can equal more clicks, which can equal more conversions, which means more return on investment.

Another matching option is phrase matching. With phrase matching, you have actually purchased a phrase as opposed to a single word. An example of this might be that you have bought the phrase "car dealer." Phrase matching will make sure that your microsite is returned in the results when people search for that particular phrase, but not variations of it. In other words, your site will show up in a search for "car dealer," but not in a search for "dealer car."

Yet another form of matching is exact matching, and, just as you might suspect, your microsite is only included in the results if a user searches for the exact term that you've purchased. Both phrase matching and exact matching will put your site in more targeted and relevant search results.

Another way to further target-specific searches is to create a negative keyword list. This list is used in conjunction with broad matching to weed out any searches that you know you don't want to be included in. Sticking with the search term "car," let's say your client is a car dealership and they don't want their site to show up in a search for "car wash." Simply add the word "wash" to the negative keyword list and the search engine will make sure that the site is omitted from those results.

Text Ads

Text ads (also known as sponsored links) are the text-based advertisements that you see (usually on the right side of the page) when your search results are returned to you. The search engine will determine which text ads to display based on a number of factors, including the amount paid for the advertisement and the relevance to the term that was searched. Although the amount you can actually say in any given text ad may change a little from search engine to search engine, the format is generally the same across the board. Typically, you'll be allowed to include a headline, a couple of lines of copy, and a URL for the advertised site. Because of the limited amount of text allowed in these ads, it's important to have good copy written that gets right to the point while still enticing the user to click on your ad instead of the others around it.

One thing to look for when purchasing text ads is the process the search engine uses in getting the ad running for the first time. Although some of them allow your ad to show up immediately after you make the purchase, some others will require you to run your ad through their approval processes before it is launched.

Contextual Advertising

Some search engines offer another extremely valuable option that you can sign up for: contextual advertising. At the time of purchasing your search terms, you can also spend a little extra marketing money to have your microsite show up in ads that are running on other sites. Blogs are a great place to find contextual advertising happening, and if you're familiar with Google AdSense, then you've seen an example of contextual advertising in action. The way it works is that the search engine has a system running that reads the content of the site on which the ad is being shown. If that system finds terms that match those that you've purchased, a link to your site will be included in the rotation of ads on that particular site. Contextual advertising is so valuable because it's a winning situation for everyone involved. Every time a user clicks on one of these ads, the site that is running the ads gets revenue, the search provider generates revenue, and your client's microsite gets another visitor and possibly a new customer. On top of that, the chances that a visitor will be interested in your client's brand are fairly high due to the search for relevant terms on the site they are already reading.

Banner Ads

Using banners to attract visitors involves more than simply creating a link in an ad and hoping people accidentally click on it. You definitely shouldn't trick them into clicking your ad by presenting them with a fake close button, a fake form to fill out, or anything else along those lines. Tricking your users into visiting your site will only turn them against your client. Instead, your viewers should be enticed or intrigued enough by your banner that they want to visit the site at their own will.

Design Matters

The design of your ads will have a huge impact on whether or not people want to interact with it and visit your site. If they find the ad "attractive," human nature makes them much more likely to be tempted to click on it to see if the destination is just as nice. They will also be quicker to click on an ad that clearly lets them know that they are going to be taken to a place they are interested in.

In addition to designing your banners in a visually pleasing manner, consistency will help attract users to the ads and subsequently to the site itself. The consistency of the banners should be thought of on a few different levels of design. Not only should you pay attention to making sure the banners all look alike, but they should also have similar animations. By doing this, you ensure that no matter what size banner users see from this campaign and no matter where they see it, they'll recognize it. If a user previously clicked on one of the banners from the campaign and liked the site, they will probably click on another one that looks and acts the same. Keep in mind that the consistency should not stop with the banners themselves, but should also tie the banners to the site. This consistency from banner to site will help ensure a smoother transition from the site a user is currently visiting into yours.

Keep Your Promise

When a user clicks on your banner ad, he or she is usually expecting something in particular at the site where he or she is being taken to. That something is whatever you have told her that she should expect when she first viewed the banner. Delivering on your promise is not only good business, but it's something that will drive traffic back to your site after the initial visit. If users click on a banner because they are expecting to fill out a form for travel reservations, then that's what they should get. However, if they get to the site and can't find the form, they may become frustrated and go elsewhere to book their travel plans. Once that happens, they'll only remember that they had difficulty on your client's site and they may not return at all.

From Main to Micro

Another form of driving traffic to a microsite is by way of the main Web site. Because your clients probably own their own main Web site, driving traffic from there to a new microsite is going to be extremely low cost when compared with a banner campaign. The fact that they won't have to pay for the actual placements on their own site is one thing that helps keep the cost down. In addition to the lower cost, you can rest assured that the people viewing the site (and the advertisement) are all but automatically your target audience. Because they are visiting your client's main Web site, you know that they are already aware of, and interested in, the brand. They can be considered the largest built-in audience of the new microsite, and all they need now is a little push in the right direction.

TIP

I made a brief mention earlier in this chapter about the often short life span of microsites, and while it would be nice to leave them up for an extended period of time, it doesn't always work out that way. This means at some point, there's going to be a virtual hole where the microsite used to live on the Internet. If users have visited the site before and found it to be useful, they may try to come back only to find it has gone missing. Rather than leaving them wondering what happened, it's a good idea to redirect them to your client's main Web site. To leave even less room for confusion, it's a better idea to redirect them right to the product's specific page. For example, if you were to visit a microsite for a certain model car and that microsite no longer existed, the best scenario would take you to the page about that car within the auto manufacturer's main Web site.

Highlight and Promote

The push users need can come in several different forms and the one that's best is dependent on the Web site and even the brand itself. One approach would be that the Web site has a section on the home page that is reserved for featured products or services. This may be an area where a client typically advertises a sale or other upcoming event. If your client has taken the time and spent the money to have a microsite built for a particular product, chances are pretty high that they won't have any problem at all using that promotional area to advertise and drive traffic to that microsite. There may be other areas within the main site that can be utilized for making visitors aware of the new microsite, but the goal is the same throughout: Highlight and promote the new product or service for which the microsite was built.

Send Them Back

Where the main site is a great source of traffic for the microsite, the same can be said in reverse. There are some clients who are naturally very good about keeping users flowing in both directions and then there are those who you'll need to explain this to. Although a microsite is focused on a particular product or service that your client has to offer, it's smart to try to influence users to also visit the client's main Web site to find more. Once they visit the main Web site, they may find products or services that your client has to offer that they were previously unaware of. And who knows, they may even be interested in buying those other items. Another advantage to driving users to both sites from within both sites is link popularity. For every link and every click from one site to the other, the destination site's link popularity grows, which, in turn, raises that site in search results. With that said, I should point out that it's a bad practice to overload your sites with links to each other just for the sake of raising their popularity.

Viral Marketing and Social Networking

If the site is designed and built right, users will walk away remembering not only the information they learned or the fun game they played, but they'll be able to tell their friends and coworkers whose microsite they were visiting and the URL to get to that site. Believe it or not, this is actually a form of advertising that goes by different names like "word of mouth" or "viral marketing," and they say it's one of the best forms of advertising available. For one thing, outside of the initial expense to get it going, it's free of cost. The other great aspect is that it seems to be in human nature to listen to and trust people we know much more than we listen to or trust typical advertising. If a friend tells you about a Web site they visited, chances are that you're going to give it a visit because if your friend liked it, it must have been good and you're guessing you'll like it as well.

One of the great things about microsites is that they are so perfectly built to accommodate viral marketing. If you think about how many times you've suggested a site to a friend or how many times you've been told about a site, you'll start to see that those sites are microsites more often than they are full corporate/company Web sites. When you have a site that is centered around one specific idea, product, or service, you're able to put more focus and energy into that one item. With that energy, your creations can dig further into the realm of entertainment and that's when you start to hit on the things that people talk about and pass around to each other.

Generating a Buzz

Before people start talking about your site, those first potential visitors will need to know it exists, right? After all, if nobody ever sees it then nobody will be able to talk about it. This somewhat wraps back around to using the other forms of driving traffic to your site previously mentioned in this chapter because those other methods can be used to generate the initial buzz. Then, once people have started talking about the site and passing the URL around to their friends, you can phase those methods out and let the site advertise itself for a while. If traffic starts to die down at any point, you always have the option of stirring up a buzz again.

Internal Kick-Off

A great first step that most companies, clients, agencies, freelance developers, and so on can (and should) do in their attempts to generate buzz about a new microsite is to kick-off the site internally. If you work for an advertising agency, send a notification out to everyone letting them know to check out the new site that your company has just launched for their client. Additionally, you may make a suggestion that your client does the same within their offices. When your client's employees start visiting the microsite, they'll most likely pass it on to their friends and family. Speaking of friends and family, let yours know about the microsite as well. After all, you should be proud that you've been a part of the huge effort that has taken place to make it happen.

Seed the Link

Another way to kick-start a little viral action is blogs. I think it's pretty safe to say that there are a large amount of people who maintain a blog of some sort. Whether they maintain it on their own Web site or they use one of the many available blogging networks, they are out there and you can utilize them. One way to do this is to find bloggers who are already writing about the brand you are promoting and make them aware of the new microsite.

> **ALERT!**
>
> Blog spamming (also known as *comment spamming*) is a very bad practice and it should be avoided at all costs. To avoid blog spamming, simply avoid talking about or posting a link to the microsite on blogs that are irrelevant to the subject matter of the microsite itself. Just remember that if you are going to plug your work in the comments of someone else's blog, either have the blogger's permission to do so or make very sure it fits within the flow of conversation.

There are several ways to find the people or interest groups that are writing about the brand and one of those ways is Technorati (http://www.technorati.com). Technorati allows you to search blog posts from all over the world for a certain term such as your client's company name. Once your results are returned to you, you have several sorting/refining options at your disposal such as topic, authority, relevance, and date. The authority option uses link popularity along with other factors to determine which blogs historically have the most (or least) authority on the subject of your search. Choosing to include those with less authority will yield a larger number of results, while choosing to show only those with a lot of authority will do just the opposite and lower the number of results shown. Trim the results further and get more targeted by changing the topic as well. These features may come in handy when you're looking for a person who manages a blog that has many readers and that has posts talking about your client's brand. After finding those individuals, you can proceed to contact them through e-mail to find out if they are interested in writing about your client's new microsite.

ALERT!

When contacting a blog owner about potentially writing a piece about, or including a link to, your client's new microsite, always be up front and honest about the fact that you work for the advertising agency that created the site (if you created the site on your own and don't work for an agency, you should still inform them as to who you are). Not only is it better business to be honest about such things, but also the blog owner will appreciate that honesty and will be more likely to want to help you out. If you decide against informing the blog owner about who you are, you run a high risk of him figuring it out later down the line. If that happens, not only will he probably remove the story/link, but you can bet he will never trust you again after that point. Additionally, it could end up completely reversing the blog owner's thinking about your client.

In addition to contacting other blog owners, you can also write to your own blog to help promote the new microsite. For example, I maintain a blog in which I talk about Flash Platform–related topics and one of the things I've blogged about in the past is Flash-based projects that my employer has launched (regardless of if I personally worked on it or not). Although my intention is simply to share the work with the online community, there have been times when people have read my blog, visited a site I wrote about, and subsequently wrote about the site on their own blog. From that point, this scenario can very easily turn into the classic "I shared it with two friends, they shared it with two friends, those friends each shared it with two friends, and so on" scenario. With that, you can see how it can spread quickly without much effort on anyone's part. As a matter of fact, it's that virus-like spreading that gives it the name "viral marketing."

Targeting Specific Blogs

Another way to advertise your microsite on blogs is by actually targeting them individually. The difference between using a contextual network and using a blog-advertising specialist such as Blogads (www.blogads.com) is that you can choose which blogs your ads will appear on. You can start out by sorting through a list of highly visible and influential blogs and then you can narrow your target down as far as you want. For example, you might want to target blogs that are only read by car enthusiasts. Or maybe you want to target Flash Platform developers. Or you could even narrow it down further by targeting Flash Platform developers who are car enthusiasts and live in Dallas, Texas. Targeting specific blogs in this way can give you visitors who are interested in topics and products that more directly relate to your client's microsite.

Social Utilities

Something that has really exploded over the last few years is all of the different social utilities that are out there. Whether you're looking at more business-based tools like LinkedIn or more personal-based tools like Facebook and Twitter, there are an uncountable number of potential visitors to your microsite and every single one of them could be a potential customer for your client. Although a tool like LinkedIn is more likely to be used for business contacts and B2B communications, there are also groups that individuals can join or be invited to. For example, your car client may create a different group for the owners of each of its models. From those groups, they can send links to featured content, updates, or special promotions that are running on their microsites.

On a more personal front, Facebook and Twitter are currently enjoying very large success in terms of number of users. Think about this: According to Facebook's statistics at the time of this writing, there are more than 400 million active users who spend an average of more than 55 min per day on the site and have an average of 130 friends. That's a pretty large amount of people spending a pretty large amount of time there, huh? So how to use this tool to your advantage? Well, you have several options of which you can do one, some, or all. One of those options is to create a "Facebook Page" for your client. Here are a couple more numbers for you: There are currently three million active Pages on Facebook, and the average user becomes a fan of four Pages each month. Once a user becomes a fan of your client's Page, they are informed of updates, events, photos, links, and anything else that your client posts to the Page. That makes for the perfect opportunity to send them to new microsites as they are built!

In addition to creating Pages, Facebook offers several other options that can and should be considered such as Widgets and paid ads. There are different kinds of Facebook Widgets for individuals, businesses, and even developers. One example of a Widget for a business is the Fan Box. The Fan Box can actually be embedded on a Web page, and it will not only show a stream of information coming from that company's Facebook Page (such as links to microsites), but also will allow a reader to become a fan of that company right from that page. That means the user doesn't even have to be on Facebook to become a fan of your client's Facebook Page! What!? I know!

So what about paid advertising on Facebook? If you're a Facebook user, go ahead and go to the site now and find a friend's name to click on. I'll wait. Okay, are you looking at your friend's profile? Do you see those three ads stacked on the right side? Those are paid advertising and you can do some pretty cool targeting with them. For example, you can target them at anyone who lives in Texas. You can also get more defined and target them at anyone who lives in Dallas, Texas. Okay, that's no big deal but how about this: You can target the ads at only fans of your client's Facebook Page. Hmm... that doesn't make sense, why target them if they are already fans? Okay, then let's target their friends. Let's target only friends of fans of your client's Facebook Page. And you can actually keep getting even more granular than that based on virtually any information that a user has entered into his or her account.

Another great tool to use right now is Twitter. Setting up a Twitter account for your client is free and takes just a few minutes. The key after that is getting followers, and there are a few ways to do that including running Twitter searches for the client's name or product and responding to the people who have mentioned it. Another way would be to place links to the client's Twitter profile on their sites (both full and micro). As the number of followers starts to climb, so do the number of potential customers. With a 140-character limit, there's only so much you can expect to do with this tool, but links to the microsite are definitely one of those things. You can also use the Twitter account to link to the Facebook Page and to make it even more powerful, you can actually tie the two accounts together in such a way that each time the clients update their status on one account, it also updates on the other.

With more and more options and features on sites like Facebook, it's definitely a good idea to keep your finger on the social pulse of the Internet as much as you can. After all, the more people you can reach and engage, the more potential customers you can generate for your client and the more your client will keep coming back to you to reach and engage more potential customers. It's like the circle of life but different.

User Interactions and Referrals

I think it's safe to say that you can learn a lot about what people like by physically watching what they do, where they go, and even who they interact with. The same is true for those people when they visit a microsite. The only difference is that you are looking at a virtual trail of actions they left behind. Although tracking the sections a user has visited in a Flash site requires a little help from another language outside of Flash (JavaSript, PHP, and so on), the benefits can be very rewarding in terms of knowing what steps you need to take next in your efforts to bring even more visitors to the site.

What Do Users Like?

You can build your own custom-tracking scripts or you can do it through one of several companies like Omniture (http://www.omniture.com) who actually specialize in this field. Using either your scripts or the products these companies have to offer, you can get various reports on items like which areas of the site were visited more. Once you know which particular areas of the microsite interest users the most, you can apply that information to the next banner campaign by highlighting those sections in the creative.

Where Do Users Come From?

Another highly valuable piece of information is to know where your visitors actually come from. A lot of Web-hosting companies will provide you with site statistics that give you a list of referrers for your site. Those referrers have a link somewhere on their Web site that directs their visitors to your microsite. If your hosting company does not provide site stats or if you (or your company) are hosting the microsite yourself, you may need to look into other ways of getting your referrer reports. There are many options out there ranging from expensive solutions that need to be installed on your server to free solutions like Google Analytics. And just as there is a range of cost for the different solutions, there is also a range of features and details with each solution (which should not actually be judged by the cost).

Regardless of which direction you use to get your list of referrers, that list can help you enhance and fine-tune your next (and even current) campaign. By reviewing the list, you can find new referrers as soon as they appear. As a kind gesture, and to open a new relationship with a potential future referrer of your work, it's not a bad idea to send certain new referrers an e-mail thanking them for linking to your microsite. Of course, this depends on the kind of site it is, what they had to say about the site, and a few other factors that you'll have to judge for yourself. Additionally, if you find that one of two sites are sending a much larger number of visitors than any of the other referrers, you may want to go ahead and plan on contacting them in the future to see if they would like to promote other projects.

Conclusion

To wrap up this chapter, remember that part of the effort that should be put into a microsite project is getting people to visit it. There are many ways to get people to come to your new site. Some of those ways cost money all the way through the project and eventually in the end, while others cost a little bit up front but resolve to no cost in the end. On top of being virtually free, viral advertising can last just as long as people are still talking about it. There are even times when the talk may die down for several months only to have someone bring it back up to their friends at a later date (which could stir the viral effect back into motion).

Don't forget that search engines can be your very best friend when you want to drive people to a microsite. By utilizing their paid search terms, you can guarantee your client a spot in the list of results returned on a search of a given word. Additionally, some search engines also tie in with blogs to offer an additional point of contact with potential customers. In the end, the benefits of using paid search far outweigh the cost involved with doing so.

Another avenue clients (and sometimes even agencies or developers) forget about is that of the client's main Web site. There are not many reasons I can think of that would prevent you from linking from the main Web site to the microsite and vice versa. The visitors are already there, they are already familiar with the brand, and they obviously like it enough to be at one of the two sites in the first place. Why not take advantage of that built-in audience and offer them a way to get to the other site to find more entertainment or information about the brand?

Don't rule out getting other people involved in your viral marketing. Send e-mails around notifying friends, family, and coworkers about the launch of the site. If you maintain a blog, write about it to let the world know of your company's wonderful work. Contact other blog owners who are already interested in your client's brand, and, after telling them your intentions and who you are, most people will be more than happy (and even thrilled) to be a part of the advertising effort. Some of those blog owners are even signed up to blog-advertising networks on which you can purchase space to run your ads. By utilizing a blog-advertising network, you can run your ads on blogs that you have targeted based on as specific of a criterion as you see fit. Let's also not forget that "social" is the current word of the day, and at the time of writing this, it is a very big word with a huge amount of advertising potential. From LinkedIn to Facebook and Twitter, you should definitely find ways to utilize these tools to their fullest.

Finally, keep an eye on what your users are doing while they are visiting your microsite. If you keep reports on areas of higher interest, you can better tailor your next campaign to fit what your visitors want to see. In addition to paying attention to what they are doing while they are on your site, you should know where they were prior to getting there. With that piece of information, you can do things like run ads on sites that have sent a high number of visitors to your microsite or contact the sites directly the next time you launch a similar project.

11

ADVERGAMING AND APPLICATIONS

Since this book is titled "Flash Advertising" and not "Flash Gaming" or "Flash Apps," I'll go ahead and state up front that this chapter is not intended to teach you the full ins and outs of building games or applications. I'll also be skipping over the discussion of topics like image compression and general optimization because those were already covered in earlier chapters, and you'll pretty much handle it all the same in your games and applications. What I would like to do instead is just take a little bit of your time to discuss these subjects at a high level in terms of how they relate to the world of advertising and maybe we'll hit on some general tips and suggestions to remember while planning and building. Also within this chapter, you'll notice several screenshots of games (Fig. 11.1 through Fig. 11.21) produced by the wonderful folks at Blockdot, Inc. (http://www.blockdot.com). As you look over these examples, note that each of them could be (and have been) very easily reskinned with a client brand to provide a fun and memorable interactive experience for the end users. With that said, let's jump in:

- Advergames
  - Branded Play
  - Play Again?
  - Modularity FTW!
- Applications
  - AIR Overview
  - Freedom of Design

Flash Advertising. DOI: 10.1016/B978-0-240-81345-5.00011-6

Advergames

I'm not sure if you've noticed or not, but over the last several years, casual gaming has really taken off and you can find people playing around at all times of day or night regardless of where they are. If they're at work, they may be playing during their lunch break (or just when the boss isn't looking). If they're at home, they may be spending a little time playing some Flash games before they go to bed at night. I've seen people playing Flash games in libraries, coffee shops, and believe it or not, I've even seen them playing while waiting to get the oil changed on their car. So with all of this interaction between these people and these games, you know that someone had to come up with the idea of branding them (the games, not the people). And if you stop to think about it, you'll see that advertising has been tied in with games of one sort or another for a very long time. Look no further than professional sports to find that evidence.

TIP

For great in-depth coverage of Flash game development, I would highly recommend "Real-World Flash Game Development: How to Follow Best Practices and Keep Your Sanity" by Chris Griffith.

Figure 11.1 "Tax Smack" – Produced by Blockdot, Inc.

Figure 11.2 "Tax Smack" – Produced by Blockdot, Inc.

Figure 11.3 "Tax Smack" – Produced by Blockdot, Inc.

Branded Play

So let's think about this for a minute. There are innumerable people who are spending an enormous amount of hours playing Flash games online at all times of the day. They play and leave, and if the developer of that game is lucky, they come back later to play again. With each user dedicating so much time to seeing the same screens over and over again, wouldn't it make sense to slap your client's logo in there? Or maybe somehow actually place their product somewhere in the game? And while we're at it, let's go ahead and alter the overall color scheme as well so that it matches with your client's branding. The point here is exposing users to the brand while they are having fun playing a game. Think about all of the Flash games you've played online. While I'm sure there are some that weren't trying to sell you on any product, service, or even a company in general, I would be willing to bet that plenty of them did and that you can name a few of the companies or products that were branded in those games.

So in case it's not completely obvious yet, the value for your client in all of this is mostly the repeated exposure to the brand, and we'll add bonus points because users are (hopefully) having a good time interacting with it in a fun environment as well. As for the uncountable ways to immerse them in the brand while playing these games, you're really bound only by imagination and creativity here (oh, and those pesky legal departments). Take a look at the brand and what it stands for or represents. Take a look at the product or service and take a look at the values and beliefs of your client. Those things combined with other things like the campaign goals and target audience should help you figure out the best way for those users to play around with the brand so to speak. In some cases, you'll find that simply placing your client's logo in a visually strategic location will suffice. For example, the best type of game to use for

Figure 11.4 "Art Thief" —
Produced by Blockdot, Inc.

Figure 11.5 "Art Thief" –
Produced by Blockdot, Inc.

the campaign may be something like tic-tac-toe or another extremely simple idea like that. In that case, maybe the logo is in the form of a watermark under the game board. You could take it a small step further in this example by using other branded elements like images of actual products instead of Xs and Os.

However, you may find that you want to build an entire game branded from top to bottom. Let's go back to our car company, Typical Motors, from earlier in the book. You could place their company logo behind a tic-tac-toe game board and you could even use individual car logos for the game pieces. But what if you took it even further? How about a racing game designed 100% around the Typical Motors branding? You could allow players to choose from their different models of cars and even give them the option of customizing with new wheels, bigger engines, and other modifications. Of course, the players would need to somehow earn those modifications, right? You can't just allow every player to put in the most powerful engine and the best looking wheels from the start. This is where you add a little data storage to the mix so you can let players log in, win points in races, and save car models and any other information that might be handy to reuse again at a later time. Tie the whole thing together in a real-time multiplayer experience, allow player A to challenge players B and C, and I'm sure you'll have a good number of users playing the game time and time again. Brand interaction score! While saving their info and allowing them to play against each other will help bring players back to the game, there are also other things you can do that will help as well.

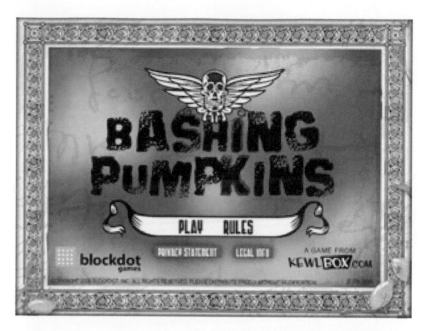

Figure 11.6 "Bashing Pumpkins" – Produced by Blockdot, Inc.

Figure 11.7 "Bashing Pumpkins" – Produced by Blockdot, Inc.

Play Again?

There are a number of fairly simple things you can do to get players to return to play a game and interact with the brand several times over, and it can really be just as easy as making sure they don't lose too easily. Let's start with something I'm sure we're all familiar with: a level-based game. In most level-based games, you'll notice that not

Figure 11.8 "Bashing Pumpkins" – Produced by Blockdot, Inc.

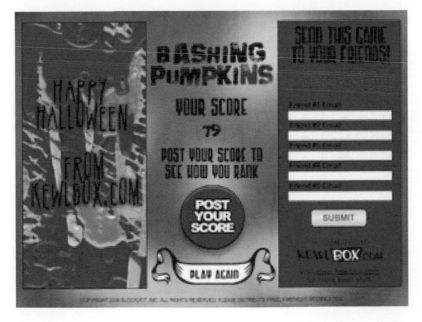

Figure 11.9 "Bashing Pumpkins" – Produced by Blockdot, Inc.

only is the first level usually very simple, but also the first few levels are often designed to teach the player how to use the controls and perform certain tasks within the game. This allows the player to get more comfortable with the mechanics of the game while also building their confidence in the game play itself. Raising that confidence will keep them from getting frustrated and leaving too quickly.

Figure 11.10 "Poker Solitaire" – Produced by Blockdot, Inc.

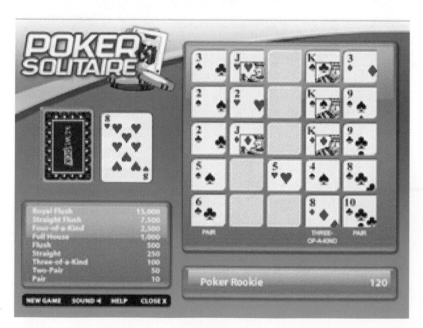

Figure 11.11 "Poker Solitaire" – Produced by Blockdot, Inc.

Once you've given them a chance to get a handle on how to play the game, you'll want to present them with a bit more of a challenge a few levels in. As I'm sure you know from your own game-playing experiences, the difficulty usually increases more and more with each level from there on. And if you do want to challenge the player, make it difficult for them to go to the next level, but you still want them to be able to get there eventually. Again, think about games you've played before where you got stuck on a level and you came back again and again to try to get past the part that was holding you back. Something you might notice is that a lot of those probably had certain steps you had to follow to get past the point where you were stuck. At some point, your persistence paid off and you moved to the next level, and you may have felt some sense of accomplishment (if even just a little bit). The goal is to make the levels get harder, but not so hard that they can never be defeated by anyone. If players stop feeling like they can advance further into your game or that they don't stand a chance of beating it altogether, a large number of them will stop trying and move on to something else. Brand interaction fail! One more important aspect I should point out here is the ability for a player to save their progress in your game or, at the very least, have pre-determined codes that will allow access to levels as they progress. Level two has its own code; level three has its own and so on. Giving a user the option to jump straight back to the level they last played alleviates the frustration of having to play the same levels over and over. And we all know that can be especially tedious the further you are in a game when you stop playing.

So let's discuss a little about another reason users would want to come back to play a game with your client's brand all over it. How about a little payoff? Or a big payoff if that's more suitable for your client. If players know that they are actually playing toward something, it can be an incredible incentive for them to come back to play again. This is especially true if they are big fan of your client's brand or even just the product for which the game was designed and built. And the payoff doesn't always have to hold a monetary value because there are plenty of players out there who consider simple recognition to be the best prize you could offer them. For example, we've all seen the contests or other challenges where the prize is something along the lines of "A chance to have your name and photograph featured in/on _____!" On the other end of the spectrum, your client may be willing to offer up a more elaborate grand prize like a television, a game console, a new car, or an all-expense-paid trip to anywhere the winner would like to visit. The extent of the prizes is really up to what the client is willing to do.

Also, it doesn't have to be just a single prize at the end of some specified time period. Something else to consider is that your client could do something like giving out smaller prizes to players during the course of the games. Maybe the game will be running for the duration of a 6-month campaign and at the end, the top scoring person wins the grand prize, but the smaller prizes are given out at regular intervals to active players. Or maybe a tournament-style game is the way to go where prizes are given to something like the top 10 players. Tenth place gets a small prize, and the prizes get

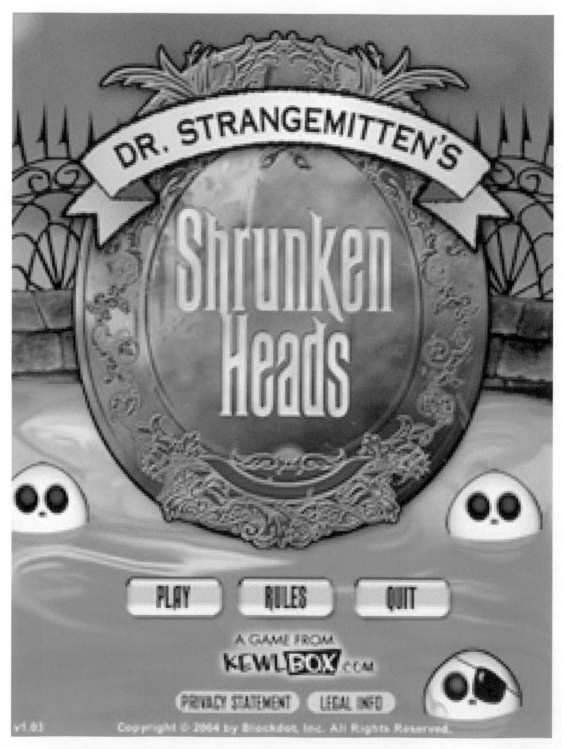

Figure 11.12 "Dr. Strangemitten's Shrunken Heads" – Produced by Blockdot, Inc.

Figure 11.13 "Dr. Strangemitten's Shrunken Heads" – Produced by Blockdot, Inc.

Figure 11.14 "Dr. Strangemitten's Shrunken Heads" – Produced by Blockdot, Inc.

progressively larger until the number one player gets the grand prize. As for those smaller prizes, they can be anything from key chains to drinking glasses to thumb drives, but the one requirement about them is that they really should have your client's brand all over them. At that point, your client has just made the transition from interacting with a potential customer in a game to being in their home and day-to-day life. Brand interaction score!

One more thing real quick before we move on: security. When you start getting into contests, prizes, winners, losers, and even just high-score tables, you'll definitely need to consider different (and possibly multiple) forms of security. There's a wide range of things you can do from obfuscating your .swfs to encrypting any data to protect from cheaters. I recommend both and a quick Internet search for "swf encryption" or "swf obfuscation" will return tools like Amayeta's SWF Encrypt and Kindisoft's secureSWF. As for encrypting/hashing the data, look no further than as3corelib, where

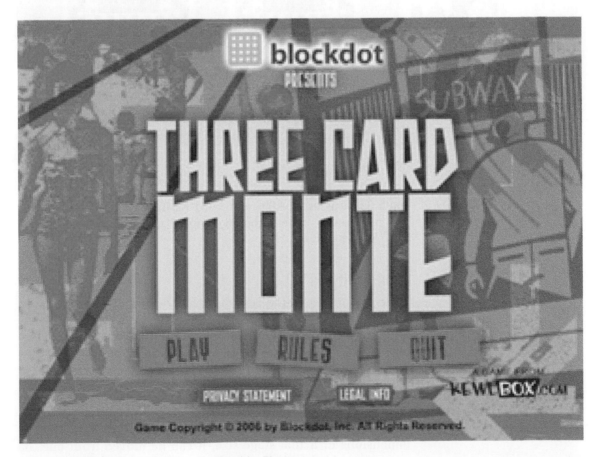

Figure 11.15 "Three Card Monte" – Produced by Blockdot, Inc.

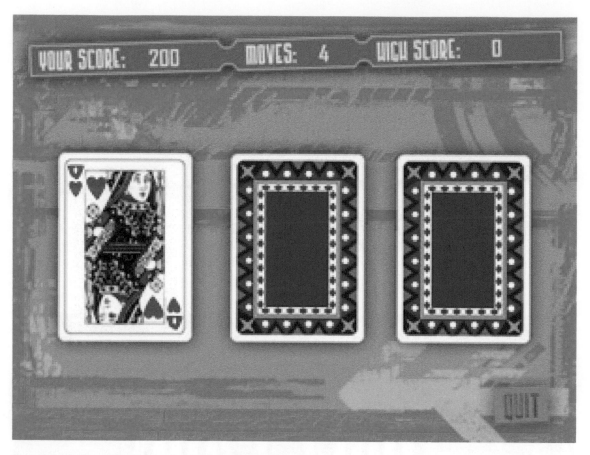

Figure 11.16 "Three Card Monte" – Produced by Blockdot, Inc.

you'll find classes for MD5 and SHA1 hashes. At the time of writing this, as3corelib can be found on Google Code at http://code.google.com/p/as3corelib/.

Modularity FTW!

When the time comes to start the actual development of the game, one big thing you should really strive for is portability of your game and its code. Regardless of its original form being in a banner, a microsite, a standalone AIR application, or an iPhone application, the more code you can use to port your client's game to the other options, the better. A big part in achieving that portability is to keep things very modular in terms of class files, .flas and assets. At a high level, you can think of it like this: If all of the logic behind your game doesn't care about things like image dimensions or actual stage size, it can be moved from one .fla to another with minimal to no changes at all. Within each different

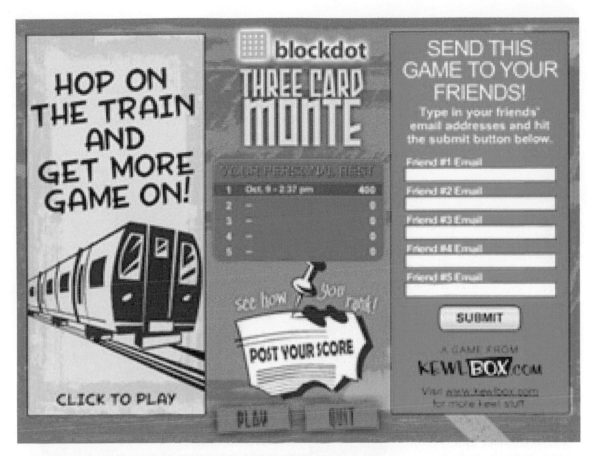

Figure 11.17 "Three Card Monte" – Produced by Blockdot, Inc.

.fla, you may have different images for assets like game pieces and your stage size may be different from file to file due to the game being shown in a microsite versus a banner versus an iPhone.

One example of that would be a memory game that I originally worked on with a friend of mine at Ovrflo Media some time ago. If you aren't familiar with the game of memory, it's a matching game where you are presented with several cards in the facedown position. For each card, there is a matching card, and the goal is to turn over two matching cards in a single turn. If you don't match cards, you turn both of them facedown and try again. Anyway, this memory game was originally built to be played within a microsite, and the core engine was written as a single class with a couple of other classes that accompanied it. Not too long after the microsite was launched, the client asked if we could build a "widget" version for Web site owners to place on their sites. Because of the decision to build the game the way we did, it was much easier to build the smaller version than it would have been if all of the code had been on the timeline and dependent on hardcoded values for things like width and height. Now to take it even further, the code base was used again more than a year later. I chose to make slight modifications to the way it played, but I was still able to use the core classes before making another version that I published for the iPhone. If you're interested, you can search the App Store for the game, which is called Memory4Kidz. Remember that at the time of writing this, I'm not sure if it will still be available due to the new iPhone developer rules dealing with building apps in anything other than Objective-C. Also due to the new rules, it doesn't seem that I'll be able to update the design as I had originally planned.

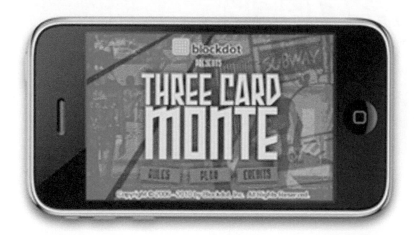

Figure 11.18 "Three Card Monte" for the iPhone (built with Flash Professional CS5) – Produced by Blockdot, Inc.

Figure 11.19 "Three Card Monte" for the iPhone (built with Flash Professional CS5) – Produced by Blockdot, Inc.

Figure 11.20 "Three Card Monte" for the iPhone (built with Flash Professional CS5) – Produced by Blockdot, Inc.

Figure 11.21 "Three Card Monte" for the iPhone (built with Flash Professional CS5) – Produced by Blockdot, Inc.

Applications

The Internet is a wondrous place with its vast fields of information and rolling hills of branded experiences all right within your browser, wouldn't you agree? And it's a great thing to be able to learn and play and discover new products and services right from within that very same browser, yes? Well let's take a few minutes and ditch that browser to talk briefly about advertising on the users' desktop through Adobe AIR.

If you stop to think about it for a second, there are a ton of ideas that could be utilized to present your client's brand to the user in an application that's running directly on their desktop. Some of those ways might tie directly in with your client's products or services, whereas others may seem a little more arbitrary but can still be related in one way or another. For example, you may present the idea of a branded weather application to an automobile company. While you may not include a form for users to customize and order a new car, it would allow them to check weather conditions before they get on the road and they would do so with your client's brand right in front of them.

Another more related example might be an application that allows users to book their travel arrangements (flight, hotel, car, and so on) without ever opening a browser. Obviously, this one would be designed around the brand of your travel company client. As you can imagine, the possibilities are pretty much only bound by your imagination … and maybe a little by deadlines. For more specific examples of how companies are using AIR to extend their brand to the desktop, go check out the Adobe AIR showcase at http://www.adobe.com/products/air/showcase/. At the time of writing this, companies listed include names like eBay, Nickelodeon, AOL, and The New York Times.

AIR Overview

So what is Adobe AIR? Well, in a nutshell it's a runtime that allows developers to create desktop applications with their choice of HTML, Ajax, Flash, and/or Flex. The compiled fruit of that developer's labor yields a single installer that can be successfully run across various operating systems in much the same way that a Flash site can be built once and viewed across various browsers. It provides a great way to keep the user engaged with your client's brand even while their browser is closed.

One of the many cool things about an AIR application is how it can work with a user's Internet connection (or lack thereof). In the weather example I mentioned earlier, the user would definitely need to be connected to get the most up-to-date weather conditions. On the other hand there are also cases, like a game of solitaire, where the user may not need to be connected at all. On the third hand (what, you don't have three?), there are plenty of good reasons that an application could work offline and then perform some action once the user gets connected.

So let's talk about a couple of benefits of AIR when it comes to your clients. Obviously, the big value is that users continue to interact with the brand even after they leave the browser, but there are some others as well. For example, if developed to do so, an AIR application can push notifications to the end user. Imagine a user is planning on booking a flight for a trip in the near future, but he or she's waiting for a good price before doing so. I'm sure the user would appreciate it very much if your client's application was kind enough to inform him or her that it had found a flight below a certain price that he or she had set in advance. Another benefit would be in the case of a business traveler. With the right "sometimes-connected" AIR application, the business traveler could go ahead and get started on something like a multipage form while on an airplane with no connectivity. That data could very easily be stored locally and then pushed online once the traveler arrives at his or her destination and gets connected.

Freedom of Design

Continuing with some of the benefits of AIR, let's move into the fact that you have a huge amount of freedom in the design of your application. Not only have you broken out of the browser by creating an AIR application, but you can also escape the boring 'ol box in which it's built. While the browser and most other applications are typically constrained to four sides, you can utilize some of the AIR features to remove that box and shape your application the way you want it shaped. The great thing about a feature like this is that you can really compliment the brand with the right window design. For example, if your client is a movie theater, your application could provide show times and be shaped like a movie ticket with the notches cut out on both sides.

> **TIP**
>
> When you are designing a custom shaped window chrome, remember not to get too crazy unless the brand truly calls for it. Someone looking for a good price on an airplane ticket doesn't necessarily need an application that's shaped like an airplane. However, a little more creative license can probably be taken when designing a game targeted at children.

User controls are another aspect to think about when you're designing your application. Although you may want them to perpetually interact with it, most users are going to want a way to close the application at some point and you really should provide it to them in the form of what? If you said a "close button," you win! In addition to the close button, think about the controls that you see on so many other applications. Controls like the minimize/maximize buttons, the handle to resize the window, the scrollbars, and scroll arrows. Although some of these are must-have controls (close button), others may not be as important and can be left out. It's up to you if you want the user to be able to do something like change the size of the window.

Something else to put on the design plate for your application is the icons. I would be willing to bet that just about every application that you work with has icons associated with it. There are the small icons you see when you come across the application in Windows Explorer or Finder on the Mac. There are the icons that represent the application in the Windows Taskbar and the Dock on the Mac. And you may even want to go ahead and think about the icon for the Windows system tray because you may just need it.

One more thing to mention before I move on is the install badge. The install badge is a .swf file that you can put on a Web site for seamless installation of your application. Not only does the badge present the opportunity to install the application directly from within the browser, it also checks to see if the user has the AIR runtime installed (which is kind of important here). If they don't, it installs it and then moves on to installing your application. If they do already have it installed, it jumps right to your application and installs it from the site without requiring the user to save it to their system first. For quick and easy creation of your installer badges, check out the Badger AIR application that Grant Skinner put together for Adobe. At the time of this writing, you could get Badger at http://www.adobe.com/devnet/air/articles/badger_for_air_apps.html. If it's not there any more, a quick search for "Grant Skinner Badger" should yield some good results.

Conclusion

Well, like I was saying earlier, this was a bit of a high-level overview of linking games and applications to your advertising. With the enormous growth that Flash-based games have seen over the last few years, advergaming is definitely something to pitch to your clients when coming up with a campaign strategy or even just for brand awareness. And because people are spending more and more time playing games in their browsers through the Flash Player, there are more and more opportunities to really get them immersed in a fun, branded experience. Remember also that the experience can be very subtly branded by just placing your client's logo in a strategic location or it can be completely designed around the brand from the ground up.

Another thing to think about is how to get players coming back to play the game again and again. Some of the tactics to achieve that goal are in features like allowing them to save their progress or collect points to spend on in-game items. Something else that is good at drawing players back in is competition. Generally speaking, people are naturally competitive and love to challenge other people to games where one of them will be a winner and the other will be a loser. Make it interesting for them by taking the competition a step or two further and offering actual prizes (client branded of course). Introducing that element into the mix will not only make more people come back more often, but also get the brand physically in their hands. Again, don't forget about security.

Security is very important in this case because you really don't want people cheating to win any prizes. Not only could it turn into a big legal issue, but also it's just not cool.

Also, you should shoot for as much portability as you possibly can in your advergames. Remember that if you build a game that is successful in terms of how often it gets played and how many users it attracts, you may be asked to build it again in another form. If you originally built it as a feature in a microsite, it might make sense to rebuild it in a banner that drives people to the microsite or to even port it to the iPhone. The best way to do that is to keep everything modular. If possible, you should have one set of classes that can drive any one of several .fla files that contain nothing more than different assets from one another.

Finally, AIR applications can be a very powerful form of advertising because you can stay engaged with the user even after they have left the browser. You can build applications that help them with their productivity, provide them with information to help them plan their day, and offer many other things that they may need to use on a daily basis. Applications that can continue to work without an Internet connection, but that will make sure that all required data is correct as soon a connection is available, are another bonus to offering AIR to your clients. And let's not leave out the designers, right? The designers get to completely (and literally) break outside the box when concepting and designing an AIR application.

12

CLASSES

Writing good classes (and reusable code in general) can sometimes be a challenge in the advertising agency world where timelines tend to be significantly shorter than a developer would like and project functionality can change at the drop of a hat during the final moments of a tight deadline. Another challenge to writing code that can be easily passed across projects is the fact that, in general, no two projects are ever the same. That said you should still strive for reusable classes in your projects.

Flash Advertising. DOI: 10.1016/B978-0-240-81345-5.00012-8

Even if they have to be slightly modified from project to project, it's always a good thing to have reusable classes at your disposal. Classes that you can grab and throw into a project at a moment's notice without having to worry too much if it's going to work correctly or not. And just in case the chapter title didn't give it away, we'll be spending the next several pages looking over different classes. Some of them have been used in actual client projects, some of them were written specifically for this book, and all of them can be found at http://www.flashadbook.com/code/.

Set Up

Before we dive in, I'd like to offer a bit of an explanation of how my files were set up while working on these classes. When you download the code from the Web site, you'll see that I placed all the separate classes in a folder structure as seen in Fig. 12.1. The structure starts with the com/flashadbook folder and then goes down to the base, display, engines, events, and utils folders. When working with these folder structures within the code of the classes themselves, these will be the structures of the packages.

Packages

By the most simple of explanations (and as we just discussed), a package is a representation of a directory path where a group of your classes is stored. When used correctly, not only are packages a great way to organize and maintain your code but they also help minimize the risk of name conflicts between classes.

Figure 12.1 Folder structure for the classes used in this chapter.

Package declaration occurs at the beginning of your class file with the directory path in dot notation. For example, using the directories mentioned in the previous section, your package declarations would be as follows: `com.flashadbook.base`, `com.flashadbook.display`, `com.flashadbook.engines`, `com.flashadbook.events`, **and** `com.flashadbook.utils`. While the display, events, and utils are pretty standard packages to use for certain kinds of classes, I also have an engines package that contains the `MemoryGame` engine from the next chapter and the base package that contains Document classes used to show examples of these classes. What's a Document class? Let's take a look.

Document Class

Rather than placing any code on the timeline of my .fla, I've created a separate Document class for each sample. For example, in order to implement the BorderButton class, I've created a BorderButton-Sample class that is used as the Document class of a .fla file. This way, you can work with a single .fla in which you only need to change the Document class to create a completely different output .swf based on the examples. There are also several other benefits to using a Document class, including the fact that it allows a developer to work on the code while a designer works in the .fla file, or that you can extend your code much more easily if it doesn't live on the timeline. How about adding the ability to do things like reuse your code in a Flex project even after it was originally written for a Flash project? When you start looking at these and the many other benefits, it's very much worth keeping the code in a Document class.

The next question then is how to tie a Document class to a .fla, and the answer is that you have two choices. One option is through the Advanced ActionScript 3.0 Settings, and the other is through the Properties window of the .fla. To set the Document class via the Advanced ActionScript 3.0 Settings, go to the File menu and select "Publish Settings." From the resulting window, make sure the box next to "Flash (.swf)" is checked and choose the tab labeled "Flash." Within the Flash tab, make sure "ActionScript 3.0" is selected in the drop-down labeled "Script" and click the "Settings…" button. Finally, in the Advanced ActionScript 3.0 Settings window, type in the path to the class you would like to use as the main code for the .fla (see Fig. 12.2).

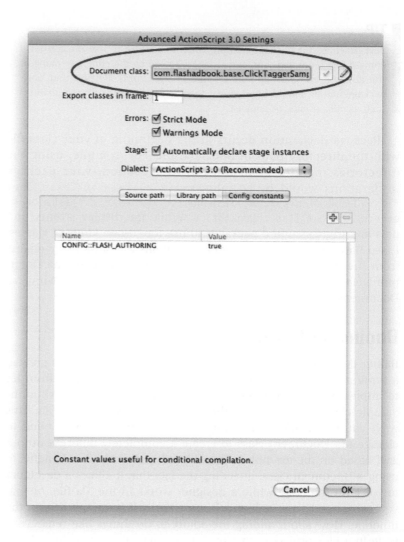

Figure 12.2 Setting the Document class from the Advanced ActionScript 3.0 Settings window.

Alternatively (and slightly more easily) you can set the Document class from the Properties window of your .fla. To do so, simply make sure the Properties window is visible by going to the Window menu and selecting "Properties." Once the Properties window is available, type the path to your class in the "Class" text field under the Publish section (Fig. 12.3). If you don't see the "Class" text field in the Properties window, make sure you don't have anything selected on the stage.

And now that we've got some of those items taken care of, let's get to the classes. Most of them are rewrites from their original ActionScript 2 versions that were in the first edition of this book. And once again, you can download all these files from the Web site at http://www.flashadbook.com/code/.

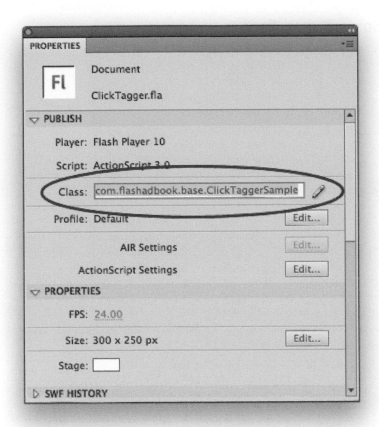

PROPERTIES

Figure 12.3 Setting the Document class from the Properties window.

The BorderButton Class

In addition to creating an invisible button that covers the stage, the BorderButton class also gives you the option to include a border of any color and thickness you need based on the design layout and specs (some sites require a border to separate banners from their content). As a matter of fact, the BorderButton class is set up to offer three different choices. One option for using this class would be a full-stage button that also draws a border around your banner. Another option would be a full-stage button that does not draw a border around your banner. The third option would be to draw a border around your banner without creating a full-stage clickable area. Each of these options has their uses, and the project at hand will determine which you would use. An example would be if you had a banner with specs that called for a border, but you also need to make three different clickable areas within the banner. In that case, you would go with the third option of drawing the banner without including the full-stage clickable area.

BorderButton Code

```
package com.flashadbook.classes {
    import flash.display.DisplayObjectContainer;
    import flash.display.Sprite;
    import flash.events.MouseEvent;
    import flash.net.URLRequest;
    import flash.net.navigateToURL;

    public class BorderButton extends Sprite{
        private var _bbParent:DisplayObjectContainer; //the
parent of the BorderButton
        private var _halfThick:Number; //half the thickness
of the border line
        private var _w:Number; //the width to draw the
BorderButton
        private var _h:Number; //the height to draw the
BorderButton
        private var _targetWindow:String; //the window in
which the targetURL will open
        private var _request:URLRequest = new URLRequest();
//the URLRequest used to get to the target url

        public function BorderButton(){
            super();
        }

        public function draw(parent:DisplayObjectContainer,
outline:Boolean = false, lineColor:uint = 0x000000,
lineThickness:int = 1):void {
            _bbParent = parent;
            _bbParent.addChild(this);
            _halfThick = lineThickness / 2;
            _w = _bbParent.stage.stageWidth - _halfThick;
            _h = _bbParent.stage.stageHeight - _halfThick;
            graphics.lineStyle(lineThickness, lineColor);
            graphics.beginFill(0, 0);
            graphics.drawRect(0, 0, _w, _h);
        }

        public function activate(targetUrl:String,
targetWindow:String = "_blank"):void {
            buttonMode = true;
            _request.url = targetUrl;
            _targetWindow = targetWindow;
            if(!hasEventListener(MouseEvent.CLICK)){
                addEventListener(MouseEvent.CLICK,
clickOut, false, 0, true);
            }
        }
```

```
    public function erase():void{
        if(_bbParent != null){
            deactivate();
            _bbParent.removeChild(this);
        }
    }

    public function deactivate():void{
        if(hasEventListener(MouseEvent.CLICK)){
            buttonMode = false;
            removeEventListener(MouseEvent.CLICK,clickOut);
        }
    }

    private function clickOut(e:MouseEvent):void {
        try {
            navigateToURL(_request, _targetWindow);
        }catch (e:Error){
            trace("An error occurred trying to navigate
to the target url.");
        }
    }
    }
}
```

BorderButton Breakdown

On the very first lines of the BorderButton class, you'll see the package declaration and the imports used within.

```
package com.flashadbook.display {
    import flash.display.DisplayObjectContainer;
    import flash.display.Sprite;
    import flash.events.MouseEvent;
    import flash.net.URLRequest;
    import flash.net.navigateToURL;
```

Next is the class declaration where you'll notice the use of the final class attribute and the fact that the BorderButton extends Sprite. A Sprite is a very basic display object that gives us access to properties like graphics, so we can draw out the border. The access to the graphics property also allows us to use drawRect a bit further in. Directly inside the class constructor, we'll set up the variables in Table 12.1.

```
public final class BorderButton extends Sprite{
```

The next item in the lineup is the class constructor that, in this case, is really just an empty function that reestablishes the call to the parent class (Sprite) with super.

```
public function BorderButton(){
    super();
}
```

Table 12.1 The Private Variables of the BorderButton Class

Variable	Purpose
_bbParent (DisplayObjectContainer)	The parent object of the BorderButton
_halfThick (Number)	Half the thickness of the border line
_w (Number)	Width to draw the BorderButton
_h (Number)	Height to draw the BorderButton
_targetWindow (String)	Window where targeted URL will open
_request (URLRequest)	Used to launch the target URL

Table 12.2 Parameters for the Draw Method

Parameter	Purpose
parent (DisplayObjectContainer)	The parent where the BorderButton will be added as a child
outline (Boolean)	Determines if the BorderButton will have the border or not; default is false
lineColor (uint)	The color of the border; default is black
lineThickness (int)	The thickness of the border; default is 1 pixel thick

Now, we'll get to the real functionality of the BorderButton class with the draw method. The draw method does exactly what you probably guessed it does: it draws the BorderButton by using the parameters (Table 12.2) passed in by you, the developer. Note the use of the _halfThick variable in this method. Because of the way that Flash draws out the lines, I've learned that I have to pull the width and height of my button in by half the thickness of the line. If this is not done and your button goes right to the edge of the stage, you'll notice half of the border getting cut off from the right and bottom.

```
public function draw(parent:DisplayObjectContainer,
outline:Boolean = false, lineColor:uint = 0x000000,
lineThickness:int = 1):void {
    _bbParent = parent;
    _bbParent.addChild(this);
    _halfThick = lineThickness / 2;
    _w = stage.stageWidth - _halfThick;
    _h = stage.stageHeight - _halfThick;
```

```
graphics.lineStyle(lineThickness, lineColor);
graphics.beginFill(0, 0);
graphics.drawRect(0, 0, _w, _h);
}
```

The next method is the `activate` method, and once again, the name should give away its role in this class. By calling the `activate` method, we're telling the BorderButton that its `buttonMode` should be active and that it should listen for the user to click on it (if it isn't already listening). Since this method only accepts two parameters, I'll cover them real quick rather than use another table. The first one is `targetURL`, and it's used to pass in the URL you want the users to visit when they click your add. `targetURL` has no default value. The other parameter is the `targetWindow` parameter. This one defaults to "_blank," but you may have some specific reason to change that value when calling the `activate` method. You'll notice a reference to the `clickOut` method in the event listener. We'll get to that one in just a bit.

```
public function activate(targetUrl:String,
targetWindow:String = "_blank"):void {
    buttonMode = true;
    _request.url = targetUrl;
    _targetWindow = targetWindow;
    if(!hasEventListener(MouseEvent.CLICK)){
        addEventListener(MouseEvent.CLICK, clickOut, false,
0, true);
    }
}
```

After the `activate` method are a couple of methods that are there to tear down the BorderButton. The first of those is the `erase` method. The `erase` method simply checks to see if the Border-Button has a parent. If it does, then it removes the BorderButton from its parent. However, before doing that, it calls another method named `deactivate`. The `deactivate` method is just as simple as the `erase` method, but this one turns off the `buttonMode` of the Border-Button and removes the mouse click event listener.

```
public function erase():void{
    if(_bbParent != null){
        deactivate();
        _bbParent.removeChild(this);
    }
}

public function deactivate():void{
    if(hasEventListener(MouseEvent.CLICK)){
        buttonMode = false;
        removeEventListener(MouseEvent.CLICK,clickOut);
    }
}
```

Last, but far from least, is the `clickOut` method that was referenced in the `activate` method. This method is called when the user clicks on the BorderButton (if the BorderButton is active). Once again, we have a very simple and straightforward method sitting in front of us. This one uses a try catch statement to make an attempt at taking the user to the targeted URL by first trying to use `navigateToURL`. If it succeeds, that's great. If it doesn't, then it currently traces out a message letting you, the developer, know about it. You may want to put some proper error handling in the catch.

```
private function clickOut(e:MouseEvent):void {
    try {
        navigateToURL(_request, _targetWindow);
    }catch (e:Error){
        trace("An error occurred trying to navigate to the
target url.");
    }
}
```

Sample Use of BorderButton

The following code is the full code from the Document class named BorderButtonSample in the com.flashadbook.base package. It's pretty simple and takes care of everything in just a few steps: a new BorderButton is instantiated, a clickTag is assigned to a private variable, and the BorderButton is drawn and activated. That's it.

```
package com.flashadbook.base {
    import com.flashadbook.display.BorderButton;
    import flash.display.Sprite;
    import flash.events.MouseEvent;

    public class BorderButtonSample extends Sprite {
        private var _borderButton:BorderButton = new
BorderButton();
        private var _clickTag:String =
"http://www.flashadbook.com";

        public function BorderButtonSample(){
            _borderButton.draw(this);
            _borderButton.activate(_clickTag);
        }
    }
}
```

The SimpleMenu Class

The following SimpleMenu class is a single-dimension (no dropdowns) menu that has limited styling properties that can be set by the developer. One of the styles that is changeable is the TextFormat used for the upstate (when the mouse is not over the button), the overstate, and the downstate. For example, you may want to show your menu using Arial font with no underlines until a user rolls his or her mouse over a button. The other modifiable style in the SimpleMenu class is the rectangle that is drawn behind the text of each button. You can control the opacity of the rectangle in the different states with the backgroundUpAlpha, backgroundDownAlpha, and backgroundDownAlpha properties to have it semi see-through (or set their value to 0 and get rid of the rectangle altogether). Additionally, you can control the color of the rectangle separately for each state as well. Once the Simple-Menu class is used to create a menu in your project, you can assign any function to any button within that menu by using the assign Action method.

SimpleMenu Code

```
package com.flashadbook.display {
    import flash.display.DisplayObjectContainer;
    import flash.display.Sprite;
    import flash.events.MouseEvent;
    import flash.text.TextField;
    import flash.text.TextFormat;

    public class SimpleMenu extends Sprite {

        // —— layout options for the menu
        public static var HORIZONTAL:String = "horizontal";
        public static var VERTICAL:String = "vertical";

        private var _layout:String; // used to hold the
chosen layout
        private var _spacing:Number; // the amount of space
between menu items
        private var _menuItem:Sprite; // used to create and
alter individual menu items
        private var _menuItemLabel:TextField; // used to
create and alter individual menu item labels

        // —— background color
        private var _upBackground:uint = 0x000000;
        private var _overBackground:uint = 0x000000;
        private var _downBackground:uint = 0x000000;

        // —— background alpha
        private var _backgroundUpAlpha:Number = 1.0;
        private var _backgroundOverAlpha:Number = 0.5;
        private var _backgroundDownAlpha:Number = 0.0;

        // —— label text format
        private var _labelFormatUp:TextFormat = new
TextFormat();
```

```
        private var _labelFormatOver:TextFormat = new
TextFormat();
        private var _labelFormatDown:TextFormat = new
TextFormat();

        // ── color, alpha and format used for different
states of the menu items
        private var _stateBackgoundColor:uint =
upBackground;
        private var _stateBackgroundAlpha:Number =
backgroundUpAlpha;
        private var _stateTextFormat:TextFormat =
labelFormatUp;

        public function SimpleMenu(menuArray:Array,
spacing:Number = 0, layout:String = "horizontal") {
            _layout = layout;
            _spacing = spacing;
            setDefaultFormats();
            menuArray.forEach(createMenuItem);
        }

        public function assignAction(itemIndex:int,
action:Function):void {
            _menuItem = Sprite(getChildByName("menuItem" +
itemIndex));
            _menuItem.addEventListener(MouseEvent.CLICK,
action, false, 0, true);
        }

        public function
setPosition(xPosition:Number,yPosition:Number):void{
            x = xPosition;
            y = yPosition;
        }

        // START PRIVATE FUNCTIONS
        private function setDefaultFormats():void {
            labelFormatUp.color = 0xFFFFFF;
            labelFormatUp.underline = false;

            labelFormatOver.color = 0xCCCCCC;
            labelFormatOver.underline = true;

            labelFormatDown.color = 0x000000;
            labelFormatDown.underline = true;
        }

        private function createMenuItem(itemLabel:String,
index:int, array:Array):void {
            _menuItem = new Sprite();
            _menuItem.name = "menuItem" + index;
```

```
        _menuItem.mouseChildren = false;
        _menuItem.buttonMode = true;

        _menuItemLabel = new TextField();
        _menuItemLabel.name = "itemText";
        _menuItemLabel.autoSize = "left";
        _menuItemLabel.antiAliasType = "advanced";
        _menuItemLabel.selectable = false;
        _menuItemLabel.text = itemLabel;
        _menuItemLabel.setTextFormat(_labelFormatUp);

        drawItemBackground(_menuItem, _upBackground,
_backgroundUpAlpha, _menuItemLabel.width,
_menuItemLabel.height);
        addItemListeners(_menuItem);
        placeItem(_menuItem, index);

        _menuItem.addChild(_menuItemLabel);
        addChild(_menuItem);
    }

    private function
drawItemBackground(item:Sprite,color:uint,alpha:Number,
w:Number,h:Number):void {
        item.graphics.clear();
        item.graphics.beginFill(color, alpha);
        item.graphics.drawRect(0, 0, w, h);
    }

    private function addItemListeners(item:Sprite):void
{
        item.addEventListener(MouseEvent.MOUSE_OVER,
alterState, false, 0, true);
        item.addEventListener(MouseEvent.MOUSE_DOWN,
alterState, false, 0, true);
        item.addEventListener(MouseEvent.MOUSE_UP,
alterState, false, 0, true);
        item.addEventListener(MouseEvent.MOUSE_OUT,
alterState, false, 0, true);
    }

    private function
placeItem(itemToPlace:Sprite,index:int):void {
        if(index == 0) return;
        var lastItem:Sprite = Sprite(getChildAt(index -
1));
        switch(_layout){
            case HORIZONTAL:
                itemToPlace.x = lastItem.x +
lastItem.width + _spacing;
                break;
```

```
                            case VERTICAL:
                                itemToPlace.y = lastItem.y +
lastItem.height + _spacing;
                                break;
                            default:
                                trace('Please use a String value of
"horizontal" or "vertical" for the SimpleMenu layout
param.');
                                break;
                    }
            }

        private function alterState(e:MouseEvent):void {
            _menuItem = Sprite(e.target);
            _menuItemLabel =
TextField(_menuItem.getChildByName("itemText"));
            switch(e.type) {
                case MouseEvent.MOUSE_UP:
                case MouseEvent.MOUSE_OVER:
                    _stateBackgoundColor = overBackground;
                    _stateBackgroundAlpha =
backgroundOverAlpha;
                    _stateTextFormat = labelFormatOver;
                    break;
                case MouseEvent.MOUSE_DOWN:
                    _stateBackgoundColor = downBackground;
                    _stateBackgroundAlpha =
backgroundDownAlpha;
                    _stateTextFormat = labelFormatDown;
                    break;
                case MouseEvent.MOUSE_OUT:
                    _stateBackgoundColor = upBackground;
                    _stateBackgroundAlpha =
backgroundUpAlpha;
                    _stateTextFormat = labelFormatUp;
                    break;
            }

            _menuItemLabel.setTextFormat(_stateTextFormat);
            drawItemBackground(_menuItem,
_stateBackgoundColor, _stateBackgroundAlpha,
_menuItem.width, _menuItem.height);
        }
        // END PRIVATE FUNCTIONS

        // START GETTERS AND SETTERS
        // —— background colors
        public function get upBackground():uint {
            return _upBackground;
        }
```

```
    public function set upBackground(value:uint):void {
        _upBackground = value;
    }
    public function get overBackground():uint {
        return _overBackground;
    }
    public function set overBackground(value:uint):void
{
        _overBackground = value;
    }
    public function get downBackground():uint {
        return _downBackground;
    }
    public function set downBackground(value:uint):void
{
        _downBackground = value;
    }
    // —— background alphas
    public function get backgroundUpAlpha():Number {
        return _backgroundUpAlpha;
    }
    public function set
backgroundUpAlpha(value:Number):void {
        _backgroundUpAlpha = value;
    }
    public function get backgroundOverAlpha():Number {
        return _backgroundOverAlpha;
    }
    public function set
backgroundOverAlpha(value:Number):void {
        _backgroundOverAlpha = value;
    }
    public function get backgroundDownAlpha():Number {
        return _backgroundDownAlpha;
    }
    public function set
backgroundDownAlpha(value:Number):void {
        _backgroundDownAlpha = value;
    }
    // —— label text formats
    public function get labelFormatUp():TextFormat {
        return _labelFormatUp;
    }
    public function set
labelFormatUp(value:TextFormat):void {
        _labelFormatUp = value;
    }
```

```
        public function get labelFormatOver():TextFormat {
            return _labelFormatOver;
        }
        public function set
labelFormatOver(value:TextFormat):void {
            _labelFormatOver = value;
        }

        public function get labelFormatDown():TextFormat {
            return _labelFormatDown;
        }
        public function set
labelFormatDown(value:TextFormat):void {
            _labelFormatDown = value;
        }
        // END GETTERS AND SETTERS
    }
}
```

SimpleMenu Breakdown

Once again, we'll start with the package and the imports for SimpleMenu:

```
package com.flashadbook.display {
    import flash.display.DisplayObjectContainer;
    import flash.display.Sprite;
    import flash.events.MouseEvent;
    import flash.text.TextField;
    import flash.text.TextFormat;
```

The next thing in line is the class declaration and a list of several variables. Most of the variables are private, and two of them are public and static. Also, most of the private variables have getters and setters further down in the class that allow the values to be set and retrieved from outside of the class itself. As with the BorderButton class, the SimpleMenu class extends Sprite. The reason I chose Sprite again for SimpleMenu was to gain access to many of the properties and functionalities available to a MovieClip, but without needing a timeline. So let's take a look at that class declaration followed by the variables in Table 12.3:

```
public class SimpleMenu extends Sprite {
```

Let's move on to the class constructor, shall we? To instantiate a new SimpleMenu, there are three parameters that need to be considered. One of them (menuArray) is required, and the other two (spacing and layout) are optional. menuArray is an array of Strings that will be used as the labels for the menu items. The optional parameter, spacing, sets the distance (or padding) between the

Table 12.3 The Variables of the SimpleMenu Class

Variable	Purpose
HORIZONTAL (public, static String)	Option for laying out the menu in the horizontal direction
VERTICAL (public, static String)	Option for laying out the menu in the vertical direction
_layout (String)	Holds the chosen layout
_spacing (Number)	The number of pixels to place between menu items
_menuItem (Sprite)	Used for the creation and manipulation of each menu item
_menuItemLabel (TextField)	Used for the creation and manipulation of each menu item label
_upBackground (uint)	The background color of the menu items in the upstate; default is black
_overBackground (uint)	The background color of the menu items in the overstate; default is black
_downBackground (uint)	The background color of the menu items in the downstate; default is black
_backgroundUpAlpha (Number)	The background alpha of the menu items in the upstate; default is 1 (100%)
_backgroundOverAlpha (Number)	The background alpha of the menu items in the overstate; default is 0.5 (50%)
_backgroundDownAlpha (Number)	The background alpha of the menu items in the downstate; default is 0
_labelFormatUp (TextFormat)	The TextFormat used for the menu item labels in the upstate
_labelFormatOver (TextFormat)	The TextFormat used for the menu item labels in the overstate
_labelFormatDown (TextFormat)	The TextFormat used for the menu item labels in the downstate
_stateBackgroundColor (uint)	Holds the background color of the current state of a menu item that is being interacted with
_stateBackgroundAlpha (Number)	Holds the background alpha of the current state of a menu item that is being interacted with
_stateTextFormat (TextFormat)	Holds the TextFormat of the current state of a menu item's label that is being interacted with

menu items. spacing defaults to 0 if nothing is passed in. The other optional parameter, layout, tells the SimpleMenu the direction in which to organize the menu items. The options are horizontal and vertical with the default being set to horizontal. Once inside the SimpleMenu class constructor, we'll make the values of the spacing and layout parameters available to the rest of the class by assigning them to the private variables through the (almost) same names of _layout and _spacing. The next line calls the setDefaultFormats method, which we'll get to in just a bit. After that call, I use the forEach method from the Array class to call the createMenuItem method with each item of the menuArray. More on that a little further in as well.

```
public function SimpleMenu(menuArray:Array, spacing:Number
= 0, layout:String = "horizontal") {
    _layout = layout;
    _spacing = spacing;
    setDefaultFormats();
    menuArray.forEach(createMenuItem);
}
```

Next are a couple of publicly available methods used to control the position of the entire menu and the behavior of each individual menu item. The setPosition method does exactly what its name claims to do: it sets the position of the SimpleMenu. There's not too much to explain there except that you pass in the x and y values where you want the SimpleMenu to live. On the other hand, the assignAction method does a bit more. The assignAction method allows you to write the functionality outside of the class for each individual menu item and then pass it in and assign it to the desired menu item. You can do so with this method's two parameters, itemIndex and action, both of which are required. Because the createMenuItem method names each menu item in a particular way using the index of that item in the menuArray, we're also able to use those index numbers here. For example, let's say you want to assign functionA to the first item in your menuArray. You would pass in 0 as the itemIndex and functionA as the action.

```
public function assignAction(itemIndex:int,
action:Function):void {
    _menuItem = Sprite(getChildByName("menuItem" +
itemIndex));
    _menuItem.addEventListener(MouseEvent.CLICK, action,
false, 0, true);
}

public function
setPosition(xPosition:Number,yPosition:Number):void{
    x = xPosition;
    y = yPosition;
}
```

Remember, we'll discuss the createMenuItem method in just a bit, but first, let's take a quick look at the setDefaultFormats method. This one is very straightforward because it's not doing anything but setting the color and underline values for the menu item labels in each state (up, over, and down). These default values could be set to match your style guide, or they could be left as they are, but the point is to have defaults in case they aren't set later when a new instance of SimpleMenu is created.

```
private function setDefaultFormats():void {
    labelFormatUp.color = 0xFFFFFF;
    labelFormatUp.underline = false;

    labelFormatOver.color = 0xCCCCCC;
    labelFormatOver.underline = true;

    labelFormatDown.color = 0x000000;
    labelFormatDown.underline = true;
}
```

And now, without further ado, the much talked about create
MenuItem method! This little chunk of code is responsible for creating
each menu item and adding it to the stage. If you remember in the
class constructor, we called this method with each item in the
menuArray. The three parameters in this method are the parameters
that get passed when you use the forEach method from the Array
class. They are the value of the item, the index of that item in its
containing Array, and the containing Array object itself. Inside
createMenuItem, the first thing that happens is the instantiation and
naming of a new Sprite, which will be the new menu item. In order
to access the menu item later (e.g., from the assignAction method),
the menu item is named by appending its index in the array to the
string "menuItem," so we end up with menuItem0, menuItem1, and so
on. Next, we'll set the mouseChildren property to false, so no
children within this menu item will be able to take over the focus of
the mouse. After that comes setting the buttonMode to true, so the
menu item will show the hand cursor and will accept a click event if
the space bar or Enter key are pressed while it has focus.

After creating the new menu item, I move on to create its label
as a new TextField. I won't go through each line of this process in
great detail, but you can see that the properties being set are name,
autoSize (set to "left", which essentially means the text is left
aligned), antiAliasType, selectable, and text. Also, we run a
setTextFormat call to set the initial formatting of the label. From
here, we call a couple of other methods for the look, interactivity,
and location of the menu item being created (those are up next).
Finally, the label is added to the menu item, and the menu item is
added to the SimpleMenu.

```
private function createMenuItem(itemLabel:String,
index:int, array:Array):void {
    _menuItem = new Sprite();
    _menuItem.name = "menuItem" + index;
    _menuItem.mouseChildren = false;
    _menuItem.buttonMode = true;

    _menuItemLabel = new TextField();
    _menuItemLabel.name = "itemText";
    _menuItemLabel.autoSize = "left";
    _menuItemLabel.antiAliasType = "advanced";
    _menuItemLabel.selectable = false;
    _menuItemLabel.text = itemLabel;
    _menuItemLabel.setTextFormat(_labelFormatUp);

    drawItemBackground(_menuItem, _upBackground,
_backgroundUpAlpha, _menuItemLabel.width,
_menuItemLabel.height);
    addItemListeners(_menuItem);
    placeItem(_menuItem, index);
```

```
    _menuItem.addChild(_menuItemLabel);
    addChild(_menuItem);
}
```

So now let's see those methods that are called at the end of the `createMenuItem` method. The first two we'll look at together are `drawItemBackground` and `addItemListeners`. `drawItemBackground` uses the graphics property of the menu item passed in (via the `item` parameter) to draw a rectangle with the color, alpha, and size that are also passed in through the method's parameters. The first thing it does is clear the graphics in case there was anything drawn in the menu item prior to this call. Once things are cleared out, the `begin Fill` method is called. This is where the background color and alpha values come in. With the fill color and alpha set, all that's left to do in this method is to call the `graphics.drawRect` method. The next method, `addItemListeners`, simply adds MouseEvent listeners to the menu item, so its look can be changed with the `alterState` method (coming up after we look at the `placeItem` method).

```
private function
drawItemBackground(item:Sprite,color:uint,alpha:Number,
w:Number,h:Number):void {
    item.graphics.clear();
    item.graphics.beginFill(color, alpha);
    item.graphics.drawRect(0, 0, w, h);
}

private function addItemListeners(item:Sprite):void {
    item.addEventListener(MouseEvent.MOUSE_OVER,
alterState, false, 0, true);
    item.addEventListener(MouseEvent.MOUSE_DOWN,
alterState, false, 0, true);
    item.addEventListener(MouseEvent.MOUSE_UP, alterState,
false, 0, true);
    item.addEventListener(MouseEvent.MOUSE_OUT, alterState,
false, 0, true);
}
```

The last method that was called from within `createMenuItem` was `placeItem`, and it's the next method we're going to look at. The two parameters this method is expecting are, of course, the item that needs to be placed (`itemToPlace`) and the `index` of that item. The very first thing we do here is check to see if `index` is equal to 0. If it is, we can jump right back out of this method because there's nothing we need to do since the very first item in a SimpleMenu gets placed at the x,y position of (0,0) within the SimpleMenu itself. Once index is anything other than 0, the code can continue on to the next line where we need to get a reference to the previously created menu item (`lastItem`). This is the second time the `index` parameter comes in handy because we can check one position beneath that `index` to get the reference we need. Finally, we'll run a quick switch statement to check the _layout of the SimpleMenu. Depending on that value, we know to place the current menu item either beneath the `lastItem (VERTICAL)` or beside it `(HORIZONTAL)`. If some other value was passed in when the SimpleMenu was instantiated, now is the time to let the developer know he or she has made a mistake and inform him or her of the acceptable values. That gets taken care of in the default case of the switch statement.

```
private function
placeItem(itemToPlace:Sprite,index:int):void {
    if(index == 0) return;
    var lastItem:Sprite = Sprite(getChildAt(index - 1));
    switch(_layout){
        case HORIZONTAL:
            itemToPlace.x = lastItem.x + lastItem.width +
_spacing;
            break;
        case VERTICAL:
            itemToPlace.y = lastItem.y + lastItem.height +
_spacing;
            break;
        default:
            trace('Please use a String value of
"horizontal" or "vertical" for the SimpleMenu layout
param.');
            break;
    }

}
```

Other than the getter and setters, there's only one method left to cover in the SimpleMenu class and that is the `alterState` method. If you recall, the `addItemListeners` method added MouseEvent listeners to change the states of the menu items. The `alterState` method handles the changing of the background color, the background alpha, and the formatting of the label as a menu item is interacted with. Again, this is a very simple method because it is just checking the type of MouseEvent that occurred and setting the values accordingly. One thing to note in the switch statement is that there is nothing for the `MouseEvent.MOUSE_UP` case (not even a `break`). You'll also notice that the `MouseEvent.MOUSE_OVER` case is directly after it. By leaving that first case blank, the outcome is the same for both the upstate and the overstate. The thinking behind that is that when you put the item in a downstate and then bring it back to the upstate, your mouse is still over the item. In that case, the upstate should be the same as the overstate. Once the mouse triggers the `MouseEvent.MOUSE_OUT` event, then I set all the styling back to the real upstate styling that was originally intended.

The last thing that happens here is another call to the `drawItem Background` method, which you'll remember clears the graphics and redraws with the desired color and alpha values.

```
private function alterState(e:MouseEvent):void {
    _menuItem = Sprite(e.target);
    _menuItemLabel =
TextField(_menuItem.getChildByName("itemText"));
    switch(e.type) {
        case MouseEvent.MOUSE_UP:
        case MouseEvent.MOUSE_OVER:
            _stateBackgoundColor = overBackground;
            _stateBackgroundAlpha = backgroundOverAlpha;
            _stateTextFormat = labelFormatOver;
            break;
        case MouseEvent.MOUSE_DOWN:
            _stateBackgoundColor = downBackground;
            _stateBackgroundAlpha = backgroundDownAlpha;
            _stateTextFormat = labelFormatDown;
            break;
        case MouseEvent.MOUSE_OUT:
            _stateBackgoundColor = upBackground;
            _stateBackgroundAlpha = backgroundUpAlpha;
            _stateTextFormat = labelFormatUp;
            break;
    }
    _menuItemLabel.setTextFormat(_stateTextFormat);
    drawItemBackground(_menuItem, _stateBackgoundColor,
_stateBackgroundAlpha, _menuItem.width, _menuItem.height);
}
```

Sample Use of SimpleMenu

The following code is the full code from the Document class named SimpleMenuSample in the com.flashadbook.base package. The first thing this class does is to declare a `_simpleMenu` variable and a `_menuArr` variable. Once inside the class constructor, we'll create the new SimpleMenu using the `_menuArr`. We'll set the padding between menu items to 10 and tell it to have a vertical layout. The next thing we take care of is assigning actions to each menu item using the `assignAction` method of SimpleMenu. After that, we'll call `setPosition` with an x value of 100 and a y value of 0, and then we'll add the SimpleMenu to the stage. Once again, nothing much to it.

```
package com.flashadbook.base {
    import com.flashadbook.display.SimpleMenu;
    import flash.display.Sprite;
    import flash.events.MouseEvent;
```

```
    public class SimpleMenuSample extends Sprite {

        private var _simpleMenu:SimpleMenu;
        private var _menuArr:Array = new Array("Menu Item
1","Menu Item 2","Menu Item 3");

        public function SimpleMenuSample(){
            _simpleMenu = new
SimpleMenu(_menuArr,10,SimpleMenu.VERTICAL);
            _simpleMenu.assignAction(0, releaseFunction1);
            _simpleMenu.assignAction(1, releaseFunction2);
            _simpleMenu.assignAction(2, releaseFunction3);
            _simpleMenu.setPosition(100, 0);
            addChild(_simpleMenu);
        }

        public function
releaseFunction1(e:MouseEvent):void{
            trace("function 1");
        }
        public function
releaseFunction2(e:MouseEvent):void{
            trace("function 2");
        }
        public function
releaseFunction3(e:MouseEvent):void{
            trace("function 3");
        }
    }
}
```

The SimpleGallery Class

There will most likely be occasions where your client wants to show off a gallery of either several of their products or multiple photographs of a specific product. The automobile manufacturer example I've used in this book would be a prime candidate for a photo gallery. Since you may find yourself making these galleries on project after project after project, it might be a good idea to have a simple base for one at your disposal. The SimpleGallery class is meant as exactly that. With control over properties to do things like move the entire gallery around and control how many columns you want to break the gallery into, it gives you a simple layout with a simple method to view each thumbnail in its larger form. You only need to tell it the directory where the images live and which ones to pull from that directory, and it will take care of the rest for you. As we go through the code, note that there is no transition from the thumbnail of an image to its full-size version.

The change in size happens instantaneously in the `imageClicked` method, and you may want to consider adding in a tiny bit of math for transitions or even looking into one of the popular tweening libraries like Tweener or TweenLite.

SimpleGallery Code

```
package com.flashadbook.display {
    import flash.display.DisplayObjectContainer;
    import flash.display.Loader;
    import flash.display.Sprite;
    import flash.events.MouseEvent;
    import flash.geom.Point;
    import flash.net.URLRequest;
    import flash.events.Event;
    import flash.events.IOErrorEvent;

    public class SimpleGallery extends Sprite{

        private var _galleryParent:DisplayObjectContainer;
// the parent of the gallery
        private var _galleryPath:String; // external folder
that holds the images
        private var _imageArray:Array; // array of image
names within the _galleryPath
        private var _columns:int; // number of columns for
the gallery
        private var _thumbScale:Number; // percentage to
shrink the image for the thumbnail
        private var _padding:Number; // the amount of space
between menu items
        private var _numberOfImages:int; // number of
images in the gallery

        private var _numberLoaded:int; // how many images
have finished loading
        private var _imageLoader:Loader; // used to load
and manipulate each image
        private var _loadedImage:Loader; // used to
reference each image as it is loaded
        private var _targetScale:Number; // used to scale
images up and down
        private var _targetX:Number; // used to move the x
position of a selected image
        private var _targetY:Number; // used to move the y
position of a selected image
        private var _halfWidth:Number; // half the width of
the gallery
        private var _halfHeight:Number; // half the height
of the gallery
```

```
        private var _imageNamePrefix:String = "image_"; //
used for naming the images
        private var _pointVector:Vector.<Point> = new
Vector.<Point>(); // vector of points for the images
        private var _imageURLRequest:URLRequest = new
URLRequest(); // used to load the images
        public function
SimpleGallery(parent:DisplayObjectContainer,galleryPath:
String,imageArray:Array,columns:int=1,thumbScale:Number=1,
padding:Number=5) {

            _galleryParent = parent;
            _galleryPath = galleryPath;
            _imageArray = imageArray;
            _columns = columns;
            _thumbScale = thumbScale;
            _padding = padding;
            _numberOfImages = imageArray.length;

            for (var r:int = 0; r < _numberOfImages; r +=
columns) {
                for (var c:int = 0; c < columns; c++) {
                    if(r+c < _numberOfImages){
                        createImage(c, r);
                    }
                }
            }
        }

        public function setPosition(xPosition:Number = 0,
yPosition:Number = 0) {
            x = xPosition;
            y = yPosition;
        }

        // START PRIVATE FUNCTIONS
        private function createImage(column:int,
row:int):void {
            _pointVector.push(new Point(column,
row/_columns));
            _imageURLRequest.url = _galleryPath +
_imageArray[row + column];

            _imageLoader = new Loader();
            _imageLoader.name = _imageNamePrefix + (row +
column);
            _imageLoader.addEventListener(MouseEvent.CLICK,
imageClicked, false, 0, true);
            _imageLoader.contentLoaderInfo.addEventListener(Event.
COMPLETE, placeImage, false, 0, true);
```

```
                _imageLoader.contentLoaderInfo.addEventListener
(IOErrorEvent.IO_ERROR, imageLoadError, false, 0, true);
                _imageLoader.load(_imageURLRequest);
        }

        private function placeImage(e:Event):void {
                e.target.removeEventListener(Event.COMPLETE,
placeImage);

                e.target.removeEventListener(IOErrorEvent.IO_ERROR,
imageLoadError);

                _loadedImage = e.target.loader;
                var pIndex:int = pointIndex(_loadedImage);
                var column:int = _pointVector[pIndex].x;
                var row:int = _pointVector[pIndex].y;

                _loadedImage.scaleX = _loadedImage.scaleY =
_thumbScale;
                _loadedImage.x = _pointVector[pIndex].x =
(column * _loadedImage.width) + (column * _padding);
                _loadedImage.y = _pointVector[pIndex].y = (row
* _loadedImage.height) + (row * _padding);

                addChild(_loadedImage);
                _loadedImage = null;

                _numberLoaded++;
                if(_numberLoaded == _numberOfImages){
                    _halfWidth = width/2;
                    _halfHeight = height/2;
                }
        }

        private function imageClicked(e:MouseEvent):void {
                _imageLoader = Loader(e.target);
                _targetScale = _imageLoader.scaleX == 1 ?
_thumbScale : 1;
                _targetX = _imageLoader.scaleX == 1 ?
_pointVector[pointIndex(_imageLoader)].x : _halfWidth -
(_imageLoader.content.width/2);
                _targetY = _imageLoader.scaleX == 1 ?
_pointVector[pointIndex(_imageLoader)].y : _halfHeight -
(_imageLoader.content.height/2);
                if(_targetScale == 1){
                    swapChildren(_imageLoader,
getChildAt(numChildren - 1));
                }

                _imageLoader.scaleX = _imageLoader.scaleY =
_targetScale;
```

```
            _imageLoader.x = _targetX;
            _imageLoader.y = _targetY;
            _imageLoader = null;
        }

        private function pointIndex(loader:Loader):int {
            return
int(loader.name.substring(_imageNamePrefix.length));
        }

        private function
imageLoadError(e:IOErrorEvent):void{
            trace("!!! There was an error loading an image
!!!");
            trace(e.text);
        }
        // END PRIVATE FUNCTIONS

        // START READ-ONLY GETTERS
        public function get numberOfImages():int {
            return _numberOfImages;
        }
        public function get galleryPath():String{
            return _galleryPath;
        }
        public function get imageArray():Array{
            return _imageArray;
        }
        // END READ-ONLY GETTERS
    }
}
```

SimpleGallery Breakdown

The SimpleGallery class package and imports:

```
package com.flashadbook.display {
    import flash.display.DisplayObjectContainer;
    import flash.display.Loader;
    import flash.display.Sprite;
    import flash.events.MouseEvent;
    import flash.geom.Point;
    import flash.net.URLRequest;
    import flash.events.Event;
    import flash.events.IOErrorEvent;
```

Now with that out of the way, let's take a look at the variables for this class because there are indeed a lot of them. All of them are private, and only one of them has a public "getter" at the end of the class. When you look at them in the code, you might notice that they appear to be in two groups separated by an empty line. The only reason I did that is because the first group are the variables that are immediately set inside the SimpleGallery class constructor. So let's take a look at these variables now in Table 12.4.

The SimpleGallery class constructor doesn't have a huge amount of code in it. The first thing it does is to set some of the private variables based on the parameters that are passed in. The six parameters used in the constructor are evenly split between required and optional. The first three (parent, galleryPath, and imageArray) need values from you when you create a new instance of the SimpleGallery. The other three (columns, thumbScale, and padding) aren't as dependent and needy. Instead, they each have default values (1, 1, and 5, respectively), which, when left

Table 12.4 The Private Variables of the SimpleGallery Class

Variable	Purpose
_galleryParent (DisplayObjectContainer)	The parent of the gallery
_galleryPath (String)	The path to the external directory that holds the images
_imageArray (Array)	An array of image names located within the external directory
_columns (int)	The number of columns in which to layout the gallery
_thumbScale (Number)	The scale the thumbnail should be in relation to the original image
_padding (Number)	The number of pixels to place between the images
_numberOfImages (int)	The number of images in the gallery
_numberLoaded (int)	The number of images that have completely finished loading
_imageLoader (Loader)	Used to load and manipulate the images
_loadedImage (Loader)	Used to reference each image as it has finished loading
_targetScale (Number)	Used to scale the images up and down when the user interacts with them
_targetX (Number)	Used to set and move the x position of an image that a user is interacting with
_targetY (Number)	Used to set and move the y position of an image that a user is interacting with
_halfWidth (Number)	Half the width of the gallery; used for placement of an image as it is interacted with
_halfHeight (Number)	Half the height of the gallery; used for placement of an image as it is interacted with
_imageNamePrefix (String)	Used as the first part of the name of each image as it is loaded and placed in the gallery
_pointVector (Vector)	A Vector containing the Points to use for the placement of each image
_imagesURLRequest (URLRequest)	Used to load each image

unchanged, will simply lay your unscaled images out in a vertical line with 5 pixels between each one.

> **TIP**
>
> If you aren't familiar with the Vector class, I would like to go ahead and recommend that you take a few minutes to look it up in the Adobe ActionScript 3.0 Language Reference online. The general description is that a Vector is like an Array, but you only put one type of data in it. You might have a Vector that contains Strings or one that contains Points as we have in the SimpleGallery class. A Vector is more efficient to work with than an Array.

Once the private variables have been set to match the parameters, we're going to run through a nested `for` loop and call out to the `createImage` method if conditions permit. If conditions permit? What do I mean by that? Well, you'll notice that I use the variables `r` and `c` in the `for` loops (yeah, yeah, I know... variable names less than three letters). These represent rows and columns, respectively, and we can use them to count which image we're currently on in our loop. For example, if we're on row 2 (`r=2`) and column 4 (`c=4`), then we know we're on image number 6 (2 + 4 = 6). However, if we only have five images in our gallery, then we don't want to run the `createImage` method, and we want to get out of the loop instead. If you noticed and were wondering about the part of the code that says `columnLoop:` prior to the `for` loop, this is where it comes in. By placing this before the `for` loop, we've labeled the loop, and we can reference it by that label from within itself or its nested children loops (`break columnLoop`). So let's look at this chunk of code on its own, and while we're at it, let's take a quick look at `setPosition` as well. We've seen this simple method in other classes earlier in the chapter, and it does the same thing here. It allows you to set the `x` and `y` positions of your newly instantiated SimpleGallery.

```
public function
SimpleGallery(parent:DisplayObjectContainer,galleryPath:
String,imageArray:Array,columns:int=1,thumbScale:Number=1,
padding:Number=5) {
    _galleryParent = parent;
    _galleryPath = galleryPath;
    _imageArray = imageArray;
    _columns = columns;
    _thumbScale = thumbScale;
    _padding = padding;
    _numberOfImages = imageArray.length;
```

```
columnLoop: for (var r:int = 0; r < _numberOfImages; r
+= columns) {
    for (var c:int = 0; c < columns; c++) {
        if(r+c < _numberOfImages){
            createImage(c, r);
        }else{
            break columnLoop;
        }
    }
}

public function setPosition(xPosition:Number = 0,
yPosition:Number = 0) {
    x = xPosition;
    y = yPosition;
}
```

Now let's take a look into that `createImage` method that was being called from the `for` loop in the constructor. Since this is an image gallery, there are images in it, and they need to be created (or loaded, actually). The two parameters required by this method are the column and row where the image will end up. If you remember from the `for` loop, we passed those in with the two variables `c` and `r`. On the very first line of `createImage`, we're going to create a new Point with an `x` value equal to the `column` parameter and a `y` value equal to the `row` parameter. That new Point is immediately added to the `_pointVector` for later use. Yes, you are correct. That means you now have a Vector filled with Points with x,y values like (0,1), (0,2), and (1,2). It may not make sense right away, but it will make more when we look at the `placeImage` method. The next way we're going to use the `column` and `row` parameters together is to grab an image name from `_imageArray` and append it to `_gallery Path`. With those two values added together, we should have a valid URL to an image for the gallery. What a coincidence! We need a value like that for the `url` property of `_imageURLRequest`. Let's use this one, shall we?

Okay, now we're going to use the `_imageLoader` variable to create a new Loader for loading the image. Once we've instantiated that new Loader, we're going to give it a name using the `_imageNamePrefix` combined (once again) with `row` and `column`. This time we're adding the values of `row` and `column` to come up with a number, so we end up with names for our images like `image_1`, `image_2`, and `image_3`. Let's add a few listeners to our images' Loaders next. First is a `MouseEvent.CLICK` listener that will call the `imageClicked` method. The second is an `Event.COMPLETE` listener that will call `placeImage` once the image has finished loading from its external location.

The last one I'm adding is an `IOErrorEvent.IO_ERROR` listener. This is in place in case there's a problem loading the image. It calls out to `imageLoadError`, which you'll need to modify to fit your particular error-handling needs. And finally, we'll use the `load` method of our Loader to attempt to load an image.

```
_imageURLRequest.
private function createImage(column:int, row:int):void {
    _pointVector.push(new Point(column, row/_columns));
    _imageURLRequest.url = _galleryPath + _imageArray[row +
column];

    _imageLoader = new Loader();
    _imageLoader.name = _imageNamePrefix + (row + column);
    _imageLoader.addEventListener(MouseEvent.CLICK,
imageClicked, false, 0, true);
    _imageLoader.contentLoaderInfo.addEventListener(Event.
COMPLETE, placeImage, false, 0, true);
    _imageLoader.contentLoaderInfo.addEventListener(IOError
Event.IO_ERROR, imageLoadError, false, 0, true);
    _imageLoader.load(_imageURLRequest);
}
```

So now that we've created the images, the next thing that happens for each one after it's finished loading is that it notifies the `placeImage` method of its load completion. The first thing the `placeImage` method then does is to release a little memory by removing the two load-related listeners (`Event.COMPLETE` and `IOErrorEvent.IO_ERROR`). Now we're going to use `_loadedImage` to reference and manipulate our currently targeted Loader (image). So here's where we get back to the Vector full of Points with x,y values that didn't make any sense earlier. Remember when we named our images and added the row and column together to append a number to the end of the name? Well that number just so happens to match the image's index in `_imageArray` and the index of the Point it will use from `_pointVector`. See where I'm going with this?

So let's take `_loadedImage` and pass it to the `pointIndex` method. We'll quickly look at that method later, but it basically just strips the number off the end of the name for us to use in the next steps. Now that we've got that number, we can use it to pull the correct Point from `_pointVector`. We'll grab the x and y values from that Point and assign them back to `column` and `row` variables for use within this method. Next is to set the image's `scaleX` and `scaleY` according to the `_thumbScale` variable and then get into a tiny bit of math.

Now that we've scaled the image, we're dealing with a thumbnail (assuming that the `_thumbScale` variable was set lower than 1). The math in the next couple of lines is where the location of the thumbnail is both determined and stored. The first part is the x value of the location, and it is realized by multiplying the column number with the width of the thumbnail and then adding that product to the product of the column multiplied with _padding. It looks like this:

```
(column * _loadedImage.width) + (column * _padding)
```

So let's say you're in column 3, the width of your thumbnail is 120 pixels and the padding between your images is 10 pixels. The x position of that particular thumbnail would be 390: (3 * 120) + (3 * 10) = 390.

That total is not only used to place the image in the correct x position but also used to change the x property of the corresponding Point in _pointVector and will be called on later when the user is interacting with the image. The same thing is then done for the y position of the thumbnail and y property of the Point but with the row and thumbnail height. Once we have the position worked out, it's time to place the image on the stage and set _loadedImage back to null to clear up any memory that was associated with it. Finally, we're going to increment _numberLoaded and test to see if it matches _numberOfImages. If it does, then all images are loaded, resized to their thumbnail sizes, and placed on the stage. With all of them in place, we can get the width and height of our gallery, and therefore, we can assign values to _halfWidth and _halfHeight (which we'll use in the imageClicked method).

```
private function placeImage(e:Event):void {
    e.target.removeEventListener(Event.COMPLETE,
placeImage);
    e.target.removeEventListener(IOErrorEvent.IO_ERROR,
imageLoadError);

    _loadedImage = e.target.loader;
    var pIndex:int = pointIndex(_loadedImage);
    var column:int = _pointVector[pIndex].x;
    var row:int = _pointVector[pIndex].y;

    _loadedImage.scaleX = _loadedImage.scaleY =
_thumbScale;
    _loadedImage.x = _pointVector[pIndex].x = (column *
_loadedImage.width) + (column * _padding);
    _loadedImage.y = _pointVector[pIndex].y = (row *
_loadedImage.height) + (row * _padding);

    addChild(_loadedImage);
    _loadedImage = null;

    _numberLoaded++;
    if(_numberLoaded == _numberOfImages){
```

```
    _halfWidth = width/2;
    _halfHeight = height/2;
  }
}
```

Now that all the images are in their correct locations on the stage, they're ready for user interaction via the `imageClicked` method. The first thing we need to do is assign the Loader (image) that was clicked to the `_imageLoader` variable (notice how we keep reusing that variable and then we clear it out when we're finished with it). After that, there's a set of ternary operators that are determining how to scale the image and where to place it. The first one assigns a value to the `_targetScale` variable by testing against the current scale of the image. If the current scale is 1 (100%), then the image needs to be sized down to the value of `_thumbScale`. If it isn't currently at a scale of 1, then it needs to be and that is the value assigned to `_target Scale`. The next two ternary operators are essentially the same as one another except for the fact that one is assigning a value to `_targetX` and the other to `_targetY`. To do so, we test against the current scale of the image again. Once again, if the scale is equal to 1, the image is on its way back to thumbnail size and therefore needs to be on its way back to its thumbnail position as well. So we'll grab the appropriate property (x or y) from the appropriate Point in `_pointVector` and assign that value. On the other hand, the current scale may not be equal to 1. If that's the case, the image is on its way to being viewed at full size and needs to be placed in the correct location. This is where the `_halfWidth` and `_halfHeight` variables come in and allow us to center the full-size image to the gallery itself:

```
_halfWidth - (_imageLoader.content.width/2)
```

Now, we have stored the values we need prior to the targeted image being altered in any way, so let's start altering it. The first thing to do here is check to see if `_targetScale` is set to 1. If it is, we know the image is about to be viewed, and we need to make sure it's in front of all other images in the gallery. To do that we'll use `swapChildren` with the image that sits at the top of the gallery's display list (`getChildAt(numChildren – 1)`). After all that is finished, it's time to manipulate the target image by assigning our stored values to set its scale and position. And finally, let's clear that associated memory up again by setting `_imageLoader` back to `null`.

```
private function imageClicked(e:MouseEvent):void {
    _imageLoader = Loader(e.target);
    _targetScale = _imageLoader.scaleX == 1 ? _thumbScale :
1;
    _targetX = _imageLoader.scaleX == 1 ?
_pointVector[pointIndex(_imageLoader)].x : _halfWidth -
(_imageLoader.content.width/2);
```

```
    _targetY = _imageLoader.scaleX == 1 ?
_pointVector[pointIndex(_imageLoader)].y : _halfHeight -
(_imageLoader.content.height/2);

    if(_targetScale == 1){
        swapChildren(_imageLoader, getChildAt(numChildren -
1));
    }
    _imageLoader.scaleX = _imageLoader.scaleY =
_targetScale;
    _imageLoader.x = _targetX;
    _imageLoader.y = _targetY;
    _imageLoader = null;
}
```

Finally, we've reached the `pointIndex` and `imageLoadError` methods. There's not much going on at all in either one of these, but I felt they still deserved a quick mention. First is the `pointIndex` method. If you remember earlier in the class, we called on this method and passed in the name of the Loader (image) whose index we were in search of. The workings inside `pointIndex` are very simple because they are doing nothing more than stripping the number off the end of the Loader's name and returning it as an `int`. As for the `imageLoadError` method, I only placed a couple of trace statements in there and thought I'd leave it up to you to handle that error in the best way you see fit for your particular needs.

```
private function pointIndex(loader:Loader):int {
    return
int(loader.name.substring(_imageNamePrefix.length));
}
```

```
private function imageLoadError(e:IOErrorEvent):void{
    trace("!!! There was an error loading an image !!!");
    trace(e.text);
}
```

One last group of items for the SimpleGallery are the "getters" I placed at the end of the class. The fact that these variables have getters but no setters makes them read-only properties. I decided on `numberOfImages`, `galleryPath`, and `imageArray` because I saw those as the most useful pieces of information that needed to be made available. Of course, none of this is set in stone, and you can obviously change it up as needed.

```
public function get numberOfImages():int {
    return _numberOfImages;
}
```

```
public function get galleryPath():String{
    return _galleryPath;
}
public function get imageArray():Array{
    return _imageArray;
}
```

Sample Use of SimpleGallery

And now a quick sample use of SimpleGallery. Just like the previous samples, this is a Document class that is located in the com.flashadbook.base package. This one uses an images directory that contains nine images named galleryImage1.jpg through galleryImage9.jpg. You can download the directory of images from the same location as the code, and it should be placed with your .fla file (or you should alter the _galleryPath variable to match its location). So let's go through this sample real quick.

Skipping the imports and jumping right into the variables, we have the declaration of _simpleGallery, _galleryPath, and _imageArray (all of which are obviously described in their names). After that is the _columns variable that I chose to do a little math on to get the number of columns and rows to come as close to matching as possible given the number of images in _imageArray. Again, set that value to meet the requirements of the project at hand. _thumbScale and _padding are set next, and again, these are self-explanatory in their names. Once we step in to the constructor, we'll create a shiny new SimpleGallery and pass it all the variables we just got finished setting up. The last two steps are to set the position of the gallery and then to add it to the stage.

```
package com.flashadbook.base {
    import com.flashadbook.display.SimpleGallery;
    import flash.events.MouseEvent;
    import flash.display.Sprite;

    public class SimpleGallerySample extends Sprite {

        private var _simpleGallery:SimpleGallery;
        private var _galleryPath:String = "images/";
        private var _imageArray:Array = new
Array("galleryImage1.jpg","galleryImage2.jpg","galleryImage
3.jpg","galleryImage4.jpg","galleryImage5.jpg","galleryImage
6.jpg","galleryImage7.jpg","galleryImage8.jpg","galleryImage
9.jpg")
        private var _columns:int =
Math.round(Math.sqrt(_imageArray.length))
        private var _thumbScale:Number = 0.15;
        private var _padding:Number = 5;
```

```
        public function SimpleGallerySample(){
            _simpleGallery = new SimpleGallery(this,
_galleryPath, _imageArray, _columns, _thumbScale,
_padding);
            _simpleGallery.setPosition(84,105);
            addChild(_simpleGallery);
        }
    }
}
```

The ReverseClip Class

Reversing a MovieClip in Flash can come in handy in many situations like animated menu buttons or really anything else that may be moving on the stage. I've included the following small ReverseClip class that I put together simply because I find myself using it to get to previous states of animations in numerous projects. It's pretty small and straightforward, so the explanation on this one is shorter, but let's take a look at the entire piece of code first.

ReverseClip Code

```
package com.flashadbook.utils{
    import flash.display.MovieClip;
    import flash.events.DataEvent;
    import flash.utils.setTimeout;
    import flash.events.TimerEvent;
    import flash.utils.Timer;

    public class ReverseClip{

        public static const REVERSE_COMPLETE:String =
"reverseComplete";
        private static var _revTimer:Timer = new Timer(0);
// the timer used to run the clip in reverse
        private static var _targetClip:MovieClip; // the
MovieClip which will be reversed
        private static var _targetFrame:int; // the frame
at which the reversal will be considered complete
        private static var _loopCount:int; // the number of
times to repeat the reversal (0 is default, -1 loops
infinately)
        private static var _currentLoop:int = 0; // the
loop that is currently playing

        public static function play(targetClip:MovieClip,
loopCount:int=0, targetFrame:int=1, speed:Number=30):void {
if(!_revTimer.hasEventListener(TimerEvent.TIMER)){
            _targetClip = targetClip;
```

```
        _targetFrame = targetFrame;
        _loopCount = loopCount;
        _revTimer.delay = speed;
        _revTimer.addEventListener(TimerEvent.TIMER,
reverseFrame, false, 0, true);
        }
        _revTimer.start();
    }

    private static function
reverseFrame(e:TimerEvent):void {
        if(_targetClip.currentFrame > _targetFrame){
            _targetClip.prevFrame();
        }else{
            targetClip.gotoAndStop(_targetFrame);
            _revTimer.reset();
            _loopCount==-1 ? _targetClip.play() :
replay();
        }
    }
    private static function replay():void {
        if (_currentLoop < _loopCount) {
            _currentLoop++;
            _targetClip.play();
        }else{
_revTimer.removeEventListener(TimerEvent.TIMER,reverseFrame
);
            _targetClip.dispatchEvent(new
DataEvent(REVERSE_COMPLETE,true));
            _targetClip = null;
        }
    }
    }
}
```

ReverseClip Breakdown

Once again, a quick look at the package and imports and then we'll
move on:

```
package com.flashadbook.utils{
    import flash.display.MovieClip;
    import flash.events.DataEvent;
    import flash.utils.setTimeout;
    import flash.events.TimerEvent;
    import flash.utils.Timer;
```

In the class declaration, you'll notice that we aren't extending
anything in this class as we have in the previous classes in this

chapter. Also like the other classes in this chapter, let's take a quick look at the variables in Table 12.5.

And now let's move on to the functionality of ReverseClip by first taking a look at its `play` method. The ReverseClip `play` method calls for four parameters. Three of them are optional, one of them is required, and all of them are listed in Table 12.6. But before we look at these, what's happening in the `play` method? The very first thing that happens is that we check to see if `_revTimer` has a TimerEvent listener attached to it. If it does, we know that ReverseClip is in use and that all the variables already have values assigned. In that case, we jump down to tell the `_revTimer` to start. However, if it doesn't have that TimerEvent listener attached to it, that means it's not being used and we need to assign some values based on the parameters before we go any further. And don't forget that we also need to add that listener that will trigger the `reverse Frame` method.

Table 12.5 The Variables of the ReverseClip Class

Variable	Purpose
REVERSE_COMPLETE (public, static String)	Passed via DataEvent to notify of reverse completion
_revTimer (private, static Timer)	Timer used to reverse the MovieClip
_targetClip (private, static MovieClip)	The MovieClip that will be reversed
_targetFrame (private, static int)	Frame at which the reverse will be complete
_loopCount (private, static int)	Number of times to allow the animation to loop
_currentLoop (private, static int)	The number of loops that have happened so far

Table 12.6 Parameters for the ReverseClip Play Method

Parameter	Purpose
targetClip (MovieClip)	The MovieClip you want to reverse
loopCount (int)	The number of times you want your MovieClip to loop; default is 0 and –1 loops infinitely
targetFrame (int)	The frame where you want the MovieClip to stop playing in reverse; default is 1
speed (Number)	The number of milliseconds between the TimerEvents that tell the MovieClip to reverse; default is 30

```
public static function play(targetClip:MovieClip,
loopCount:int=0, targetFrame:int=1, speed:Number=30):void {
    if(!_revTimer.hasEventListener(TimerEvent.TIMER)){
        _targetClip = targetClip;
        _targetFrame = targetFrame;
        _loopCount = loopCount;
        _revTimer.delay = speed;
        _revTimer.addEventListener(TimerEvent.TIMER,
reverseFrame, false, 0, true);
    }
    _revTimer.start();
}
```

The `reverseFrame` method that gets called as a result of `_revTimer` firing off a TimerEvent makes a simple decision to either move the MovieClip back by one frame or not. So, first it compares the `currentFrame` property of `_targetClip` to the value of `_targetFrame`. If `_targetClip` hasn't reached that point on the timeline yet, we'll tell it to go backwards by one frame (`prevFrame`). Remember, we're testing to see if `currentFrame` is greater than `_targetFrame` because the MovieClip is playing backwards at this point. So if it's not greater, then we need to stop rewinding. The first thing to do in this case is to force the MovieClip to `gotoAndStop(_targetFrame)`. This step is really just a fallback to make sure the timeline didn't go too far. Since we're forcing the frame number, we're accounting for the possibility that the playhead reversed too far by at least one frame. Next, we'll `reset` the timer, so it will be ready to go when/if we need it again. At the end of this piece, let's check to see if `_loopCount` is equal to –1 (remember, that means infinite looping). If it is equal to –1, all we need to do is tell `_targetClip` to `play` again. On the other hand, if `_loopCount` is not equal to –1, we'll call the `replay` method.

```
private static function reverseFrame(e:TimerEvent):void {
    if(_targetClip.currentFrame > _targetFrame){
        _targetClip.prevFrame();
    }else{
        _targetClip.gotoAndStop(_targetFrame);
        _revTimer.reset();
        _loopCount==-1 ? _targetClip.play() : replay();
    }
}
```

And now for the `replay` method. The replay method also consists of a pretty simple if/else statement. Our test this time is to see if `_currentLoop` is less than `_loopCount`. If it is, we increase `_currentLoop` and tell `_targetClip` to play again (or loop). If `_currentLoop` is not less than `_loopCount`, it's time to stop everything and move on. The first of the last steps is to remove the TimerEvent listener, so we can clear up a little memory. Next, we'll dispatch a DataEvent and pass our REVERSE_COMPLETE variable from earlier as the type.

> **TIP**
>
> For dispatching a simple event where you just need to listen for a custom name but you don't need a full blown custom event class, consider dispatching a DataEvent and using your custom event name as the type parameter.

```
private static function replay():void {
    if (_currentLoop < _loopCount) {
        _currentLoop++;
        _targetClip.play();
    }else{
_revTimer.removeEventListener(TimerEvent.TIMER,reverseFrame
);
        _targetClip.dispatchEvent(new
DataEvent(REVERSE_COMPLETE,true));
        _targetClip = null;
    }
}
```

Sample Use of ReverseClip

For this sample, place a MovieClip in your library and give it a Class/Linkage of "ball" (or use the .fla available in the downloads from the book's Web site). After creating a new instance of ball named myBall, we jump straight into the action by adding a REVERSE_COMPLETE listener to the ReverseClipSample itself. Next, we're going to use the wonderful addFrameScript to add a function to the final frame of myBall. That method, rewindBall, can have any code in it that you need, but let's be sure to include the line that tells ReverseClip to play and target myBall for 1 loop (or as many as you'd like). Now that we're all set up, let's add the ball to the display list using addChild. Lastly, reverseCompleteHandler simply traces out a notification that it has indeed been called. Again, use the code that best suits your project here.

```
package com.flashadbook.base {
    import com.flashadbook.utils.ReverseClip;
    import flash.display.Sprite;
    import flash.events.DataEvent;
    import flash.events.EventDispatcher;
```

```
public class ReverseClipSample extends Sprite {

    private var myBall:ball = new ball();

    public function ReverseClipSample(){
addEventListener(ReverseClip.REVERSE_COMPLETE,reverseComplete
Handler,false,0,true);
        myBall.addFrameScript(myBall.totalFrames - 1,
rewindBall);
        addChild(myBall);
    }

    private function rewindBall():void {
        trace("rewindBall");
        ReverseClip.play(myBall,1);
    }

    private function
reverseCompleteHandler(e:DataEvent):void{
        trace("reverseCompleteHandler");
    }
  }
}
```

The ClickTagger Class

ClickTagger is a class that was primarily built to solve for the case sensitivity issue that Flash developers may run into when using the clickTag variable in their banners. Without a current standard in place for ad-serving companies, some use clickTag, while others use clickTAG, and still others use ClickTag or even clicktag. In ActionScript 2, this wasn't/isn't an issue, but as soon as Flash Platform developers or agencies start creating banners with Action-Script 3, they may very quickly encounter the problem by having their ads kicked back for not working correctly.

While writing ClickTagger, I also decided to add a bit of functionality to it to allow the developer to not only assign the clickTags to the proper interactive elements but assign a fallback URL as well. The fallback URL works for local testing from within the Flash IDE (where clickTags aren't passed in) and is also used in the unfortunate event that there's a problem loading the clickTags at runtime. If the clickTags fail to load, at least the user will still be taken to the URL you provide.

ClickTagger Code

```
package com.flashadbook.utils{
    import flash.display.LoaderInfo;
    import flash.events.MouseEvent;
```

```
import flash.external.ExternalInterface;
import flash.net.URLRequest;
import flash.net.navigateToURL;
import flash.system.Capabilities;
import flash.display.InteractiveObject;

public class ClickTagger {

    private var _clickTags:Array = new Array(); //
Array of clicktag objects
    private var _clickObjects:Array = new Array(); //
Array of clickable items
    private var _targetWindow:String = "_blank"; //
window to lauch the url in
    private var _tagName:String = "clicktag"; // used
in solving for case sensitivity
    private var _playerType:String =
Capabilities.playerType.toLowerCase(); // check for local
testing
    private var _extInterfaceAvailable:Boolean = false;
// true if in browser AND ExternalInterface.available
    private var _securePattern:RegExp = new
RegExp("^http[s]?\:\\/\\/([^\\/]+)"); // RegExp for
security check on clicktag url

    public function ClickTagger(loaderinfo:LoaderInfo){
        for(var p:String in loaderinfo.parameters){
            // solve for case sensitivity (clickTag,
ClickTag, clickTAG, etc)
            if (p.toLowerCase().indexOf(_tagName) == 0)
{
                var tagPosition:int = 0;
                if(p.length > _tagName.length){
                    tagPosition =
int(p.substr(_tagName.length))-1;
                }
_clickTags.push({tagIndex:tagPosition,tagUrl:loaderinfo.para
meters[p]})
            }
        }

        _clickTags.sortOn("tagIndex", Array.NUMERIC);
    }

    public function
assignClickTag(element:InteractiveObject,failSafeUrl:String,
tagNumber:int=1):void{
        tagNumber = tagNumber < 0 ? 0 : tagNumber-1;
element.addEventListener(MouseEvent.CLICK,clickOut,false,0,
true);
```

```
_clickObjects.push({clickElement:element,fallBack:failSafeUrl,
tagIndex:tagNumber});
        }

       private function clickOut(e:MouseEvent):void{
           var clickedIndex:int;
           var destination:String;

           clickLoop: for(var obj:Object in
_clickObjects){
               if(e.target ==
_clickObjects[obj].clickElement){
                   clickedIndex =
_clickObjects[obj].tagIndex;
                   destination =
_clickObjects[obj].fallBack;
                   break clickLoop;
               }
           }

           if(_playerType=="activex" ||
_playerType=="plugin"){
               if(_clickTags[clickedIndex]){
if(secureTag(_clickTags[clickedIndex].tagUrl)){
                   destination =
_clickTags[clickedIndex].tagUrl;
               }
           }
           _extInterfaceAvailable =
ExternalInterface.available;
           }

           if (_extInterfaceAvailable) {
ExternalInterface.call('window.open',destination,target
Window);
           }else{
               navigateToURL(new
URLRequest(destination),targetWindow);
           }
       }

       private function
secureTag(targetURL:String):Boolean {
           var resultObj:Object =
_securePattern.exec(targetURL);
           if (resultObj == null || targetURL.length >=
4096) {
               return false;
           }
```

```
                return true;
            }

        public function get targetWindow():String{
            return _targetWindow;
        }
        public function set
    targetWindow(value:String):void{
            _targetWindow = value;
        }
    }
}
```

ClickTagger Breakdown

Okay, are you ready to break this down? Because based on the rest of this chapter, it's time for that step, so let's start out by taking a look at Table 12.7 and the variables that are instantiated at the top of the class.

And now let's jump right into the ClickTagger constructor, which requires only one parameter of type LoaderInfo, which is very creatively named `loaderInfo`. The LoaderInfo class provides plenty of information about our .swf including the parameters that have been passed in to it like flashvars with clickTags. To get to those parameters, we need not look any further than, you guessed it, the `parameters` property of our `loaderInfo` to get the object that contains all the name-value pairs that have been sent in to the banner. Once we have those name-value pairs, we're going to run through them, convert them to lowercase, and test them against our `_tagName` of "clicktag." If we catch one that matches, we check

Table 12.7 The ClickTagger Variables

Variable	Purpose
_clickTags (Array)	An Array that will be filled with Objects containing all the clickTags and their positions as they are passed in to the banner
_clickObjects (Array)	An Array that will have an Object added to it each time the assignClickTag method is called
_targetWindow (String)	The window in which the target URL will be launched
_tagName (String)	A String used to handle the case sensitivity issue
_playerType (String)	A String used to determine if the ad is being played in the browser or not
_extInterfaceAvailable (Boolean)	A Boolean that will be set to true if the ad is in a browser and ExternalInterface is available
_securePattern (RegExp)	A RegExp used to check for "http://" or "https://" in the clickTag

it for an `int` on the end, so we'll know if it's clickTag1, clickTag2, and so on. From that `int`, we get the "position" of the clickTag, and we wrap it up in an object with the associated URL and put that object in out `_clickTags` Array. Finally, after we're finished checking the parameters for clickTags, we sort the `_clickTags` Array based on the `tagIndex` we pulled from the end of each clickTag name. Next in this class is the `assignClickTag` method, which calls for the parameters in Table 12.8, but first, here's the constructor:

```
public function ClickTagger(loaderinfo:LoaderInfo){
    for(var p:String in loaderinfo.parameters){
        if (p.toLowerCase().indexOf(_tagName) == 0) {
            var tagPosition:int = 0;
            if(p.length > _tagName.length){
                tagPosition =
int(p.substr(_tagName.length))-1;
            }
_clickTags.push({tagIndex:tagPosition,tagUrl:loaderinfo.
parameters[p]})
        }
    }
    _clickTags.sortOn("tagIndex", Array.NUMERIC);
}
```

This particular method is very short (three lines), but don't judge its value by its size because outside of the constructor, this is the most important method in this class. The first line is reassigning the value of the `tagNumber` parameter. The reason for this is because before all is said and done, `tagNumber` is going to be used to call on a position in our `_clickTags` Array. Since arrays are zero based but our clickTags aren't, we need to drop the value of `tagNumber` down

Table 12.8 Parameters for the ClickTagger assignClickTag Method

Parameter	Purpose
element (InteractiveObject)	The InteractiveObject that will accept the click event from the user's mouse
failSafeUrl (String)	The URL to be used during testing and also in the event that the clickTags don't load for some reason
tagNumber (int)	The clickTag to use for this particular InteractiveObject (clickTag1, clickTag2, and so on); default is 1

by one (unless it's negative and then we set it to zero). After setting that, we add a click listener to the `element` InteractiveObject (which can be a SimpleButton, MovieClip, and so on) that was passed in. On the third line, we create an object that consists of all the parameters and add that object to our `_clickObjects` Array.

```
public function
assignClickTag(element:InteractiveObject,
failSafeUrl:String,
tagNumber:int=1):void{
    tagNumber = tagNumber < 0 ? 0 : tagNumber-1;
element.addEventListener(MouseEvent.CLICK,clickOut,false,0,
true);
_clickObjects.push({clickElement:element,fallBack:failSafe
Url,tagIndex:tagNumber});
}
```

Oh wait, did I say that the `assignClickTag` method was really, really important? Because so is this next method called `clickOut`. If you noticed in the click listener that we added in the `assignClickTag` method, `clickOut` is the method that gets called when the user clicks on that `element`. First up, we create a couple of variables for the index of the clicked item in the destination the user will be taken to. Next, we use a `for` loop with a label of `clickLoop` to run through our `_clickObjects` Array and find the object that was clicked on. Once we have a match, we pull the `tagIndex` and `fallBack` out of that object we created and added to the `_clickObjects` Array, and we break out of the `clickLoop`. In the following if statements, we check `_playerType` to see if we're in the browser, and make sure that there is actually an object at the `clickedIndex` position of the `_clickTags` Array and then check the `tagUrl` of that object for "http://" or "https://" with the `secureTag` method. Once we obtain all of that clearance, we can change the value of `destination` from the fallback URL to the clickTag that was passed in. If it doesn't pass any of those tests for some reason, `destination` remains set to the fallback URL. From there, we check to see if `ExternalInterface` is available. If it is, we use its `call` method to take the user to the destination. If not, we go ahead and use `navigateToURL` instead.

TIP

Assigning labels to loops is a handy little tool that was introduced with ActionScript 3. By placing a label directly before the loop statement, you gain the ability to break out of a specific loop. This comes in extremely handy in nested loops where you might need to break out of the parent loop because the child loop has found what you're looking for. Consider this example: `myLoopLabel: for(var obj:Object in myVector){...}.` Now you can break out of that loop by simple calling `break myLoopLabel.` Pretty nifty, huh?

```
private function clickOut(e:MouseEvent):void{
    var clickedIndex:int;
    var destination:String;

    clickLoop: for(var obj:Object in _clickObjects){
        if(e.target == _clickObjects[obj].clickElement){
            clickedIndex = _clickObjects[obj].tagIndex;
            destination = _clickObjects[obj].fallBack;
            break clickLoop;
        }
    }

    if(_playerType=="activex" || _playerType=="plugin"){
        if(_clickTags[clickedIndex]){
            if(secureTag(_clickTags[clickedIndex].tagUrl)){
                destination =
_clickTags[clickedIndex].tagUrl;
            }
        }
        _extInterfaceAvailable =
ExternalInterface.available;
    }

    if (_extInterfaceAvailable) {
ExternalInterface.call('window.open',destination,
targetWindow);
    }else{
        navigateToURL(new
URLRequest(destination),targetWindow);
    }
}
```

The final items in ClickTagger are the secureTag method and a getter and setter to allow the _targetWindow to be changed. We've already pretty much covered what secureTag does ("http://" or "https://" in the clickTag), and it either returns true or false based on its findings.

```
private function secureTag(targetURL:String):Boolean {
    var resultObj:Object = _securePattern.exec(targetURL);
    if (resultObj == null || targetURL.length >= 4096) {
        return false;
    }
    return true;
}
public function get targetWindow():String{
    return _targetWindow;
}
public function set targetWindow(value:String):void{
    _targetWindow = value;
}
```

Sample Use of ClickTagger

Much like the ReverseClip sample, this one requires you to add a couple of things to the stage of your .fla. Also like the ReverseClip sample, you have the option of downloading a .fla from the book's Web site (ClickTaggerTest.fla). If you choose to create your own .fla, you'll simply need to add three buttons to the stage and give them instance names of button1, button2, and button3. Once you have them in place, use the following code for your Document class. If you have downloaded the code from the Web site, this is the code from ClickTaggerSample.as in the com.flashadbook.base package. Within this code, the first couple of things we do are create a new instance of ClickTagger named _clickTagger and three fallback URLs (one for each button) called _fallback1, _fallback2, and _fallback3 (again with the crafty names). Finally, we get to the constructor of our Document class where we are just calling ClickTagger's assignClickTag method once for each button and passing in the variables as described in the ClickTagger Breakdown section. Obviously, there would be more if this was the Document class for an actual banner ad, but since it's not, that's all there is to it.

```
package com.flashadbook.base {
    import com.flashadbook.utils.ClickTagger;
    import flash.display.Sprite;
    import flash.events.MouseEvent;

    public class ClickTaggerSample extends Sprite {
        private var _clickTagger:ClickTagger = new
ClickTagger(stage.loaderInfo);

        private var _fallback1:String =
"http://www.flashadbook.com";
        private var _fallback2:String =
"http://www.jasonfincanon.com";
        private var _fallback3:String =
"http://www.adobe.com";

        public function ClickTaggerSample() {
_clickTagger.assignClickTag(button1,_fallback1,1);
_clickTagger.assignClickTag(button2,_fallback2,2);
_clickTagger.assignClickTag(button3,_fallback3,3);
        }
    }
}
```

Conclusion

Well, this is definitely the longest chapter in this book, and we just finished up with a good amount of code here. As I said earlier, some of these classes were pulled over from the first edition of this book and rewritten for ActionScript 3, and some of them are completely new. All of them are available on the book's Web site and will be updated if errors are caught later or if any new methods/functionality are added to any of them. Hopefully at least one of them will come in handy for some of your projects. In the next chapter, we're going to continue with some more classes, but these will all be used together to build a memory card game. See you there!

13

THE MEMORY GAME

The memory game in this chapter was originally built for a site that was targeted at children. The site itself emulated a board game that had checkpoints along the way, and there was a spinner for the users to click to determine how many spaces their game piece would move. As they passed over each checkpoint, they would be taken into one of six different secondary games. The memory game was one of the six. Since then, this same engine has been used to create a small memory game "widget" that Web site owners could put on their sites, as well as a slightly modified version for an iPhone memory game application (Fig. 13.1).

I've divided this chapter into four sections, and each one is needed to build the game. The first three sections are the classes that make up the core of the game, and the fourth section describes how a .fla file would be set up to utilize the engine. Don't forget, as I've mentioned before, all these files are available to download at http://www.flashadbook.com/code/.

The DeckArray Class

The DeckArray class is used to hold the deck of cards in the memory game. It's a pretty simple extension of the Array class that adds the ability to shuffle. In addition to wanting the shuffle feature,

Flash Advertising. DOI: 10.1016/B978-0-240-81345-5.00013-X

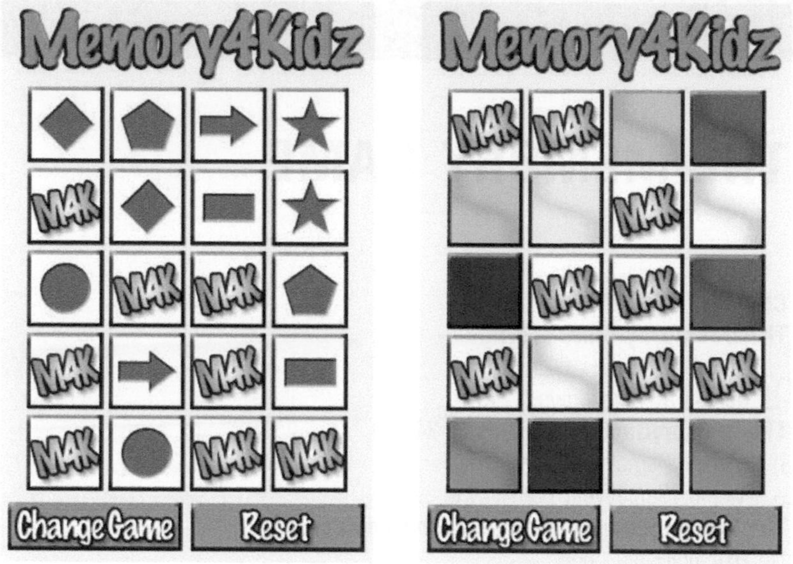

Figure 13.1 The iPhone application "Memory4Kidz" was built in Flash Professional CS5 using a slightly modified version of the memory game.

my intention for this class was (and is) to add new functionality to it as needed. If I do happen to add anything to it, I'll be sure to keep it updated on the site.

DeckArray Code

```
package com.flashadbook.utils{

    dynamic public class DeckArray extends Array{

        private var _deckCount:uint; // the number of
cards in the deck
        private var _shuffleNumber:int; // how many
times the deck has been shuffled in a single call
        private var _shuffleCard:Object; // the card
currently being shuffled

        public function DeckArray(...args){
            for each (var val:* in args){
                super.push(val);
            }
        }

        public function
shuffle(timesToShuffle:int=2):Array{
            _deckCount = this.length;
            _shuffleNumber = 0;
            while(_shuffleNumber < timesToShuffle){
                for(var c:int=0; c<_deckCount; c++){
                    // remove a random card from the
deck and place it back on top
```

```
                        _shuffleCard =
this.splice([Math.floor(Math.random()*_deckCount)],1);
                        this.push(_shuffleCard);
                    }
                    _shuffleNumber++;
                }
                return this;
            }
        }
    }
```

DeckArray Breakdown

First, the package. Since DeckArray is a utility, we'll go ahead and place it in the com.flashadbook.utils package. The first thing we do inside the class is to declare a few variables that will be used by the shuffle method. First is _deckCount, which is used to hold the number of cards in the deck (also known as the objects in the array). The reason we'll need this is because we're going to reference it in a for loop in the shuffle method. By referencing this variable instead of the .length property of the array, we save the virtual machine the trouble of having to actually get the length on each and every loop. The next variable is _shuffleNumber and is used to count how many times the deck has been fully shuffled in a single call to the shuffle method. The third variable is the _shuffleCard variable. The _shuffleCard variable will be used as the card that's being pulled from the deck and then immediately put back in a new position. The next item in the DeckArray class is the constructor. Since it's a pretty standard Array constructor, I'll just say that it's there and it fills the DeckArray with the items passed in via the ...args parameter. And finally, we get to the shuffle method.

You'll notice that the shuffle method returns an Array and has a single optional parameter named timesToShuffle. This parameter allows you to determine how many times the deck should be fully shuffled, and it defaults to 2. Once inside this method, we'll immediately (re)set the values of two of the variables that were declared at the top of the class: _deckCount and _shuffleNumber. Now for the actual shuffling of the cards. The while loop keeps track of how many times the deck has been fully shuffled by comparing _shuffleNumber against timesToShuffle, and the for loop contained within does the shuffle. Inside the for loop, a single, random card is assigned to the _shuffleCard variable, pulled from the deck (this.splice), and placed back on top of the deck (this.push). Once the number of cards that have been shuffled matches the number of cards in the deck (_deckCount), _shuffleNumber is increased, and the deck is shuffled again if needed.

The MemoryGameEvent Class

Each time a user turns over two cards in the memory game, the game needs to know if the two cards match or not. That's where the MemoryGameEvent class comes in. The MemoryGameEvent class extends Event and is pretty specific to the memory game since the events it dispatches are directly related to matching cards and completing a game.

MemoryGameEvent Code

```
package com.flashadbook.events{

    import flash.events.Event;
    import flash.events.EventDispatcher;

    public class MemoryGameEvent extends Event{
        public static const INCORRECT_MATCH:String =
"incorrectMatch";
        public static const CORRECT_MATCH:String =
"correctMatch";
        public static const GAME_COMPLETE:String =
"gameComplete";

        public function MemoryGameEvent(type:String,
bubbles:Boolean = false, cancelable:Boolean = false) {
            super(type, bubbles, cancelable);
        }

        public override function clone():Event{
            return new MemoryGameEvent(type, bubbles,
cancelable);
        }
    }
}
```

MemoryGameEvent Breakdown

Once again, the package for this class mirrors that of the class it extends. In this case, MemoryGameEvent is in the com.flashadbook.events package. Since it does extend Event and we want it to behave as an Event would, the first thing we do is import `flash.events.Event` and `flash.events.EventDispatcher`. The next items in MemoryGameEvent are the constants that represent the events that can be dispatched. They are pretty self-explanatory in their names: `CORRECT_MATCH`, `INCORRECT_MATCH`, and `GAME_COMPLETE`. I'm sure you can guess what each one represents. The only two things left in this class are the standard Event constructor and the overridden `clone` function.

ALERT!

If you are creating a custom event class that extends Event, remember that it's very important to override the `clone` function. By overriding the `clone` function, you allow the event to be redispatched if needed.

The MemoryGame Class (the Game Engine)

And now for the core of this chapter and the engine of the game itself: the MemoryGame class. The MemoryGame class uses an array of images that are passed in to create, shuffle, and deal the cards. It also handles user interactions, checks for card matches/mismatches and game completions, and sends out a notification of each event using the MemoryGameEvent class.

MemoryGame Code

```
package com.flashadbook.engines{

    import flash.display.BitmapData;
    import flash.display.Bitmap;
    import flash.display.Sprite;
    import flash.display.MovieClip;
    import flash.events.MouseEvent;
    import flash.utils.getDefinitionByName;
    import flash.utils.setTimeout;
    import com.flashadbook.DeckArray;
    import com.flashadbook.events.MemoryGameEvent;

    public class MemoryGame extends MovieClip{

        public const GRID_LAYOUT:String = "gridLayout";
        public const CUSTOM_LAYOUT:String = "customLayout";

        private var _cardsToCompare:Array = new Array();
        private var _memoryCards:DeckArray = new
DeckArray();
        private var _numberOfCards:uint;
        private var _cardPadding:int;
        private var _matchesComplete:int;

        private var _tempCard:Class;
        private var _frontBmd:BitmapData;
        private var _frontSkin:Bitmap;

        private var _tempCardBack:Class;
        private var _backBmd:BitmapData;
        private var _backSkin:Bitmap;
```

```
private var _allowClick:Boolean = true;

public function
MemoryGame(cards:Array,cardBack:String=null,spread:int=10):
void{
        var cardsLen:uint = cards.length;
        for(var d:int=0; d<2; d++){
            for(var e:int=0; e<cardsLen; e++){
                _memoryCards.push(cards[e]);
            }
        }
        _memoryCards.shuffle();
        _numberOfCards = _memoryCards.length;
        _cardPadding = spread;
        _tempCardBack = cardBack==null ? null :
Class(getDefinitionByName(cardBack));
    }


public function
deal(layoutType:String=GRID_LAYOUT,customCoordinates:Array=
null,rows:int=2):void{
        var c:int;
        switch(layoutType){
            /*case YOUR_LAYOUT:
                CREATE OTHER LAYOUTS HERE
                "gridLayout" is only an example name
but you could use something like "circleLayout",
"lineLayout", etc.
                Be sure to set the name as a public
const. For example: GRID_LAYOUT = "gridLayout"
                break;*/
            case CUSTOM_LAYOUT:
                if(customCoordinates == null ||
customCoordinates.length != _numberOfCards){
                    trace('ERROR: When using layoutType
"custom", your customCoordinates array must contain twice
as many coordinates as your array of images.');
                    trace("If you have 4 images, you
must have 8 sets of coordinates.");
                }else{
                    for(c=0; c<_numberOfCards; c++){

buildCard(_memoryCards[c],customCoordinates[c].x,custom
Coordinates[c].y);

                    }
                }
                break;
            case GRID_LAYOUT:
```

```
                        /* The default GRID_LAYOUT places one
instance of each card in each row
                        The default GRID_LAYOUT uses 2 rows
and the number of columns is equal to the number of cards
passed in*/
                        for(var r:int=0; r<rows; r++){
                            for(c=0; c<_numberOfCards/rows;
c++){
                                var cardPos:int = c +
((_numberOfCards/rows)*r);

buildCard(_memoryCards[cardPos],(_frontSkin.width*c)+(_card
Padding*c),(_frontSkin.height*r)+(_cardPadding*r));
                            }
                        }
                        break;
                }
        }

        // showCard draws a card to the game
        private function
buildCard(cardName:String,cardX:int=-1,cardY:int=-1):void{
            _tempCard =
Class(getDefinitionByName(cardName));
            _frontBmd = new _tempCard(0,0);
            _frontSkin = new Bitmap(_frontBmd);

            _backBmd = _tempCardBack==null ? new
BitmapData(_frontSkin.width,_frontSkin.height,false,0xCCCCCC) :
new _tempCardBack(0,0);

            _backSkin = new Bitmap(_backBmd);

            var cardSprite:Sprite = new Sprite();
            cardSprite.addChild(_frontSkin);
            cardSprite.addChild(_backSkin);
            cardSprite.x = cardX;
            cardSprite.y = cardY;
            cardSprite.buttonMode = true;

_cardSprite.addEventListener(MouseEvent.CLICK,showCard);
            addChild(cardSprite);
        }

        // showCard completes the card flip and shows the
player what card they have chosen
        private function showCard(e:MouseEvent):void{
            if(!_allowClick){
                return;
            }
```

```
                     var cardObj:Object = e.currentTarget;
                     cardObj.buttonMode = false;
                     cardObj.getChildAt(1).visible = false;
_cardsToCompare.push({bitmap:cardObj.getChildAt(0).bitmapData,
card:cardObj});
                     if(_cardsToCompare.length == 2){

if(_cardsToCompare[0].bitmap.compare(_cardsToCompare[1].
bitmap) == 0){
                             dispatchEvent(new
MemoryGameEvent(MemoryGameEvent.CORRECT_MATCH));
                             correctMatch();
                         }else{
                             dispatchEvent(new
MemoryGameEvent(MemoryGameEvent.INCORRECT_MATCH));
                             _allowClick = false;
                             setTimeout(hideCards,1000);
                         }
                     }
                 }

        // hideCards hides the cards if they are not a
match
        private function hideCards():void{
            for(var c:int=0; c<_cardsToCompare.length;
c++){

_cardsToCompare[c].card.getChildAt(1).visible = true;
                     _cardsToCompare[c].card.buttonMode = true;
                 }
                 _cardsToCompare.splice(0);
                 _allowClick = true;
             }

        /* correctMatch adds to the number of total matches
found and, if all matches
        have been found, dispatches a custom event of
"GameComplete"*/
        private function correctMatch():void{
            _matchesComplete++;
            _cardsToCompare.splice(0);
            if(_matchesComplete == _numberOfCards/2){
                dispatchEvent(new
MemoryGameEvent(MemoryGameEvent.GAME_COMPLETE));
                 }
             }
         }
 }
```

MemoryGame Breakdown

I'm going to skip past explaining the imports for the MemoryGame class, and I'll just quickly go over the variables that are declared at the top. The first variables are a couple of publicly available constants that will be used later to help the engine determine the pattern in which to layout the cards. The ones I've included are GRID_LAYOUT (to place the cards in a grid pattern) and CUSTOM_LAYOUT (used when you want to pass in your own set of coordinates for each card). The rest of the variables are private, and while I tried to make their names self-explanatory, let's still take a quick look at them in Table 13.1.

Now, let's move on to the MemoryGame constructor. The constructor calls for three parameters (cards, cardBack, and spread) with two of them being optional (see Table 13.2 for more details). Once inside the constructor, we'll assign the length of the cards Array to a new variable called cardsLen. Just the same as before, we're assigning it to a variable, so the virtual machine doesn't have to go and get the length of the array each and every time it goes through the upcoming for loop.

Up next is a nested for loop that creates duplicates of all the cards in the cards Array. The whole reason I set it up this way was in case I wanted to create some new kind of game where you had to match more than two identical cards. By changing the 2 in the outer for loop (for(var d:int=0; d<2; d++)) to a variable, you could set it

Table 13.1 The Private Variables of the MemoryGame Class

Variable	Use
_cardsToCompare (Array)	Holds the two cards that are being compared for a match
_memoryCards (DeckArray)	The deck of cards
_numberOfCards (uint)	How many cards are in the deck
_cardPadding (int)	The number of pixels between each card that is placed on the stage
_matchesComplete (int)	How many cards the player has matched
_tempCard (Class)	The raw Class representation of the front of each individual card
_frontBmd (BitmapData)	The BitmapData for the front of each individual card
_frontSkin (Bitmap)	The Bitmap representation of the front of each individual card
_tempCardBack (Class)	The raw Class representation of the back of each individual card
_backBmd (BitmapData)	The BitmapData for the back of each individual card
_backSkin (Bitmap)	The Bitmap representation of the back of each individual card
_allowClick (Boolean)	Determines whether or not the user should be able to click on a card

Table 13.2 MemoryGame Constructor Parameters

Parameter	Explanation
cards (Array)	The Array of BitmapData objects (images) that will be used as the cards for the game
cardBack (String)	A String that represents a BitmapData object to use as the back of each card; if null, a gray box is drawn to show the card (optional, default is null)
spread (int)	The number of pixels between each card that is placed on the stage (optional, default is 10)

Table 13.3 The Deal Method Parameters

Parameter	Explanation
layoutType (String)	A String representing the pattern in which the cards will be presented on the stage (optional, default is GRID_LAYOUT)
customCoordinates (Array)	An Array of Points or Objects with x and y values for each card (optional, default is null)
rows (int)	The number of rows to use when laying out the cards in a grid-style pattern (optional, default is 2)

to any number you might want to user to match. Now that we've got all the duplicated cards in our deck, we'll call the shuffle method from the DeckArray and then assign values to _numberOfCards, _cardPadding, and _tempCardBack (if one if available).

The next item in this engine is the deal method. This one has three optional parameters (Table 13.3) and is essentially just a switch statement that can be added for different card patterns on the "table." This is where the GRID_LAYOUT and CUSTOM_LAYOUT variables I mentioned earlier come into play. Depending on which one of these (or any others you may choose to add later) you pass in to the deal method, the cards will be dealt and arranged on the screen accordingly. To do this, you'll notice we're calling the buildCard method as we loop our way through the deck.

The buildCard method is where the cards actually get created and placed on the stage, and it does this with the use of three parameters. Those three parameters are cardName, cardX, and cardY. I didn't include a table for these parameters because I think they do a good job of explaining themselves with their names. The first thing that happens here is that we create a new temporary card (_tempCard) based on the cardName, which was passed in from the _memoryCards DeckArray earlier (this will make more sense when we get to the .fla example in a little bit). After we have the temporary card, let's go ahead and use it to create a new Bitmap called _frontSkin, which we'll use as the face of the card. The next thing we need to do is check to see if an image is available for the back of the card. If it is, we'll take the appropriate steps to use it to create another Bitmap called _backSkin (the back of the card).

Now that we have something to use for both the face and the back of the card, the next thing we're going to do is create a new Sprite called cardSprite. Once that's instantiated, we add the _frontSkin and _backSkin, set the location of the card (cardSprite.x and cardSprite.y), and set its buttonMode to true, so the hand cursor will show up giving the users a visual clue that they can click on the card. Finally, we add a click listener to fire the showCard method and add the card to the stage with addChild(cardSprite).

Now let's take a look at this little interaction method named showCard. Before I explain this one, let me point out that while there aren't any animated transitions happening during the card flip, it wouldn't be hard for you to add one of your choosing. I thought if I left it out, you would have more freedom to play and experiment with things like animating the card flip or fading from the back to the front. Now that we have that settled, let's take a look over this method. The very first thing that happens is that we check to see if the _allowClick variable is true or false. If it's false, then return kicks the user out of the method. However, if it's true, then we jump right in to turn off the buttonMode, so the user can't click on it again and hide the back of the card to reveal the front (this is where you would want to insert a transition). Next, we add the card we just clicked to our _cardsToCompare Array. After the user clicks on a second card, the _cardsToCompare Array has a length of two, and we can check those two cards to see if they match by using the BitmapData .compare method. If the cards match, we dispatch the MemoryGame Event.CORRECT_MATCH event and call the correctMatch method. If they don't, we call the MemoryGameEvent.INCORRECT_MATCH event, set _allowClick to false so the user can't keep clicking cards, and then run a setTimeout to give the user time (1 s in this case) to realize he or she was wrong before calling the hideCards method.

TIP

The compare method of BitmapData compares the width, height, and pixel values within two BitmapData objects. If all three of those items are equivalent, the compare method returns 0. Check out the Adobe LiveDocs for more information.

The two last methods in this engine are pretty short, so I'll breeze through them real quick. First, the hideCards method does exactly what it says by hiding the cards (or turning them over). It takes the two cards in the _cardsToCompare Array, covers the face of the card with the back of the card (another opportunity for a transition here), and makes the card interactive again by setting its buttonMode to true. After that, we just empty the _cardsToCompare Array with splice(0) and return _allowClick to true. Finally, we have the correctMatch method, which we fired earlier when there was what? Yes, a correct match. The first thing this method does is increment _matches Complete. After that, it clears out the _cardsToCompare Array and checks to see if the number of cards matched is equal to the original number of cards in the deck. If it is equal, a MemoryGameEvent.GAME_ COMPLETE event is dispatched, and that's all there is to it.

Sample Use of MemoryGame

Within the com.flashadbook.base package, you can find this sample code in MemoryGameSample.as, and here's the quick breakdown of what's happening within that class. First, there are several variables that get set up. _memoryGame is an instance of MemoryGame, and _gameCards is an array of the Linkage names for some images that are in the library of the .fla. These are the card faces. Next up are some variables that hold the coordinates for the rows and columns that we'll use to place our cards. We'll use those coordinates to fill the _coordArr Array with x and y values. Next in line is the constructor method, which, at this point, does nothing more than fire off the new-Game method and passes in _gameCards for the required cardsToUse parameter and _coordArr for the optional locationArr parameter. The result of this sample is a game like the one in Figure 13.2.

> **TIP**
>
> Note that I populated the _coordArr with Objects containing x and y values, but you could just as easily populate it with Points.

Now let's take a quick look at the newGame method. This one is another very straightforward method that instantiates a new MemoryGame with the array of cards (cardsToUse), and if you have one to use, the Linkage name of the image in the library that will be the back of the card. After the game is instantiated, it's added to the stage, and the cards are dealt with the MemoryGame.deal method. In this case, we're using the custom layout and passing in that array of coordinates we created earlier. The last thing we do in this method is to add listeners to the game for each of the MemoryGameEvent events. The last three methods in this class are simply the handlers for each of those listeners.

```
package com.flashadbook.base {
    import flash.display.MovieClip;
    import flash.events.MouseEvent;
```

```
    import com.flashadbook.engines.MemoryGame;
    import com.flashadbook.events.MemoryGameEvent;

    public class MemoryGameSample extends MovieClip{
        private var _memoryGame:MemoryGame;
        private var _gameCards:Array = new
Array("cardFace1","cardFace2","cardFace3","cardFace4");

        /*The x and y values for the rows and columns of
the custom layout of the cards
        The visual layout looks like this:
        card   card   card
        card          card
        card   card   card*/
        private var _row1:int = 5;
        private var _row2:int = _row1 + 172;
        private var _row3:int = _row2 + 172;
        private var _col1:int = 5;
        private var _col2:int = _col1 + 136;
        private var _col3:int = _col2 + 136;

        //The array used to place the cards
        private var _coordArr:Array = new
Array({x:_col1,y:_row1},{x:_col1,y:_row2},{x:_col1,y:_row3},
{x:_col2,y:_row1},{x:_col2,y:_row3},{x:_col3,y:_row1},{x:_col3,
y:_row2},{x:_col3,y:_row3});
        public function MemoryGameSample() {
            newGame(_gameCards,_coordArr);
        }
        private function
newGame(cardsToUse:Array,locationArr:Array=null):void{
            _memoryGame = new
MemoryGame(cardsToUse,"cardBack");
            addChild(_memoryGame);
            //Deal the cards

_memoryGame.deal(_memoryGame.CUSTOM_LAYOUT,locationArr);

_memoryGame.addEventListener(MemoryGameEvent.CORRECT_MATCH,
correctMatchHandler,false,0,true);

_memoryGame.addEventListener(MemoryGameEvent.INCORRECT_MATCH,
incorrectMatchHandler,false,0,true);

_memoryGame.addEventListener(MemoryGameEvent.GAME_COMPLETE,
gameCompleteHandler,false,0,true);
        }
        private function
correctMatchHandler(e:MemoryGameEvent):void{
```

```
            trace("HANDLE CORRECT MATCH HERE");
        }
        private function
incorrectMatchHandler(e:MemoryGameEvent):void{
            trace("HANDLE INCORRECT MATCH HERE");
        }
        private function
gameCompleteHandler(e:MemoryGameEvent):void{
            trace("HANDLE GAME COMPLETION HERE");
        }
    }
}
```

Figure 13.2 The result of the sample use of MemoryGame.

Conclusion

This chapter was focused on a set of classes used for the singular purpose of creating a memory game. However, like I was saying at the beginning of this chapter, it's also an example of a real-world project that was reused to create multiple versions of the game (including a version for the iPhone). Remember that not only can you get all this code on the book's Web site, but the site is set up for discussion as well.

CASE STUDIES

This case studies chapter is exactly what it sounds like: a chapter containing case studies from a couple of companies (Eyeblaster and Blockdot) who were kind enough to share their experiences with the rest of us. There's not a lot more to say to set it up, so we'll get right to the case studies. Thanks for reading and don't forget to visit the book's Web site at http://www.flashadbook.com.

Eyeblaster

In 1999, Eyeblaster (see their logo in Fig. 14.1) was among the pioneers in rich-media communication. Today, Eyeblaster extends its inventive heritage in digital advertising to ad-serving and global campaign management. As the leading provider of digital advertising solutions, Eyeblaster empowers marketers to engage consumers online. The company's flagship product, MediaMind, is the only ad-serving and campaign management solution built from the ground up for agencies and advertisers. MediaMind includes critical functions that simplify campaign process, enable cross channel analytics, and streamline integration with other technology components.

    Headquartered in New York, Eyeblaster has over 35 offices across all major markets worldwide. This footprint allows Eyeblaster

Flash Advertising. DOI: 10.1016/B978-0-240-81345-5.00014-1

eyeblaster

Figure 14.1 Eyeblaster.

customers to deploy global campaigns with guaranteed service levels, publisher acceptance, and integrated metrics. The company is the only publisher-independent provider in the field, as well as the only one certified for compliance with the three Interactive Advertising Bureau (IAB) measurement guidelines: ad serving, video, and rich media.

In 2009, Eyeblaster delivered campaigns in a variety of ad formats including rich media, in-stream video, display, search, and mobile for over 8500 brands serving approximately 3400 agencies across over 5200 global Web publishers in 55 countries worldwide. Learn more at http://www.eyeblaster.com.

Case Study: Suzuki Race Fans Stay Up to Date with Dynamic Ads

- Advertiser: Suzuki
- Agency: Questus
- Campaign: Motor Race Win
- Eyeblaster Solution: Smart Versioning

As one of the leading motor racing teams in the United States, Team Suzuki is accustomed to speed. While Suzuki dominates on the track, its agency of record, Questus, races each week to update the team's ads with fresh race data. Until recently, making any changes took hours and required a cumbersome process using Microsoft's Atlas and an XML solution. Since then, Questus switched to Eyeblaster and is using its Smart Versioning solution to create, serve, and measure all dynamic content and ads for Suzuki motorcycle and ATV race teams. Suzuki has strengthened the brand's bond with race fans by establishing its advertising as a relevant and up-to-date source of race information. See Figures 14.2 and 14.3 for example images from the Suzuki case study.

Goals

- Inform Suzuki fans of weekly race winners through frequent updates made directly within Suzuki's motor racing online banner ads.
- Deliver fresh and relevant content to motor sports fans.
- Reduce the time it takes to update and deliver dynamic content to Suzuki race fans.

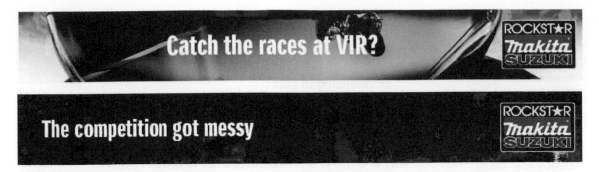

Figure 14.2 Smart Versioning enables the creation of ads that contain dynamic elements, such as text, images, and videos, which can later on be used to quickly update the ad's content.

Figure 14.3 Suzuki has strengthened the brand's bond with race fans by establishing its advertising as a relevant and up-to-date source of race information.

Strategy

- Simplify the operational process associated with making dynamic updates to online ads.
- Develop creative that enables dynamic updates to easily be made each week.
- Adopt advanced tools that increase accuracy and efficiency within Questus.

Tactics

- Leverage Smart Versioning to improve the process of making live updates.
- Implement dynamic text fields within creative.
- Make weekly changes to text to reflect the most recent Suzuki motor race winner.
- Manage all dynamic content under one unified reporting and campaign management platform.

Results

- The new process of dynamic updates increased efficiency by 30% compared with the XML solution with Atlas.
- With Smart Versioning, weekly updates were made in minutes as compared to hours.
- More than 75 changes were made to a single piece of creative throughout the 2009 Suzuki race season.

Case Study: 2–3 Minutes of Dwell Time: The Power of Online Branding

- Advertiser: L'Oréal
- Campaign: L'Oréal Derma Genesis
- Media Buy: MSN Homepage Skin with Video, MSN Hotmail ROS Expandable Showcase with Video
- Creative Agency: Compass Interactive
- Media Agency: Carat Media Services (M) Sdn Bhd

The Objective

Derma Genesis is a new product line from L'Oréal designed to revitalize and illuminate the skin. In order to promote brand awareness, L'Oréal launched a campaign in the Malaysian market to promote the range of products.

L'Oréal has a reputation for their forward thinking, and this was further proven by their first foray into online advertising. Rather than "test the waters" with a minimum buy campaign, L'Oréal decided to pull out all the stops with Derma Genesis and teamed up with Eyeblaster, MSN, and Carat Media in Malaysia. Free samples, a video contest, and interactive product information were made available to connect consumers to the full Derma Genesis product line. See Figures 14.4 and 14.5 for example images from the L'Oréal case study.

The Execution

The campaign utilized a premium brand format – the MSN Homepage skinner. The presence of the brand clearly caught the attention of MSN Homepage and Windows Live Hotmail visitors, with L'Oréal spokesmodel Penelope Cruz prominently featured on the home page. Highlights of the campaign included the following:

- An auto-initiated skinner, which branded the user's browser and created a full L'Oréal environment.
- Information on the range of products was cleverly placed to maintain the look and feel of the brand while targeting the online audience suitable for L'Oréal Derma Genesis.
- A broadcast of the L'Oréal TV commercial in the banner and an opportunity for users to gain a free sample using data capture.

Figure 14.4 L'Oréal Paris.

The Results

Combining eye-catching animation, great interaction including video streaming, and a savvy use of data capture, the Derma Genesis campaign provided very positive results for the client.

The campaign reached nearly 460,000 users, targeting users who are more affluent and who regularly visit the MSN Homepage, as well as the audience of 25–34-year-old females who use Windows

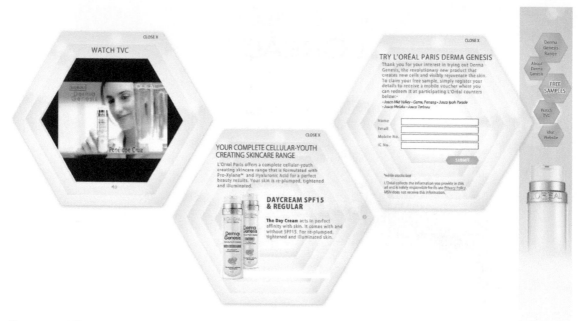

Figure 14.5 L'Oréal Derma Genesis.

Live Hotmail. Eyeblaster analytics enabled L'Oréal to measure the dwell time of the users, which was recorded as up to nearly 3 full minutes on the MSN Homepage Skinner and 2 min on the Hotmail Banners. This is where interactivity was used in the best possible manner. It provided the brand 100% attention from its users and provided users an avenue to experience the brand.

The campaign also managed to generate high brand awareness among the intended audience with a large number of exposures (1,801,638 impressions) reaching each user an average of 3.96 times each. This optimum frequency placed the brand on top of their mind. Over and above that, online was also used as an extension to broadcast the TV commercial at a minimal cost where 53,433 video views were recorded. And of that, more than 52% of the videos were viewed fully.

"In terms of post-campaign analysis, Eyeblaster's capability to provide tracking services made our task easy to justify L'Oréal's spend on this campaign," said Rueben Vijaratnam, MSN Malaysia. "The high dwell times demonstrated to the client the true value of online advertising when compared to the regular 30-second TV and radio commercials that the client had relied upon previously."

Finally, using free samples as a means to collect contact data, the campaign had provided L'Oréal a total of 825 quality leads of potential future customers who had clearly expressed interest in their product.

Blockdot

Blockdot (see their logo in Fig. 14.6) is a leading producer and provider of casual games and company-sponsored advergames. Blockdot has created over 800 games for a broad range of leading brands and companies, including American Airlines, AT&T, General Motors, Kimberly-Clark, Kraft, LEGO, Microsoft, Motorola, M&Ms, Nokia, Universal Pictures, and Verizon.

Case Study: Orlando/Orange County Convention & Visitors Bureau, Inc.

Blockdot built "Find My Smile," a truly unique game engine in which players are challenged to find the photo of an iconic Orlando hotspot hidden inside a picture montage. The picture montage itself is made up of thousands of smaller photos.

Blockdot used ActionScript 3's Client Library to create an experience that allowed players to access pictures from their Facebook account to use in the game, save their own picture montages created within the application, post their scores on their Facebook walls, and send gameplay notifications to their friends. See Figures 14.7 and 14.8 for example images from the Orlando/Orange County Convention & Visitors Bureau, Inc. case study.

Figure 14.6 Blockdot.

Figure 14.7 "Find My Smile" game for Orlando/Orange County Convention & Visitors Bureau, Inc.

Figure 14.8 Find the hidden photo in a mosaic of many other photos.

The game, which appeals to adult couples looking for "getaways" and adult females planning a "girls' weekend," became an integral part of Orlando's CVB Q3 marketing campaign. The game was released on the Orlando Convention and Visitors Bureau Web site and on Facebook.

Case Study: Three Card Monte on the iPhone

Blockdot released Three Card Monte, one of the first iPhone applications to be created with Adobe Flash. By using technology available with the release of Adobe Flash Professional CS5, Blockdot's game developers greatly reduced the turnaround time it takes to release an application compared with traditional iPhone development.

In Three Card Monte, you must keep your eyes on the prize as the dealer flips, shuffles, and rearranges the cards! When the dealer stops, choose the queen of hearts by touching a card on the screen. Pick the correct card to earn points, and move on to the next round! The fast-paced action becomes increasingly challenging as you play ... but be careful: get fooled by the dealer and the game comes to an end!

After you play, you can post your high score directly to the Kewlbox.com worldwide leader board – letting you see how you stack up against other grafters. See Figures 14.9 and 14.10 for example images of Blockdot's Three Card Monte on the iPhone.

Case Study: Kewlbox.com

Blockdot's Kewlbox.com (http://www.kewlbox.com) is one of the top gaming portals on the Internet, with more than a hundred Flash games on the site. See Fig. 14.11.

With so many gaming options on the Internet, Blockdot makes Kewlbox.com stand out from the pack by creating a true networking/social component for gamers. The site includes arcade, card, puzzle,

Figure 14.9 The main screen for Blockdot's Three Card Monte on the iPhone.

Figure 14.10 Gameplay in Blockdot's Three Card Monte on the iPhone.

Figure 14.11 Blockdot's Kewlbox.com.

word, and casual flash games. Daily, weekly, and all-time scoreboards provide a competitive environment for gamers and office workers who are looking to goof off. The site also features community-building activities like chat, polling, and an avatar and reward system.

Blockdot designers tricked out Kewlbox.com by using Flash Media Server to add multiplayer gaming capability to many of Blockdot's titles.

INDEX

Page numbers followed by *f* indicates a figure and *t* indicates a table